D1347998

As a child I grew up not far from the motorway, and I recall asking my father to drive me two junctions down the M1, so I could feel closer to London by gazing at its bright lights. In perhaps one of the few ways that a young girl can express her aspirations, the M1 was my yellow brick road and London my Oz. Like many of the contributors to this book, I couldn't wait to escape from small town to big town and find fellow day-dreamers anxious to find a place big enough to accommodate their imaginations.

For any creative individual the lure and excitement of the capital was, and still is, unavoidable. So it seemed interesting to think about creating a kind of gauge, a measure of the effect London has had on fashion practitioners past, present and future.

Under the inspirational guidance of my tutors on the MA Fashion Curation course at London College of Fashion, Alistair O'Neill and Judith Clark, my mind had been opened not only to what fashion can be, but how our understanding of it can be altered by the perspective we use when we look at it. And this idea of perspective in relation to London is reflected in the publication's title.

The Measure has grown from a commission received in the closing weeks of my MA. I have always made books as the means to express my ideas, albeit in an amateur way, so this was to be my first publication. The original brief was to create a

graduate project in the form of a book that would mark the college's centenary. But I wanted to see if I could stretch this brief by commissioning articles, interviews and first-hand narratives around the concept of looking more broadly at the creative capital. Reflecting on how I was encouraged as a student, it seemed important to me to create something that looked outwards from the college, beyond its buildings and into the city.

London has become home to creative practitioners from all over the world, and as this book reveals, the longer you stay in the capital, the more you become part of London and the more London becomes part of you. This is confirmed by a range of recently published academic texts that have explored the relationship between London and fashion in cultural and historical terms.

As Londoners we draw our own individual maps of the city that delineate our inspirations, daily life and routines. This book, can therefore, be seen as an alternative atlas, a creation of individual maps of experience and effect, each person in some way influenced by the multifarious qualities of the capital. The book itself reflects the very fabric of London.

The eclectic nature of submissions in terms of content and approach, size and accent, mimics the very place of which they speak: a cacophony of voices, some still students when the

pieces were written; some industry leaders at the pinnacle of their careers – but all with the same passion for place, celebrating the effect the capital has had upon their work.

This multifaceted perspective reflects an ongoing interest in how viewpoint can alter our perception. Continuing a long-standing collaboration with the graphic designer William Hall, these ideas have become part of the book's design: Hall has designed an object that insists on movement in order to engage with its contents. By presenting text and image at converse angles, the book can be read either as a visual essay, a continuous text or, if you are willing to keep moving, as the world of fashion insists, you can obtain an all-encompassing vista of the voices and ideas that make up *The Measure*.

The input and enthusiasm of those who have contributed to the book has been extraordinary. Contacting leading figures in the world of fashion as a recent graduate and asking them to place faith in the project was obviously not an easy task, but I was met with outstanding generosity. As the political and economic conditions for students and graduates alike become ever harder, the need to support creative talent in what is now considered to be one of the most expensive cities in the world is imperative. The contributors to *The Measure* have generously given their time and energy to help raise funds through sales of this book. This will allow a future generation of students to make their own journeys towards this unique capital city.

Anomalies from the London College of Fashion archive: *fashion for industry*, garments made by final year students from the department of clothing and technology, 1978

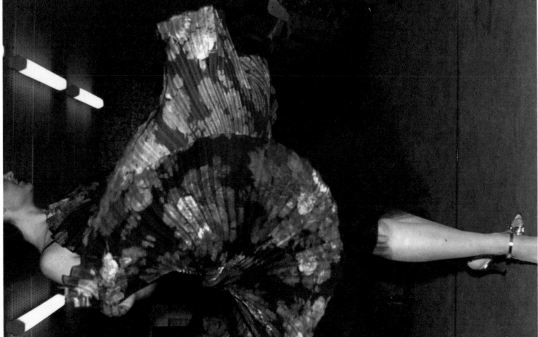

Introduction
Giles Deacon

I am often asked in interviews, why do you stay in London? This almost incredible question quite amazes me as the answer seems so obvious. I find London one of the most culturally and artistically diverse and exciting cities in the world – of all the places I have worked and travelled in I am constantly excited by the city. Nowhere in the world can you go so quickly from looking in a fantastic bookshop such as Claire de Rouen on Charing Cross Road to a museum and a sex shop, all within five minutes walk of each other.

Music, clubs and streets are continually reinventing themselves with new tribes appearing at the most unlikely of junctures. Throw in some of the best music venues and cinemas and you have a start in understanding why colleges such as London College of Fashion, where I am Designer in Residence, continue to produce such exciting and influential students.

It is this innovative city that inspires so much that is key to the future of the students who graduate. Living and working within London, senses are sharpened, opinions are formed and expressions are given the opportunity to be displayed. Individuality is welcomed and encouraged so as not to kill a spirit young, which often occurs elsewhere, and together with inspirational lecturers, skilled technicians and science-lab-like technology, students are given a hard-core base to launch from. I really think they are like ships operating in an inspirational Milky Way.

Giles Deacon: Look 37,
The Sonic Dress, A/W 2007

Introduction
Frances Corner

The Measure is an apt title for a publication celebrating the centenary of London College of Fashion and its role in the education of fashion students and the development of the London and UK fashion industries. Of the six constituent colleges within University of the Arts London, which include Camberwell, London College of Communication and Wimbledon, Central Saint Martins, Chelsea and London College of Fashion have a rich tradition of producing fashion graduates of world-class standard. These graduates, along with those from other London colleges such as the Royal College of Art, Kingston and Westminster, have helped London develop its great reputation for an approach to fashion that is creative, dynamic and at times irreverent. It is this approach and reputation that this publication seeks to celebrate.

These days we are all conscious of the part that fashion plays in our lives and the measure of its influence. Fashion is global in nature, it involves both high-tech manufacturing as well as craft skills, it embraces new technologies and in many ways drives their development, it encompasses major brands as well as niche designers, it involves the media and celebrity, yet it is inherently creative, imbuing us with our sense of identity and making us feel as though we as individuals are anticipating the future. What we have witnessed over the past hundred years is the development of an industry that at the outset of the twenty-first century makes a sign-ificant contribution to the economic, social and cultural life of the country.

London College of Fashion has played a significant role in the growth and development of fashion as an industry and a socio-cultural force. The college shares a proud history with constituent colleges whose names demonstrate their close relationship with the London fashion industry: Cordwainers, Leather Trade School, Barrett Street Technical College, Barrett Street Trade School, Clapham Trade School, Shoreditch Technical Institute Girls Trade School, Shoreditch College for the Garment Trades, Shoreditch College for the Clothing Industry and London College for the Garment Trades. These were all colleges whose purpose was to develop students who could confidently build careers in an industry that has many forms: from design and manufacture to styling, management, photography, footwear, accessories and journalism, to name but a few. London College of Fashion has thereby played a key part in the development of the fashion industry not only through its close connections to the fashion industry itself, but most particularly through the education of creative, dynamic and enterprising graduates.

This great college has thereby fashioned its future as well as those of its students and the industry. The measure of its success is that its current status reflects the great changes that have taken place over the past hundred years, both with

Janet Hanlon: *Future Body Connection*, London College of Fashion MA, 2007

Sooy Pak: *Duality*, London College of Fashion MA, 2007

Yoni Pai: *s/he*, London College of Fashion MA, 2007

regard to the higher education sector but also the fashion industry itself. It has students from further education to research and from all parts of the world. Its subject areas encompass all aspects of the fashion industry and its staff are active industry specialists and researchers. Yet in many ways London College of Fashion is true to its original founding principles. It is passionate about all that fashion is and can be. It has excellent links to industry ensuring it is at the cutting edge of what the industry is and needs to be. It is committed to providing students with excellent teaching and learning opportunities with access to the latest technology and it keeps in contact with its graduates as they move through the industry so that they can provide opportunities for current students and ensure that the college keeps its fingers on the fashion pulse.

Like the original constituent colleges, London College of Fashion has ambitious plans for its future and the next hundred years. The aim is to be the foremost higher educational institution for fashion education, research and practice in the world. A leading partner and advisor to the creative industries, government and policy makers, it will be an influential shaper in the debate about the powerful role that fashion plays in contemporary life.

London College of Fashion recognises that part of fashion's power is the fact that it is a collective activity, composed of a chain of interlocking and intersecting components dedicated to production and consumption. Maintaining its central role in all these activities will be a crucial aspect of the college's future, but more particularly will be the leading part that the college will play in the debates about sustainability, ethics, the social and environmental costs of fashion, the relationship between fashion and the nation's well-being, the incorporation of new technologies into clothing, marketing and distribution processes and the effects of globalisation. The college has the chance to exploit its leading position by incorporating these new agendas into the education of its students and the research and consultancy of its staff, thereby spreading the influence of fashion and supporting its establishment as a vital academic discipline for the coming century.

Qian Yu: *Meridian*, London College of Fashion MA, 2007

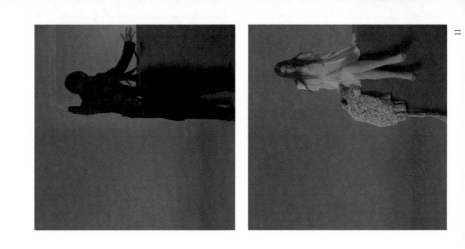

Fashion Captial

Golden Talents without Sliver Spoons
Colin McDowell

Compared to Paris, Milan and New York, its upmarket fashion siblings, London seems a bit of an upstart, a cheeky chappy. The reason isn't difficult to find. Whereas the other fashion capitals are driven by profit, London designers have always been driven by creative radicalism, without ever compromising their extreme originality simply in order to make money.

It's an attitude bred in the bone and comes from our uniquely stratified social system which, coupled with an egalitarian approach to education, means that students do not necessarily need rich parents in order to go to college. In fact, even now I suspect that a high percentage of fashion students are the first generation in their family to receive tertiary education.

This gives them a huge advantage and also quite a large disadvantage. The advantage is that they enter the system with few preconceived ideas and are therefore creatively free. The disadvantage is that they are usually dirt poor. In fact, both states are excellent for the radical new thinking, which leads to extreme creativity. I am much more inclined to believe that something really exciting and important will come out of the student whose family live in Byker or work in local factories and supermarkets than one who remembers the smell of his mother's perfume and the touch of her mink as she picked him up for a kiss before stepping out into Sloane Square.

And I know I am right because history supports my theory. Not one of the great London designers who have stormed the fashion world in the last thirty years came from a privileged background. Most of them knew, if not poverty, then certainly no luxuries in their youth. And that was important because it enabled them to dream, to imagine a different world, a world they could make for themselves alone. There is no more potent catalyst for creativity.

Vivienne Westwood, Bill Gibb, Ossie Clark and Zandra Rhodes all came from very normal, ordinary backgrounds. John Galliano's dad was a plumber; Alexander McQueen's was a taxi driver. The list could go on but, instead, I want to go back. To the class system that I mentioned earlier. Of course, to judge people by their wealth, or their family background, is limited and stupid, but that does not mean that a rigid social system (and it is still much more rigid than we are prepared to admit) is necessarily stultifying for creativity.

In fact, I believe it is the opposite. Whether in the field of the arts, society or humanities, creative, original thinking stems from the desire to change the known way, to question the accepted norms and to find new paths. If you perceive yourself as being an outsider, the desire is stronger – so much so that true originality can be seen as a battle cry against the old system.

Did Wagner want to write music like Beethoven's? Was Picasso overshadowed by Rembrandt? We all know the answer. And, just like them, each great creator begins with a desire to do something which will make all that has gone before seem irrelevant.

This doesn't mean that they are barbarians intent on smashing the system. All creators know that there is no such thing as a vacuum. They must use what has gone before, not to copy but to make their own bricks which will eventually create their entirely unique and modern edifice. And they always do it better if they stand outside the system. The artist starving in a garret rather than compromise his integrity is a nineteenth-century cliché, but it is a truism that it was because those artists were outside society and rejected its values that they made their mark and in some cases changed things – not forever, but until the next radical genius came along. I believe that students – poor and misunderstood, blah, blah (we've all heard the moans a thousand times) – are today's artists in a garret.

What they have in common with their predecessors is the public's total indifference to them and what they are doing – until they do something so stupendous that it can't be ignored. Then people will sit up and take notice and, after a while, somebody will take a chance and give money – not much! – to some young hopeful to take an idea forward.

And the long haul begins. There are no quick fixes in London fashion and very few pots of gold at the end of the road. Vivienne Westwood lived for years in a council flat and cycled to work; John Galliano used to sleep on mates' floors because he didn't have the bus fare home. Even today, London designers whose names are well known and whose careers seem successful spend sleepless nights worrying about cash flow. There are no easy paths, and neither should there be. Like nature, which scatters pollen everywhere in the hope that some will connect, fashion colleges overproduce and their graduates and postgraduates have to be tempered in the furnace of life and experience if they are to turn their skills to gold.

And that is the most exciting part for me. The watching, the waiting, the hoping and praying that a young designer in whom you believe will actually be able to fulfil a potential. That is why London Fashion Week, even at its worst – and it has at times been very bad – is often more challenging and stimulating than Paris, Milan or New York. It is the very slickness and guarantee of success you find in those cities – who can afford to be allowed to fail when so much money has been invested? – which makes them so predictable, even in excellence.

Just as we know that Miuccia Prada or Jean Paul Gaultier will never fail to stimulate and will always be technically superb, so, in London, we know that there are no guarantees. And you know what? I prefer it that way. And here's why. The big international fashion names predictably follow their well-formed creative personae. Our young hopefuls are like little children learning to walk. Their pace is not consistent. Two steps can be followed by a fall. But as long as we allow then to make their mistakes, whilst helping them to recover, London fashion will be just fine, and some day might learn to run again.

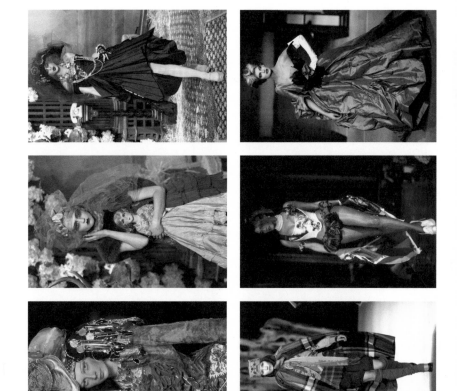

Fashion Capital
Alannah Weston

'I have heard that something very shocking indeed will soon come out in London,' wrote Jane Austen; but it could just as easily have been a foreign fashion editor writing in anticipation of London Fashion Week.

Throughout the last century, London has been the nursery of the *enfant terrible*, whether in art, fashion, music, books or architecture. It is the place to say the unsayable, wear the unwearable, build the unbuildable.

Irreverence, imagination, innovation, these are what make London different from other cities, and Selfridges has always been part of that distinctive personality. From Gordon Selfridge's flying fashion show in 1909, to Spenser Tunick's photograph of hundreds of naked people on the escalator, Selfridges has never been afraid to surprise, entertain and even shock.

But to sustain this kind of creative energy, we are constantly in search of real talent, the kind of people that London College of Fashion nurtures: you will find the college's graduates amongst the designers that we carry, but also amongst our salespeople, window designers, buyers, and graphic designers.

Fashion show in the Water Garden. Roof of Selfridges deparment store, Oxford Street, London ca. 1929

Fashion Capital

London: a right proper place that finally 'made me'
Wayne Hemingway

Wayne in Camden, 1980

I was born in Morecambe, on the north-west Lancashire coast, and whilst you wouldn't recognise the town as being an overly cultural hub now, throughout the '60s it was a cultural hot spot, a seaside town that didn't just attract retirees, but also a creative young crowd. My mum and her cool bunch of friends would hang out at Brubeck's coffee bar on the prom. There was the iconic Oliver Hill's art deco, Eric-Gill-interior-designed Midland Hotel (where in room sixteen, yours truly was conceived!), and there were a couple of wonderful structures that, at the time, filled me with dread as I was coerced into talent contests and amateur dramatics: Harry Graham's art deco bandstand and the Victorian Winter Gardens concert hall.

Approaching secondary education my family moved to a Lancashire mill town, Blackburn. It was Blackburn and a clutch of other Lancashire towns that were formative in building my cultural DNA and influencing my career in the creative industries. Apart from my beloved Blackburn Rovers (which I don't think counts as culture does it?), my memories are all built around a stimulating local youth culture. At the time, it wasn't the brooding architecture of King George's Hall that made it so attractive, and back then I couldn't see that this impressive building built in Blackburn's textile heyday might one day form a 'placemaking' icon in the town's regeneration. It was being an eleven-year-old and starting to find my

musical and fashion feet by going to see the Sweet and Slade, it was David Bowie on his Ziggy Stardust tour in 1972, and the furore surrounding the fact that he sang 'Life on Mars' wearing just some white Y-fronts and make-up, and it was Blondie and Stiff Little Fingers up on King George's Hall stage that give me my home town's cultural resonance.

There was Ribchester, a little village outside Blackburn. As a teenager I would walk six miles to Roxy and Bowie Nights and to see early performances of the Sex Pistols, Boomtown Rats and the Rezillos. When I visit family, Ribchester has become a place to walk by the Ribble, or visit a newfangled gastropub, or the Roman Museum, but it is its musical cultural legacy that has cemented Ribchester in my conscience and which draws me back.

Wigan is another Lancashire town that has a special attraction for me. As a thirteen-year-old, it provided a venue, the youth culture holy grail that was the home of Northern Soul, Wigan Casino, where I would stand on my tiptoes wearing platforms (which I would put into my badge-covered, check shopping bag and replace with flat leather-soled dancing brogues once safely past the bouncers). One of the aims of my company, HemingwayDesign, is to get involved in the regeneration of Blackpool and this stems from the fact that it housed my favourite disco; of all time, the legendary Highland Room at the Blackpool Mecca, where

Wayne and Diversen, 1981

disco and modern dance music developed in the UK. Actually maybe the Mecca wasn't my favourite disco; maybe I should say it was Wednesdays at Angels in Burnley, where I met my wife, Gerardine, twenty-six years ago!

With some ten O levels and four A levels (mostly at A grade may I add) I left school to study in London. I had no vocational desire to pursue a career in my chosen field of study, Geography and Town Planning, but rather a burning desire to immerse myself in London's youth culture that hitherto I had watched and read about from 250 miles up the M6. I dived head first into London's club culture, moving nightly from soul clubs to rockabilly to electronic. Every night was like a mass public catwalk show and half the fun, as someone obsessed with visuals, was looking at the crowds in the queues outside pleading for doormen like Boy George to let them in. Today I still navigate my way around central London by the location of the clubs where Gerardine and I developed our style and culture knowledge that would serve us so well in the development of Red or Dead and latterly HemingwayDesign. It was the Beat Route on Greek Street, and we navigated and were drawn to Covent Garden via the Blitz Club rather than the Opera House.

It was the vibrant and fast-moving late '70s and early '80s youth-culture scene that enabled Gerardine and I to establish Red or Dead in Camden Market. After punk, Joy Division and the New Romantic movement, the important and lucrative world's youth culture was looking to England and in particular London. A new form of cultural tourism was starting to rival those coming to view Britain's cathedrals and historic buildings. We were able to capitalise on this by selling sack loads of Dr Martens to French, Spanish, German, Italian and American tourists. Buyers from Macy's New York were seduced by London's youthful cultural vibrancy and visiting our little stall in Kensington Market, where Gerardine would sit sewing individual items on her little machine, they placed Red or Dead's first big export order, and a business was born that would ultimately employ hundreds of young people, have shops around the world, and which we would eventually sell for a substantial sum. It was London Fashion Week that became our window to the world.

In the sphere of design where HemingwayDesign now spends most of its time, placemaking, the places that we have been inspired by – the regeneration schemes of Malmö in Sweden, Freiberg and Kronsberg in Germany, Ijberg, Almere and Leidsche Rijn in the Netherlands – have become design and cultural tourism brands in their own right. But the liveability that London has given us through its great parks, easily navigable streets and great public transport system, the easy mix of cultures and social strata has been our 'education' and helped us to formalise and deliver the housing development that has catapulted us into the most exciting, fulfilling and meaningful part of our career, the Staiths South Bank in Gateshead.

Keeping our office and a bolthole in London, a decade ago we moved out of the city and built a home near the sea on the south coast. It's been a wonderful place to bring up our four children, but now that the elder three are well into their clubbing and gigging years, the cultural magnet of London has become stronger for them and they are choosing to study and work there. But one thing I can't do is support a London football club!

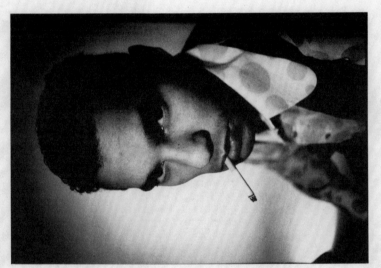

The New Red Or Dead Collection
With Love , McKitterick

Stand B81 British Designers Show , Olympia 11-14 March

the new shop is now open at:
61 neal street, london w.c.2.
other shops at:
22 rupert street, london w.1.
186 camden high street, london n.w.1.
52 church street, manchester

Fashion Capital
Jane Shepherdson

I started out working as an allocator for Topshop in the late '80s. Fresh from college, I was super keen and eager to do anything that was asked of me, so desperate was I to get to the revered status of buyer. The buyers at Topshop in those days were a frighteningly glamorous group of women who wielded a huge amount of power, and let everyone know it. They power dressed like an '80s woman should, with tight black Lycra and large shoulder pads. Harvey Nichols was the place to shop; none of them would have been seen dead in Topshop. Hair was big, and so was the jewellery – there was no subtlety here. I, on the other hand, had been a student until recently, and had no money – and had no desire to emulate these creatures.

Best-sellers meetings, the weekly staple of any fashion retailer – where the best-selling garments from the previous week are held up for all the buying community to look at and digest – were an occasion for the buyers to hold up each item, and look pityingly at it, as if it was unbelievable that someone would have bought it, followed by a laugh as if to say, fooled them again! Not all the buyers were like that; some were conscientious and professional, but nearly all lacked a real passion for what they were doing, which I found incredible, as this seemed to me the best career in the world. That was my introduction to buying, twenty years ago, and I've been doing it pretty much ever since, at various levels within Topshop.

Things have changed significantly since the '80s. For one thing, it has got tougher. In those days the competition was such that a relatively cheap, basic T-shirt in a few easy colours would sell tens of thousands each week, for a whole season. In fact they probably sold at pretty much the same price that they sell for today, due to the continued deflation of clothing prices over the years.

The '90s saw the emergence of the discount retailers for the first time, and many retailers went out of business, as their large overheads meant that they couldn't compete with these new pared-down traders buying up cancellations and selling them to ecstatic customers who couldn't believe their luck. That rather forced the large retailers to decide what they were going to be, as going for price alone wasn't an option.

This was a great opportunity for Topshop, as we decided that we would become the 'World's Fashion Authority' – a very grand vision for what was then a slightly shabby teen retailer, but we had passion, we were creative, and we knew that we could do it. We decided that we would never offer anything that we weren't proud of, even if it was selling very well, and in that way our customers would begin to recognise that our clothes were different, and that they could trust us to deliver.

This decade has brought with it a new breed of discounters, who have realised that just being cheap isn't

Window display at Topshop,
The Strand, 1988

enough, and they have added catwalk fashion to the mix. It's an addictive combination, throwaway fashion that is so cheap that it can be cast aside even before it becomes passé. Alongside this rampant consumerism, another sector is emerging: the ethical fashion retailer, for the growing number of consumers who want to wear fashionable, well-designed clothes, but not at someone else's expense. There is a lot of work to be done if these companies are to achieve any kind of scale, and the clothes themselves need an injection of excitement to live up to the expectations of a newly aware consumer, but the will is there, and I'm behind it all the way.

Indeed many other retailers took the same route, in that they decided they needed a vision to survive, and the ones that followed it through succeeded. Chelsea Girl became River Island, and established a handwriting that works for them today. French Connection became the epitome of cool, laid back style for many years, until the unfortunate fcuk got in the way.

The last few years have seen the emergence of European retailers entering the market, and teaching us all a thing or two. H&M made the first move, selling very cheap casual clothes, with an outrageously expensive ad campaign that changed the whole dynamic. They were followed by Zara, whose faultless retail execution, and quick, cheap catwalk copies made everyone sit up and listen.

Every new entry into the market helps to move it forward, and forces existing retailers to try new and different concepts and innovations.

The growth of e-tailing is having a double effect. Not only are retailers now investing heavily in their websites – Topshop employs a young team of professionals to come up with new ideas every day, including blogs, podcasts of London Fashion Week, and interactive competitions – but they also need to make sure that their actual stores are exciting enough to warrant a real instead of a virtual visit. This has seen a resurgence in the use of visual and creative in-store talent, which has led to some very exciting retail concepts throughout the sector.

I think that looking to the future, we should expect to see greater and greater creativity in stores, and in the way they are merchandised, purely to tempt us into them. Retailers with a clear vision of what they are and where they are going will be the winners, and the followers and copiers will suffer. The discounters are back again, probably not for too long, as they are sucking choice out of the market, but as long as they are, competing on price alone isn't an option. That said, the UK high street is an amazing and constantly changing place, and I wouldn't be anywhere else.

Window display at Topshop, Oxford Circus, 2007

NEWGEN SPONSORED BY TOPSHOP

Christopher Kane, Danielle Scutt, Duro Olowu, Eley Kishimoto, Gareth Pugh, Louise Goldin, Marios Schwab, Noki, Emma Cook, Roksanda Ilincic, Basso & Brooke, Marios Schwab, Todd Lynn, Bora Aksu, Erdem, Sheila la Marca, Meadham Kirchhoff, Modernist, Osman Yousefzada, Peter Pilotto

LONDON FASHION WEEK

In his writings on life in Paris in the nineteenth century, the philosopher Walter Benjamin produced what he described as 'unofficial history' by sifting through 'the debris of mass culture'. These days this is common practice and I make no claim for original philosophical intent behind my book *The Look: Adventures in Rock & Pop Fashion* by adopting the same approach. However, I became aware during *The Look*'s seven-year gestation that, by scrutinising the detail where fashion and popular music intersect, I was discovering an alternative narrative to the by now standard story of pop from Elvis to Emo.

It's apposite – since London College of Fashion perches on its northwestern corner and has developed many and varied associations with the area over the last century – that Soho emerges as a rich seam in this narrative, one which runs in my book from the Lithuanian émigré Cecil Gee providing for lindy-hopping forties spivs in Shaftesbury Avenue to Shop at Maison Bertaux supplying the new millennial demi-monde in Greek Street today.

When considering time and space, another of Benjamin's concerns was transformation, and again Soho has played a role; the laissez-faire attitude engendered here over hundreds of years has allowed freedoms of every sort – social, educational, economic, racial, religious, sexual, creative, criminal – and so transformed thousands, if not millions, of lives.

One aspect of this is the inherent duality of the square mile-and-a-half. While it is set within solid and readily defined boundaries (Oxford Street and Shaftesbury Avenue to the north and south, Regent Street and Charing Cross Road to the east and west), once inside Soho, there exists an elasticity of time, gender, class, legality and attitude. This was first expressed in the all-day immigrant coffee houses of the seventeenth and eighteenth centuries, then the music halls, theatres and brothels of the nineteenth century and the nocturnal clip joints, 'kayfs', drinkers and spielers of its heyday from the 1920s to the '60s, where the consecutive strictures of the Depression, World Wars and austerity were flouted in a never-ending spree of wreckless living.

From Karl Marx to Dylan Thomas to Francis Bacon, from Thomas de Quincy to Quentin Crisp to Jimi Hendrix, from Huguenots and Maltese to Poles, Greeks, Russians and Chinese, all these and more – students, strippers, day-trippers, thrill-seekers, boozers, losers, office workers on the tear and hapless tourists – have descended daily, many these days attracted by Old Compton Street, which was granted London's 'gay village' status when pedestrianised in the mid-nineties, just as Carnaby Street was confirmed as the centre of Swinging London when paved over three decades earlier.

The geographical demarcation which makes Soho a destination was first outlined in 1536, when the area

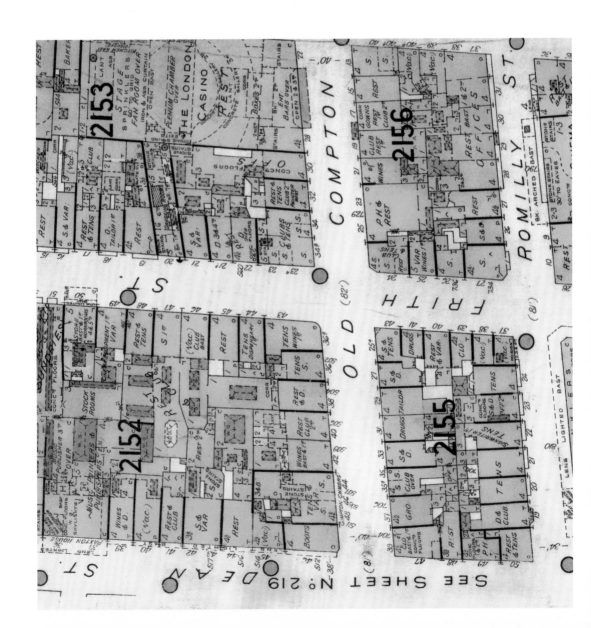

was declared a royal hunting ground by Henry VIII, with borders marked by blue-painted posts. These points were subsequently occupied by inns and lodges named Blue Posts, some of which exist as pubs of the same name to this day, notably in Kingly Street and Berwick Street. Popular say-so has it that the name is derived from the hunting cry 'So-ho!' though it has also been credited to the Duke of Monmouth's battle rally to his troops; he was one of the area's first landowners and named an early home here Soho House.

In 1660 the Crown granted Soho patricia to Henry Jermyn, the Earl of St Albans, and in 1677 builder Richard Frith embarked on substantial property development. Soho wasn't taken up by society and the fashionable moved into neighbouring Mayfair and Belgravia, leaving room for settlement by London's first substantial arrival of immigrant occupants, French Huguenots. Protestants fleeing religious persecution, in time they built properties of their own in the Huguenot style. Some of their architecture remains; there are fine examples in Meard Street.

Throughout the 1700s and the 1800s, theatres, tailors, restaurants, pubs, coffee houses and prostitution thrived as fresh waves of immigrants imprinted their nationalities on thoroughfares such as Poland Street and Greek Street.

Piccadilly boomed when the Ritz was opened in 1906, spilling its swanky residents into the Soho hinterland. The same year saw the opening of Shoreditch Technical Institute Girls Trade School (which was eventually brought together with Barrett Street Trade School in 1967 to form London College of Fashion and Clothing Technology).

In 1907 the young Arthur Ransome published his first book, *Bohemia in London*, the introduction to which neatly summed up the aspirations of Soho's denizens: 'I wanted to write a book that would make real on paper the strange, tense, joyful and despairing, hopeful and sordid life that is lived in London by young artists and writers.'

Of course much of this innocence was dashed by the grim experiences of the First World War, but nevertheless by the mid-twenties Soho expressed the spirit of the bright young things with the opening of the Gargoyle, a rooftop venue overseen by the exquisite David Tennant at the corner of Dean and Meard Streets and entered by a rickety lift. This drew fresh swarms of madmen and misfits, as the late Michael Luke described in his book *David Tennant and the Gargoyle Years*. While the Moorish interior was adorned with fragments of eighteenth-century glass in tribute to founding member Henri Matisse, notables such as Augustus John, Dylan Thomas, Tallulah Bankhead and Noel Coward cavorted.

Time is ever fluid in Soho, even during the most pressing circumstances. Let's not forget how the Blitz was insouciantly ignored by the Windmill Theatre, whose wartime motto 'We Never Close' was stubbornly upheld by owner Vivien Van Damm so that pretty ingénues and leathery harridans could unburden themselves of their clothing for the light relief of rain-coated gentlemen while V-2s buzzed outside.

A decade-and-a-half after the end of the war the pop singer and actor Adam Faith was exclaiming: 'There's a place for you!' in his 2/6d 'candid' paperback self-portrait *Poor Me*. Although Faith may as well have been enthusing about Soho, he was in fact referring to the Two I's at 59 Old Compton Street. Named after the original owners, the Irani brothers, this opened during the coffee-bar boom of the post-war years stimulated by the arrival in this country of 15,000 Italians escaping Mussolini and his henchmen. Coffee bars embodied much-needed exoticism in those austere times; Soho can claim Britain's first espresso bar opening, Pino Riservato's the Moka, at 29 Frith Street in 1953.

Since National Service wasn't finally phased out until 1958, these were also the years when the nation's young were afforded tiny windows of leisure time between school-leaving and embarkation on employment in jobs expected to last their entire working lives. Imported American jazz, blues, folk and rock 'n' roll – from shops such as Harlequin on the corner of Old Compton and Dean Streets –

Architect's drawing of the proposed London College of Fashion building superimposed on a photograph of Oxford Circus, 1959

sparked the fad for home-made skiffle. When Australian former wrestlers Ray Hunter and Paul Lincoln bought the Two I's in 1956, they surfed the craze by encouraging teens into performances for regular customers.

That same year the first phase of Britain's original youth cult, Ted, had reached its apotheosis, according to the social observer Nik Cohn. The young peacocks who had mimicked the Savile Row fashions of 1949 by adopting and adapting the garb of the last golden age of our history – the Edwardian era – were soon replaced by beetle-crusher-wearing, flick-knife-wielding creeps who espoused racist, sexist and homophobic views and resisted any change beyond the primal rock 'n' roll hewn by originals such as Elvis and Jerry Lee Lewis.

As so often in Britain, the class divide came into play as the upwardly mobile and plain middle class skiffle-ites, students, beatniks and coffee-bar habitués developed a more inclusive attitude, delighting in discussing politics, art and literature while listening to roots and Americana, paving the way for the three distinct youth groups who replaced Ted: buffoonish trad jazz fans, 'bohemian' folkies and the Europe-embracing modernists.

That's why Vince Man's Shop – arguably the world's first menswear boutique – stressed Continental styles from its premises on the corner of Newburgh and Ganton Streets. The Vince ad which appeared in *What's On In London* in 1957 featured then-model and Mr Universe finalist Sean Connery in Capri shirt, pale-blue-denim cuffed jeans and espadrilles.

Vince was another person transformed by Soho. He was in fact 'physique photographer' Bill Green, who started his rag-trade career by adapting and tightening M&S swimming trunks for his muscle-flexing models at his studio. A mail order business led to the opening of Vince's at the same site in 1954, with stock including hipsters and matelot shirts. Such fashions fitted perfectly into the Soho atmosphere and inspired John Michael Ingram to open Sportique in Old Compton Street, offering flat-fronted voile shirts and Madras jackets.

Sean Connery in advertisement for Vince Man's Shop. *What's On In London*, 12 July 1957

Article: John Stephen and the Carnaby Street Revolution, *Life* magazine, 13 May 1966

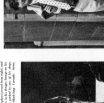

John Stephen turned from right) and customers in his London lounge as his Cadillac, parked by one of his shops in fast-thickening Carnaby Street.

A a fashion shot of John Stephen clothes at Saxs Brothers in New York, London has taken up to McGregor for a shirt (right, 67), then in with-the-season no-to-the-contrasting collar and cuffs.

Pete shoes, popular along Carnaby Street, are taken up by McGregor.

T[...body text...]

It all started in London
and it's making a smash here

McGregor's version of the Mod's fitted newlearth sweater (above) is called the London row and costs 55/. The side bib comes with the corduroys.

Hair-riving collar and the flared pattern are Carnaby trends in shirts. This McGregor collar row a full turn higher than normal. The shirt costs 47.

McGregor's Moddy blade (opposite) in this outfit. The sloped double-breasted jacket (65) of herringbone tweed has speaks on the shoulder.

McGregor's snazz blazer (left) has deep side vents, costs 6 6/6. The checked wool pants (59) are shin-lipped but still bear enough width to flare loose.

CONTINUED

1956 also witnessed the double death-blow to Britain's claims to political hegemony when Atlee's government eschewed the opportunity to become a signatory to the Treaty of Rome and simultaneously plunged the country into the unwinnable Suez Crisis. Thus our political leaders stuck their heads in the sand while the denizens of Soho made the wise choice and quietly clung to the Continent; after all, many had no choice as first generation Brits. Espresso was sipped at Bar Italia, wine was guzzled at the French and goulash consumed at the Gay Hussar.

Back at the Two I's business boomed, and the newly attuned British music business came a-hunting – 'Soho!' – with TV cameras and newspapermen joining the chase. In the process the small downstairs space became the crucible of British rock 'n' roll, spawning the mainstream likes of Tommy Steele and Cliff Richard (groomed into changing their respective names from Thomas Hicks and Harold Webb) as well as Faith himself (real name Terence Nelhams). By the time he came to publish *Poor Me* at the age of twenty-five, Faith boasted of raking in £50,000 a year, having scored hits such as the hiccoughing *What Do You Want?* and having starred in the John Barry-scored exploitation movie *Beat Girl*.

Faith was an early customer of showbusiness tailor Dougie Millings, whose cutting rooms were a couple of doors down from the Two I's. When Brian Epstein escorted the Beatles to Millings' first-floor premises at 63 Old Compton Street in November 1962, John Lennon instructed Dougie: 'Don't make us look like the Shadows.' So he came up with the classic collarless Beatles jacket based on a thirties railway attendant's jacket, helping along the transformation of the four surly ex-rockers into the greatest pop group of all time.

The Two I's transformed the lives of many: future Led Zeppelin manager, the tougher-than-tough Peter Grant, worked the door, while Rolling Stones' schemer Andrew Loog Oldham was a washer-up there. Glam-pop producer Mickie Most served up 'froffy' coffee and the teenage Lionel Bart, Oscar-winner for *Oliver!*, swept the floor. All of

The Beatles surround tailor Dougie Millings and his family, with son Gordon far left, 1964

these were baptised in Soho: toothy ex-merchant seaman Steele; Lucknow-born, curled-lip Richard; oversized, aggressive Grant, who weighed in at twenty-three stone by the time he had notched up as many years; ambitious Most (in reality north Londoner Michael Hayes); epicene Oldham; and gay, working class, Jewish, left-wing East-ender Bart (real name Lionel Begleiter).

Having wormed his way into Tin Pan Alley via the Two I's, Bart knocked out groundbreaking British rock 'n' roll hits before embarking on the musical *Fings Ain't Wot They Used T'Be* for the socialist impresario Joan Littlewood's British People's Theatre Workshop. This was based on the writings of Frank Norman, whose street-level memoirs *Bang to Rights* and *Stand On Me* remain as ripe texts of Soho living from a tantalisingly recent bygone age. Just as rewarding is Wolf Mankowitz's bitter cinematic masterpiece about the pop process, *Expresso Bongo*, starring Cliff Richard as the immortally-named Bongo Herbert. Just as 1956 proved a landmark in our political and social lives, so 1959 was a very good year for Soho; *Expresso Bongo* hit cinemas, *Fings* opened and Norman published *Stand On Me*.

That same year an ex-employee of Vince Man's Shop, the Glaswegian John Stephen, opened his second boutique in Carnaby Street. Within half a decade he and partner Bill Franks were operating a clothing empire which fired Swinging London and clad the British Invasion of groups into the US. Among his biggest ventures was the 1965 opening of 25–55 Carnaby Street as his 'teen' store. 'Carnaby Street is my creation,' said John Stephen in 1967, the year Westminster Council paved Carnaby Street over, such was the tourist traffic. 'I feel about it the way Michelangelo felt about the beautiful statues he created.'

As London swung, Soho was taken over by the figures who exported British fashion and music all over the world. David Bowie would hang at La Giaconda coffee bar among the Tin Pan Alley music publishers and demo studios of Denmark Street, as the likes of the Rolling Stones and the Small Faces trouped past to record at Regent Sound in the same thoroughfare. While Mark Feld used his parents' fruit stall in Berwick Street for forays to establish himself as pop star Marc Bolan, Rod Stewart started his career busking in the area as harmonica player to folkie Wizz Jones.

It's also worth noting that the Jimi Hendrix Experience made their debut at the Bag O'Nails in Kingly Street in late 1966, and that the guitarist gave his very last perform-ance jamming with Eric Burdon & War at Ronnie Scott's in Frith Street on 16 September 1970. Hendrix died two days later. During his London sojourn, however, he was just another Soho regular, haunting the bars and shops, buying such regalia as the famous Hussar's waistcoat he wore for a shoot with friend and photographer Bruce Fleming in Carnaby Street.

Hendrix was a prodigious shopper who purchased far and wide, often crossing town to visit Chelsea's King's Road. A particular favourite was the extraordinary boutique Granny Takes a Trip, one of whose founders, John Pearse, started his working life as a Savile Row apprentice. More than two decades ago Pearse returned to his spiritual home, Soho, and since that time has established his reputation as one of England's greatest and most innovative bespoke tailors from his discreet premises in Meard Street.

While the breeding grounds for London punk in the seventies can be traced to the King's Road (where Malcolm McLaren, Vivienne West-wood and their coterie hatched their plans behind the shopfront façades of SEX and Seditionaries) and Ladbroke Grove (where the Clash coalesced), Soho naturally played a major part in that movement.

Central Saint Martins student and Sex Pistols bassist Glen Matlock recalls accompanying McLaren to such faded coffee bars as Le Macabre in Meard Street, while the group was set up with dingy rehearsal space just across Charing Cross Road in Denmark Place and socialised at the lesbian bar Louise's in Poland Street with such associates as style pioneer Philip Sallon. Sallon haunted the café of London College of Fashion with his sparring partner Boy George,

who worked in punky shops Fans in Old Compton Street, the Regal in Newburgh Street and the Foundry at 12 Ganton Street. These days George collaborates with another London College of Fashion alumna, singer Amanda Ghost.

Having tolerated punks at Wardour Street clubs the Marquee and Vortex, Soho opened its arms to the swarms of fashion students, musicians and oddballs who formed the post-punk New Romantic movement. Among them were Robert Elms and Melissa Caplan, respectively chronicler and designer of the style, while Elms and art students Graham Smith and Chris Sullivan also ran one of the first New Romantic club nights, on Mondays at St Moritz, 161 Wardour Street. Today Elms is a broadcaster, travel writer and style commentator, while Sullivan reinvented Soho nightlife in 1982 with the Wag club at the Whisky-a-Go-Go premises, 33–37 Wardour Street, which became a club culture phenomenon, eventually closing in 2001.

Another character who emerged in the mid-eighties, Mark Powell opened his own gentlemen's out-fitters at 11 Archer Street, championing traditionalism with flamboyant flourishes. These days he occupies an eyrie at the top of 12 Brewer Street, attracting clientele from Bryan Ferry and Kevin Rowland to Usher and Naomi Campbell.

With a more glam take on attire, the Glaswegian Pam Hogg proffered sexually alluring and confrontational designs at her outlet at 5 Newburgh Street in the nineties, helping regenerate that part of Soho which had become swamped by tourists and novelty stores.

For at least the last decade Soho style has been embodied in the partnership between Pippa Brooks and Max Karie, who met while the former was singing and the latter DJ'ing at Wardour Street haunt Fred's. Together they opened Shop at 4 Brewer Street in 1995, attracting a worldwide clientele, and today they have intriguing outlet Shop at Maison Bertaux, underneath the fabled patisserie at 28 Greek Street.

Soho's place as the centre for fashion

has too often been elbowed aside, not only by attention-grabbing professions such as sex and advertising, but also by the grander tailoring businesses occupying neighbouring Savile Row. It's ironic that the technical skill of the clothing is – and has been for centuries – realised in the sweatshops and the cutting rooms of Soho.

For an exhibition of Soho-related images from my book – some of which are reproduced here – I chose the French House in Dean Street, itself a haven for outsiders, not least when it became the London centre of the French resistance during the Second World War. General De Gaulle camped out at the French for long periods just as succeeding generations have camped it up there ever since.

Collectively these photographs tell the tale of the development of rock and pop fashion in the area over the last six decades. It is also my belief that they supply proof positive of the truth behind Adam Faith's claim that, in Soho, at least, there's a place for you.

Mark Powell in his Brewer Street studio, 2006

Chris Sullivan in New York, 1981

Pam Hogg live on stage, 1993

Fashion Capital

London and the Cinema
Pamela Church Gibson

The notion of 'London on film' does not, perhaps, possess the same resonance as, say, the idea of Paris on screen – or Rome. The Thames does not have the historical significance of the Tiber, whilst its bridges and banks do not offer the same romantic associations as those of the Seine, so carefully nurtured through photography and popular song. London's monuments and memorable squares are widely scattered; there is no visual coherence to its centre. Tourists are forced to negotiate a journey involving crowded streets and several bus rides if they are to see everything on their list.

Yet while London is not as photogenic nor glamorous a city as other European capitals, it has a complex and interesting relationship with cinema – complicated and even flawed, possibly, for a number of reasons which this essay will try to tease out. The physical nature of the city itself is part of the problem. Another is the sheer volume of films made once the British film industry was established with London as its epicentre, some of which were less than memorable, and others in a format – that of documentary, say – which was time-specific. For many, 'London on film' probably means a series of shots used to inform the viewer of the location, which include a glimpse of Big Ben, a Routemaster bus, and a black cab. Others might think, instead, of some of the better-known products of the British film industry – documentaries, the Ealing comedies, the so-called 'Swinging Sixties' films.

Arguably, London is too problematic a city to serve simply as a backdrop, though it has been used in this way by foreign directors. But its complex history and sprawling topography make for a different interplay between city and cinema. Its sheer size and sprawl create particular difficulties. London expanded at an extraordinary, relentless pace after the Industrial Revolution made Britain the 'workshop of the world'; in the 1780s it had a population of a few hundred thousand, while a hundred years later it was closer to two million. And the population expanded so much in so short a time that the city became – as it still is – vast, amorphous, muddled.

In nineteenth-century Paris the medieval remnants of the old capital were razed to the ground and replaced by a strategically planned city with wide boulevards and radial patterning, carefully designed by Haussmann to contain any civil insurrection. In New York, which also grew at a rapid pace, the slums of the early immigrants were demolished and then replaced by a grid-based, comprehensible city. London, however, simply evolved – and accommodated its new population by the simple strategy of overcrowding. This generated manifold and dreadful social problems – which in their turn created a climate of crusading criticism, into which cinema emerged. This tradition, partly bred within literature and the visual arts during the 150 years preceding its invention, gave a particular shape to indigenous British cinema – and to its depictions of the capital.

St Pauls Cathedral by Night engraving by Gustave Doré, 1857

Some of the most indelible images of London are found in the drawings of Hogarth, which form a fierce critique of life in the newly prosperous, swiftly growing city of the eighteenth century, to which the poor flocked in their thousands to find work. In his pictures we see the entire social spectrum, from the squalor and poverty of 'Gin Lane' to the self-regarding and amoral behaviour of the beau monde. Hogarth's centennial contemporary, William Blake, provided a similarly dark depiction of the chaotic city in 'London', one of the *Songs of Experience* (1794) where the narrator finds 'in every face I meet / Marks of weakness, marks of woe'.

The next century saw the continuation, within literature and the visual arts, of moves to highlight inequity, injustice and deprivation. Gustave Doré, who visited London in the late nineteenth century, produced one especially evocative image that would later be used by the set designer John Bryan in his work for David Lean's film *Great Expectations* (1947). In this engraving Doré shows St Paul's Cathedral at night; spectral and pure in the moonlight, it rises above the dark hotchpotch of brick back-to-back houses below, which seem to huddle together in the shadows, the chasms between them spanned by primitive wooden bridges. This picture seems to suggest two separate, coexisting communities – and to make visible the nature of these two 'Londons' was a central concern of both contemporary novelists and the film-makers who followed them.

In the later novels of Dickens the overcrowded, divided city provided not only the central subject matter, but gave the novels their particular form; his intricate plots revealed unexpected links between characters seemingly divided from each other by social status and economic situation. This was part of his growing determination that his devoted middle-class readers should fully understand the particular nature of their situation – and their consequent responsibilities. For his depiction of the different strands within the underworld of Victorian London, he drew heavily upon the writings of Henry Mayhew.

Mayhew was a pioneer of what we would call today 'investigative journalism'; he saw his role as revealing to his readers the nature – and the lower depths – of the city in which they lived. He conducted an extensive, exhaustive series of interviews with the poor and the petty criminals who made their living on the streets. They were published in book form in 1851 as *London Labour and the London Poor*. Charles Kingsley's sentimental novel *The Water Babies* (1863) dramatised the way in which Blake's infant chimney sweeps were still working – and dying – in London. And if Mrs Gaskell, in *North and South* (1855), had shown the sufferings of factory workers in the north, Dickens, Mayhew and Kingsley revealed that their poverty was mirrored within the heart of the capital itself.

So the use of print culture to ensure social awareness – and hopefully to bring about change – was firmly entrenched by 1896, when cinema came to London, and would lead to a particular strain of hard-edged realism within British urban cinema. Indeed, the best-known British directors working today are Ken Loach and Mike Leigh, who have both won prestigious awards at various European film festivals during their long careers – both continue to portray a bleak but instantly recognisable London. Leigh's film *Naked* (1993) finds its homeless protagonist Johnny spending his first night in London slumped in a shop doorway; Loach, whose career spans four decades, made *Poor Cow* in 1967 to puncture the myth of 'Swinging London' and show how for one impoverished young mother in the capital, life was dismal and difficult. Over twenty years later, Loach's film *Riff-Raff* (1990) focused on a group of regional labourers, working illegally in the capital under dangerous conditions – and won the International Critics Prize at the Cannes Film Festival.

Interestingly, the very first display of the Lumière Brothers' 'cinematograph' in London was at what we would now call a press screening, in February 1896, and it took place in the Polytechnic Institute in Regent Street, now the University of Westminster. Its home-grown rival, the 'Theatograph' of Robert Paul, was displayed in the extravagant Egyptian Hall in Piccadilly – whose doors

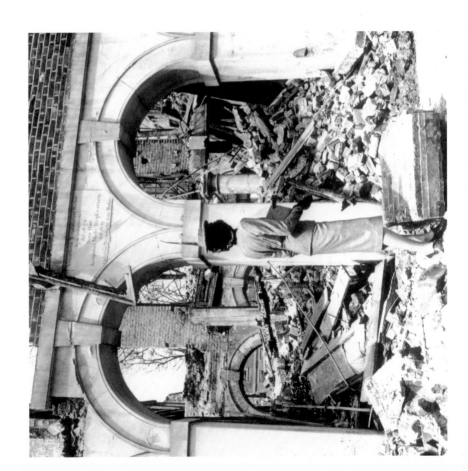

were guarded by statues of Isis and Osiris, now standing outside the doors of the Museum of London – and afterwards at the Alhambra Music Hall. So from the beginning screenings in the capital reflected what was to become the dual nature of British cinema – the escapism of the music hall and 'Egyptian' extravagance is matched by a pedagogic strain, an awareness that cinema's power can be fruitfully deployed.

In the same year the brothers themselves came to London to make two short films, *Pont de Westminster* and *Pont de la Tour* – the building of Tower Bridge had just been completed. Both bridges would go on to play their part in the developing iconography of London on film. Westminster, and of course Big Ben, is always part of the panoply of London landmarks in the 'establishing shots' within feature films – in fact, there seems to be a favourite place on the South Bank from which to film both the bridge and Big Ben.

Tower Bridge has had a varied life on camera. Its particular location meant that it appeared together with Bob Hoskins in *The Long Good Friday* (1980) in which he played a gangland boss with plans for the profitable development of the now-deserted dockyards. The wave of inferior crime films that followed all seemed to star ex-singers – Roger Daltrey as John McVicar, Phil Collins as Buster Edwards, and the Kemp brothers from Spandau Ballet as the Kray Twins. Ronnie and Reggie Kray had already been woven into the visual history of London when David Bailey included their portrait in his *Box of Pin-ups* (1965), a series supposedly intended to immortalise the key figures on the 'Swinging London' scene. Bailey's desire to find glamour within the grimier side of urban life might also have prompted his own earlier use of Tower Bridge in one of his first *Vogue* shoots in 1961; he photographed Shrimpton there, making her look dishevelled and hungover.

And Bailey himself inspired – if indirectly – one of the many films made in London by Continental directors following the example of the Lumière Brothers. *Blow-Up* (1966) is probably the best-known 'Swinging London' film, and the first film to be made by its director Antonioni

outside his native Italy. Adapting a popular novel of the time, he changed the profession of its anti-hero Thomas from painter to photographer, on the grounds that fashion photographers were 'of the moment'. He and his co-workers 'shadowed' Bailey; actor David Hemmings, who played Thomas, imitated Bailey's mannerisms and behaviour throughout. But the London we see is the London of the *fictional* photographer, who is happier taking photographs in a dosshouse and a deserted London park than working on a fashion shoot; he complains to his agent that he can't stand the fashion industry much longer. And despite the presence of Verushka, Jane Birkin, Peggy Moffitt and the Yardbirds, despite the mews flat that serves as a studio, the white Rolls-Royce convertible and the racks of Biba dresses, it is his misogyny and ennui that inform the film and its picture of London life.

Native British cinema worked in a rather different way to show the superficialities of fashionable London life. However, during the most productive years of the British film industry, film-makers with an active sense of social responsibility were – then as now – working side by side with those who had a simple fascination with the fantasy lives of the very rich. While the feature film *Dinner at the Ritz* (1937) shows just that – and stars a young David Niven in a dinner jacket – *Piccadilly* (1929) and *Kensington Calling* (1935) are documentaries which set out to show how, within the very heart of the West End, there was still hardship and even squalor for those lower down the socio-economic register.

The social documentary tradition has retained a role within British cinema. *The London Nobody Knows* (1967), narrated by actor James Mason, features the meths drinkers and malnourished children of the capital. In Patrick Keillor's *London* (1990) a narrator again leads us through lesser-known parts of the city, making us conscious of the complexity of contemporary London and its 'dark imperial past'. But arguably the 'finest hour' of the documentary film was the body of work directed by Humphrey Jennings for the Ministry of Information during the Blitz. And feature films of the time played their part – they too showed Londoners

heroic, stoic, coping and carrying on. A photograph by Cecil Beaton shows actress Valerie Hobson picking her way across a bomb site; this image appeared on the cover of the *Sketch* in December 1941, and has been reproduced endlessly. Those who have taken it for a fashion photograph are mistaken; it is in fact an image created on the set of the film *Unpublished Story*, which would be released in 1942. The heroine played by Hobson had abandoned her career for the duration – no longer a fashion writer, she is now a war reporter.

Post-war reconstruction was slow and piecemeal; bomb sites remained a distinctive feature of the London landscape for many years. They form a perfect playground for the East-End children of *Hue and Cry* (1946), the first Ealing comedy, and in a memorable climax hundreds of them swarm across a devastated 'wharf' to foil fur thieves. The ruins of the City represent the mythical wharf in Wapping. And it is bomb damage, too, which reveals to Stanley Holloway an ancient document proving that Pimlico is, in fact, a part of Burgundy – its prompt secession from London and its rationing restrictions causes the bureaucratic confusion of another Ealing comedy, *Passport to Pimlico* (1949). The last of these films, *The Ladykillers* (1955), was a very black comedy, involving the railway network, the Copenhagen tunnels behind King's Cross, and a truly menacing black-clad gangster, played by Herbert Lom. The house of the gentle old lady, Mrs Wilcox, which a gang of crooks use as the base for an elaborate robbery, was specially constructed at the end of Frederica Street in Barnsbury.

Until very recently British actors and actresses have rarely found success in Hollywood; Peter Sellers, who played one of the gang in *The Ladykillers*, was an exception. But the first British actors to be heralded as international stars both emerged from the 'Swinging Sixties' films – and have kept a distinctive London identity throughout their ensuing careers. Michael Caine achieved stardom with his portrayal of Harry Palmer – a cool, proletarian alternative to the suave public-school-and-Oxbridge figure of James Bond – in *The Ipcress File* (1965). He cemented his screen persona as the libidinous *Alfie* in 1966

David Bailey: Jean Shrimpton, *Vogue*, 1961

and is happy to be regarded as the archetypal East-End boy made good – provided that all letters are addressed to 'Sir Michael Caine', otherwise he will not open them. Julie Christie, who won an Oscar as the deceitful, ambitious fashion model in *Darling* (1965), is situated at the opposite end of the political spectrum – her image has always been that of the sixties bedsit bohemian, the middle-class hippy, commune dweller and free spirit. She dislikes publicity but has given financial backing and public endorsement to many low-budget left-wing films.

Never have young film-makers been more in need of help. In the eighties, British cinema fled backwards – into the eternal summer of Edwardian mythology and the safety of period drama – while official funding for new projects disappeared. Many directors looked to America for backing – and it was provided for *Four Weddings and a Funeral* (1994). This was the first Working Title film to star both Hugh Grant and a bizarre fantasy London, inhabited only by the young, photogenic, white and middle class. Its unprecedented success in America meant a raft of romantic comedies, all showcasing this same strange vision of London – locked private gardens in *Notting Hill* (1999), a gleaming tube train in *Sliding Doors* (1998), even Hugh Grant as Prime Minister in *Love Actually* (2003).

But London deserves more than this. Many film-makers have attempted to show the complexities of a city where currently thirty-six languages are in use. And despite funding difficulties, there are films to praise. Jamie Thraves' first film *The Low Down* (2000) showed a recognisable picture of life in today's radically altered East End, complete with studios; Gurinder Chadha's more widely distributed and deservedly successful *Bend It Like Beckham* (2002) offered a sympathetic picture of generational conflict within a Sikh family in Southall. The screenplay was sent to Beckham himself for approval – he liked it so much that he asked for a cameo appearance, and is duly glimpsed at Heathrow. And Stephen Frears' *Dirty Pretty Things* (2002), though it has its flaws, is set amongst London's illegal immigrants; as one of them says, 'We're the people you never see – who do the jobs you don't want to do.' Dickens and Mayhew would be proud of Frears' attempt to delve into this new underworld.

Whatever the problems for English film-makers, it seems that London as a location still has a future.

Michael Caine at the Plaza Hotel, New York City, 1966

Fashion Capital

Patricia Field in conversation with Marketa Uhlirova

MU   I would like to start with an open question. How do you see the difference between fashion and costume design?

PF   Fashion and costume are not radically apart but they are different. Costume comes out of the script. The script can also deal with fashion, but that's a different thing.

MU   Gloria Swanson wrote in the early 1930s about the difference between fashion and costume, and she made an important point about costume being or not being 'in fashion'. She said that film couldn't, and shouldn't try to be fashionable because of the delay between film production and film release. Are you concerned with being 'in' – with defining the moment in fashion terms?

PF   I am never trendy. The costume follows from three things – the script, the actor and the character. They are most important. You have to work with the actor because after all, you are dressing them. You can't try to be fashionable. You can't worry about the delay. And after all, there will always be a delay a few years down the line.

MU   Do you consider yourself a costume designer or a stylist?

PF   I'd say I'm a stylist. I also do other things apart from movies. I do commercials and photo shoots. Stylist suits me because it's a broader category.

MU   When did you first become aware of the stylist as a profession?

PF   That's an interesting question to ask me because I do remember this very well. It was in 1960 and I was at college. I had a summer job working for a commercial photography studio. My job was to keep the books and pay the models. The word stylist was used there in connection with photo shoots.

MU   In 1960?

PF   Yes. That was the first time I heard the word.

MU   I want to talk about *Sex and the City* now. What I think was powerful about it was that it showed off fashion together with a lot of attitude from those who wore it. Plus it connected fashion with the city in a very explicit way. But I would like to know how you see the development of the characters from your own point of view. Take Miranda for example. She went though changes.

PF   OK, let's start at the beginning. First of all, Darren Star (the show's creator) described to me how he saw the characters. He was very articulate about it and had a clear vision of who they were. This was something I could work from. And then there were the girls … they were a good part of the characters.

MU   Can you expand upon this?

Following page: Anne Hathaway in *The Devil Wears Prada*, directed by David Frankel, 2006

Patricia Field S/S 2007

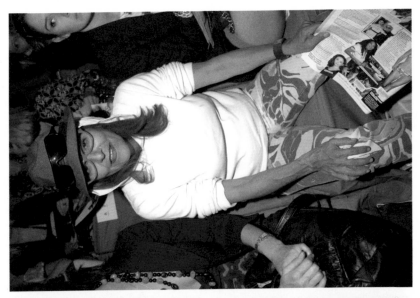

PF There was a big crossover between the girls' real-life personalities and their characters. In fact, the casting was a big part of the success of the series because ultimately you can't fight your character. OK – actors can wear anything and be anything. But there are not that many great actors. Cynthia (Nixon) and her character Miranda are the same… At the end of the series I did a questionnaire with the girls about their experience with fittings. They had to evaluate them on a scale from 1 to 10. Cynthia rated them at 6 or 7 whereas Sarah Jessica (Parker) and Kim (Cattrall) rated them at 10. Cynthia isn't all that interested in fashion. She has other interests. She has a life outside of her profession, and is very involved in a number of things such as the school education system. And she does a lot of theatre. She is probably the best of the actresses. But for me, Miranda was difficult. Trying to find a look for her. She didn't have that much fashion consciousness. She didn't have a real style. She sometimes looked good and sometimes didn't. The others stayed in shape more easily.

MU Can you say more about this staying in shape?

PF Sarah Jessica has always been in perfect form. For her it's part of the profession. When you are in front of the camera all the time, you try to look as good as you can. At least that's one philosophy… Anyway, Sarah Jessica and I had worked together before…

MU On *Miami Rhapsody*…

PF Right. And so with *Sex and the City* we had an advantage because we already knew each other. With the other girls we had to get to know one another, in every way. I think Sarah Jessica was really the leader of the pack and affected the other girls because right from day one she was looking good. And gradually they all started to fall into line, getting serious about their look. The only one that didn't care was Cynthia. And so her body played a role. It was much softer; she didn't try to sculpt it. It was a handicap for me not to have the magazine look to work with – in a way.

MU Yes, but it added complexity to the character, and the series generally (I speak as a fan of Miranda).

PF It definitely worked. I made it work to my advantage.

MU Yes. Miranda was believable because she didn't always look good. Do you enjoy dressing characters to look bad, by the way?

PF I did a pilot for *Ugly Betty* which was a new experience. I had to consciously make this character look, let's say, unfashionable. But it still had to have *something*. And that had to come from the actress who has such a personal charisma. I could only trim it. I am a trimmer!

MU That's such a nice metaphor. But let me return one more time to *Sex and the City*. Did you consider Carrie Bradshaw your alter-ego? You could say she is a stylist of sorts in her own right…Was she your special project?

PF Well, I saw all the girls as my project but all in a different way. Did I see Carrie as my alter-ego? Interesting question when you put it that way. This is what I felt about Sarah Jessica: she was using her character to make these little fashion trips with me. Her personal style is much more classical and designer-oriented. I felt that Carrie was an opportunity for her to take little experimental trips that Sarah Jessica wouldn't normally take. It was fun. But towards the end of the show she started reverting back to herself, dressing more classically. I think we did a beautiful job, but it was much more one-dimensional. But you know, you have to work with an actor. Ultimately they are the one before the camera and my job is to support them. This is different when styling for a magazine where it's not about supporting the actor: it's about supporting the clothing.

MU You just answered my earlier question about the difference between styling for film, and styling for photographs.

PF Yes, but there are also commercials which are in film…

MU Fair enough. Another thing I have always wondered about is how you dealt with the overwhelming influence you gained as *Sex and the City* progressed. How was it to find yourself with the power to launch global trends by putting together looks and endorsing clothes and accessories? Did you play with it?

PF It only happened gradually. I just wanted to dress the girls as well as I could. Then I became aware that it was starting to be this worldwide phenomenon (laughs). I just tried to stay away from it. I didn't embrace it, unless it was meant to be a parody. You can't play to your audience. You can't prejudge. When you become conscious of your audience, you get into trouble because you begin to anticipate what they want. And then you give it to them and of course that's not what they want. They want something surprising, something that they've never seen before.

MU How did you find following *Sex and the City* with *The Devil Wears Prada*, which was more conservative and designer label-led?

PF Yes. And again, this was determined by the script.

MU Of course…

PF But the experience was enjoyable. I have worked with the director (David Frankel) many times. We are very close. I also loved working with Meryl Streep and we had a very good relationship. I guess the challenge here was the sheer volume of clothes. They kept writing in new scenes as we went along and every time he put in a new scene, he added about fifty new costumes…

MU Do you travel a lot for your work? Are there any particular cities you draw inspiration from?

PF I travel a lot and I like a lot of cities: London, Tokyo, São Paolo and, of course, New York. They are all great. My inspiration comes from cities loaded with people who bump up against each other. When this happens, creative sparks start to fly. I also love Paris but not for the obvious reason. I am inspired by life, not so much by designers.

MU Really?

PF Creating a garment is a different process to creating a style. Creating a style is like collaging pieces together. It's a bigger picture. Creating a

garment is more sculptural, more focused. It's not about an overall look.

MU   Do you make drawings as part of your work at all?

PF   I hire a friend if I need to do drawings. I don't do patterns either. I don't want to know. I don't have any formal education in anything to do with fashion.

MU   How do you see London in fashion terms?

PF   What I have noticed about London over the years I've been going there – which has been since the early '60s – is that it's like a hill that goes up and down, up and down. I think a lot of the inspiration in London fashion comes from current life, mainly from the youth which is more energised. London has a real signature.

MU   So what exactly is this signature?

PF   It's based on contemporary life. The attitude of the present situation is interpreted by fashion. You see a sense of humour in British fashion. You see it with the use of fabrics, or the approach to history – take Vivienne Westwood for example. Culture is embodied in fashion, and it's true in punk or Matthew Williamson's use of colour. I never see any humour in Paris, other than with Galliano … and he isn't French. French fashion is much more serious and self-involved. American fashion also has a distinct signature: utilitarian, simple, practical…

MU   But you don't necessarily adhere to it.

PF   I do. On a personal basis, I have always been a typical American dresser. When I go to work I am a jeans, T-shirts, trench coats and loafers kind of dresser. But there is always a little twist to make it interesting.

MU   Yes, exactly. This is your DIY approach to fashion. To go back to Carrie from *Sex and the City* – she is certainly not your typical American in the way she dresses.

PF   No, but she isn't anything else either. She isn't French. She isn't British. She is an original. She is very eclectic. Her co-ordination of clothes is always interesting. Women loved Carrie because of that. It's funny but men didn't like Carrie. They loved Samantha or Charlotte. You wouldn't believe how many guys wanted me to introduce them to Charlotte! She was the girl they could introduce to their mother … Men don't really get fashion. Unfortunately, over the last 200 years men have been relegated to boring dressing. They haven't had the opportunity to get fashion. And in such a long time you lose the ability to appreciate it. I feel sorry for men. The minute they do something original they are labelled homosexual. I remember one male character told me he couldn't wear a pink shirt. He told me he loved my styling but he personally couldn't wear it. A year later I met him at a party and he confessed: I have a pink suit now. Pink somehow became fashionable for men. I hate it when things become trendy because most people will wear it wrong. And then it becomes terrible … There was a period in the '80s when everyone had to wear a deep slit in their skirt. And of course if you have fat legs, it's going to look shit. It got to the point when I thought, if I see another deep slit… There are only a couple of things you can't ruin. A name necklace is one. Everyone has a name, so it has integrity. Then a flower. A flower comes from nature …

MU   Recently I saw an article in *The New Yorker* running a profile on London. It portrayed London as a hot city, suggesting that New York should watch out because London is coming up. The underlying message was obviously that London is coming up, only to be as cool as – New York! So what is it about these two cities that makes them want to measure up the whole time?

PF   They have a close cultural relationship. They understand each other better than they understand other cities. The two are like family. But this 'New York watch out, London's coming' is so predictable. It's journalistic bullshit. Both cities have a style and both are sophisticated in their own individual way. There is room for both. They take turns in being in the spotlight.

MU   I guess journalists often have their own agenda and they make things fit in. They make you fit in …

PF   I always get asked, what's next? I mean, what do I know? I'm not a fortune teller! I suppose I'm a bit of an intellectual snob when it comes to interviews.

MU   Things like who's your icon …

PF   Exactly. I always say it's Cleopatra. And they say, but why? Because she's been around for 2000 years and we still have an image of her.

Sarah Jessica Parker in *Sex and the City*, final day of filming, Fifth Avenue, 2004

Fashion Capital
Erin O'Connor

'More than any other fashion capital, London celebrates the character and individuality of models. Here, I can be myself and working with British designers always feels like a collaborative process.'

David Downton: Erin O'Connor, in Dior Couture, 2002

Footprints Manolo Blahnik

London to me is the most exciting city in the world. It was when I first arrived here more than thirty years ago and it still is. It's an amazing city – which can sometimes be frustrating – but that is probably why we love it so much.

From a fashion point of view, it remains the hotbed in which the most exciting talent starts to take shape, thanks mainly to our outstanding fashion colleges. Only London – with its mix of old and new, of thousands of people of different origins come together, with its anti-establishment stance – can produce the likes of Galliano and McQueen, two of its best ambassadors.

Dior Couture illustration by
Manolo Blahnik

the manolo blahnik for ceinez Dior conture: 1977

Time and speed are two of the key elements in an industry that thrives on newness and a constant state of change. Fast fashion just gets faster and faster. But what would happen if we slowed down the fashion cycle, why might it be desirable and what does it mean for design practice?

There could be a new model for fashion design where the ideas of the Slow Food movement – small scale production, a link between ethics and pleasure, integrity and education – might inform future design practice and innovation; allowing time for the generation of a different kind of pleasure in fashion.

SP   How did you come across the idea of the slow movement?

TN   I read an article in one of the architectural magazines. Just the thought of it felt wonderful and especially coming from Italy, because having produced shoes for so long there, I really related to the concept.

SP   I think how you started your practice is of conceptual relevance here – can you talk about that?

TN   I'm Canadian and I come from quite a small town. I came to London and I was really, really disappointed in terms of high-street fashion. I had this perception that everything would be different, and in fact I felt like you could knock down all the walls and all the labels would be the same. That really bothered me. When I was in Canada there were no foot-wear schools or anything. When I was nine years old I was making shoes out of toilet-paper rolls for heels and walking around town, and so to not actually pursue it seemed absolutely ridiculous, and so living in London I thought I would go for it.

SP   How did you get into making shoes in Italy? That's still a centre of designer shoemaking isn't it?

TN   I did a final show with Cord-wainers, and Tracy Mulligan really liked the shoes and asked if I could do a catwalk collection for her. That went really well and she said, 'Why don't we try producing them in Italy?'

SP   How big was this factory you were working with?

TN   It was tiny and a lot of handma-king went on. I think what is quite common is you take in a shoe that someone else has done and you say you want to copy it and you put it out there. But we were not doing that. It was like, OK, I'm really looking for the sole to do this and get some movement. So it was a bit of a challenge.

SP   Were you taking drawings in to the factory or presenting them with examples of materials?

TN   The material was quite simple – when you start out, minimums are a factor, just like in fabrication. The simpler it is, the smaller the mini-mum and so it was more about the

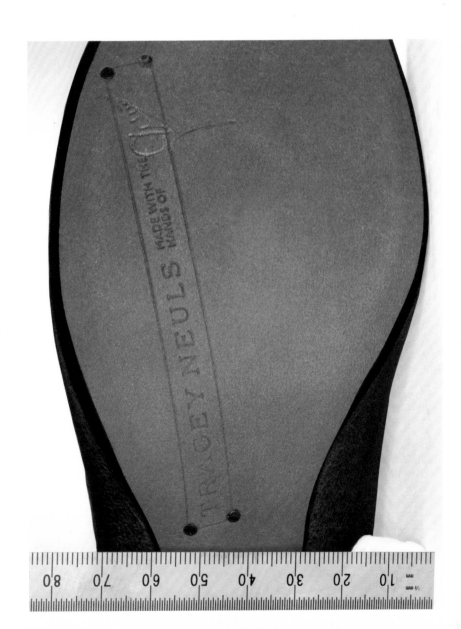

treatments and the last itself and how the soling was too.

SP   Did you have your own lasts made?

TN   Yes. For me that's almost one of the best parts of it – getting in there and sculpting it. I do a mock-up first and I use just basic plasticine. I love the smell of it.

SP   We've talked a little bit about the idea of 'slow fashion'; could you pinpoint a time when you think you were coming around to that way of thinking?

TN   I think it's something that is in you. I will be walking along the street and I often bump into people because I'm looking at the ground or I'm looking in the sky, and it's the teeny-weeny little things I'm looking at. I really love the small things in life. I think that idea of slow comes in because to really appreciate something small, you have to take the time. It's not some big Las Vegas glance.

SP   It's more the minutiae, it's the little details and the little nuances?

TN   Yes. For example, one time I was in New York, and in Soho in particular there is not a patch of green anywhere and this poor dog is looking for a pee, and you could see this sprig of grass, probably the only one for miles, and he went and sniffed that out – and that whole scenario, that theme, the story around it, I totally love. It's almost like finding that one piece of beauty or it's not even as raw as something that the human hand has done. I really do like the teeny little details.

SP   English fashion has become very high-street driven and it seems to have become more so in the last four or five years, where the high street has a sort of stranglehold almost on English fashion and the way we dress. Do you think that's true?

TN   Certainly more than the French, yes. Italians have a bit of that I think but it's a bit more driven by the classics. Everyone is buying into design and I think the high street has bought into emulating that. English fashion is sort of urgent high-street shopping.

SP   What I think is interesting is how the high street has driven this idea of speed within fashion, and the speeding up of the cycle, but it seems to me what the high street is doing is saying, 'This week we will have Marni-flavour garments, and next week we will have Prada and the week after that we will have Dries Van Noten', so in fact the idea that fashion is fast and that ideas are generated fast is crazy. What the high-street shops are doing is copying faster. They are just borrowing ideas from other designers more and more quickly and fashion shopping is being driven by the desire to consume and the high street's desire to sell you things rather than design and ideas.

TN   And I think that's shocking. The quality level is so low because people don't want it for more than three months at a time. I get emails from people who have a pair of shoes from seven years ago from the very first collection and they are distraught, like it's a pet that's gone missing or something, and they are like, 'What can I do? The sole has worn out', and I'm like, 'It's OK, we can resole it.'

SP   It seems to me that you would feel more satisfied as a consumer if you had bought something that you really loved and you knew someone had spent a lot of time over the design and making it, and also loved it.

TN   But also the idea that goes hand in hand with that is the price level, and I think America is particularly bad where the quality of something is concerned. If you think of your purchases over a lifetime instead of thinking, 'Oh, it's £300', you then think you can wear that until you're dead, not until it's dead. And it's almost like a whole new education that goes hand in hand with that idea.

SP   I think this idea of education is absolutely key for thinking about 'slow fashion'. You need to re-educate people to think about the real value of things and value beyond the thing you have in your hand. Thinking about the making of it, your consumption of it and then your continued pleasure in it, as opposed to 'I've worn it once and now I'll throw it away'.

TN   I think with a lot of things these days your pleasure needs to be a bit more considered. It's almost like we

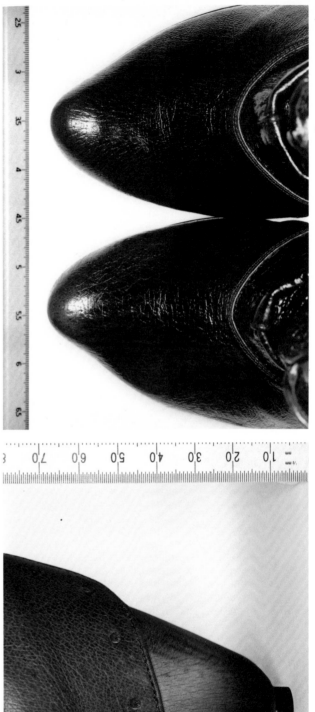

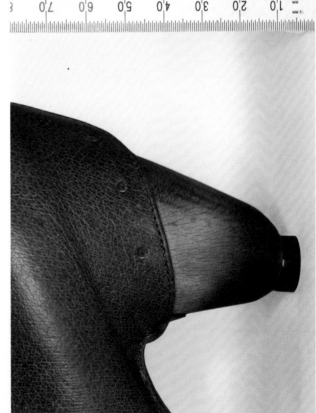

can't be that spontaneous really any more, in terms of energy, the whole gamut of environmental concerns and so on.

SP   Where do you get your ideas from, how do you start designing?

TN   I think I'm a little bit like a sponge – like I say, I'm always looking, and when it comes time to wring me out, then it all comes out. But it's not like I sit down and go OK, the fairy tale, it's so not that at all. Probably every three seasons I end up doing a new shape, and that can be quite a starting point because I love the idea of sculpting and the shape. It's almost as if the form dictates everything else in terms of inspiration. For example, stationery – I absolutely love stationery – and you get the little closes and clasps and I put them on shoes instead of lacings. So just the very small things… Making people look at things that they take for granted in a slightly different way. For me I think the stuff that I do is different, but it's not because I've thrown a bag of jewels on the top or have lots of other embellishments; I still think it's good design. Maybe it's an old way of thinking about it, but I still think that those reasons for why things are beautiful haven't changed.

SP   I'm quite interested in the idea that fashion is over, in fact, because it is so self-referential now, fashion repeats itself so quickly.

TN   I've never heard anyone declare that before!

SP   Well, it is an idea that I have been toying with, and when you tell people they are very shocked, but I think fashion as we have known it, with its six-month cycle, is definitely over. And also because there's such diversity of looks and overlapping of styles.

TN   I like that idea. It's like a dictator who's died or been overthrown or something. I get people who come in and they love the shoes and then *Vogue* is in the background going, 'you need a pair of high-heeled stilettos', or 'those aren't wedges', and you can almost sort of see the fight going on within them. But if they could learn to trust themselves and have their own personal taste and just say, 'I love that.'

SP   This is one of the things that Matilda Tam talks about in her research. The high-street consumer is very unconfident, so buys something, wears it and then thinks, 'I don't know if this is quite me, I don't know if I like it.' It's cheap enough to throw away and you can buy yourself a whole new persona for the following weekend. I think for young women it's terribly confusing, because in a way you don't get to develop your own fashion identity as you're having all this stuff forced on you all the time. You have to try it out, you have to play the game, and it's unsatisfying because you end up looking like everybody else and you find your decision has actually been manipulated by somebody else, by magazines or stylists.

TN   Yes. Even more than the designers creating the outfit.

SP   I'm quite interested in this idea that London fashion, London's designer fashion, always seems to be in this terrible crisis. Our designers are either moving to Paris or abandoning ship or the businesses just go under because it's so difficult to get finance, and it seems to me that the way you work – in a way that is removed from that very fast cycle, having direct contact with your customer and your factories and your makers – seems to me to be the only model for designer fashion that can really survive in London.

TN   It's interesting that you say that because a woman came in the other day and she said, 'This is such a find. You would never be able to make it on the high street; people have to find you.'

SP   That's a nice idea.

TN   I was thinking about London Fashion Week itself. We participated when we were first starting and we won a Marks & Spencer award and, you know, little things like that. But the fact of the matter is that it's not representative of what's going on in London and it's very strange. I mean, my wholesalers don't come to London any more whereas seven years ago, five years ago, it was on the map, and now it's not. Like right now London Fashion Week is just about a few stockists who are based in the UK.

JA805

JB825

TNA14

TNB15

EVIDENCE

TRACEY NEULS

WINTER 07

SP   I was talking to Julian Roberts not so long ago and he is really interested in London becoming not just about fashion in clothing but about film and video and graphics and fine art, and instead of having just catwalk fashion it becomes a more multimedia approach to showing design, and a showcase for everything that we do really well. Involving all the fantastic magazines that we have got and showcasing new ideas, and for it to be much livelier and much richer in its content.

TN   Last September what we did is, instead of saying that we are showing over London Fashion Week, we joined the *Design Week* trail and the *Icon* trail. We had an article in *Elle* magazine and another one in *Blueprint* magazine – we had people writing in from Australia and all over on the back of this, and it was just such a good match. Proper attention is so fantastic.

SP   It must be so nice to place yourself outside the normal fashion route.

TN   Yes, it got to a point four years ago and I'm thinking, I'm not growing fast enough, and you get so caught up in what your peers are doing, and look, there is that model wearing her shoes and that sort of stuff – and I feel so healthy now. I feel like, you know, I've gone to footwear yoga or something. And if you're true to what it is you believe in, it sort of goes back to the beginning where I can't help myself looking at tiny little details, and being fascinated

by a beautiful crack in a building or something. If it takes twenty years to build the business then fine, because I also want fun along the way.

SP   For you it sounds like going to the factory and meeting the craftsmen and being involved in all of that is actually one of the joys of the design process.

TN   Yeah, I think that your fingers are just as important as your eyes and you can't be entirely creative just looking at something. In one of my previous design jobs, when I first moved here, there were designers, and then there were buyers or design co-ordinators who would go out and basically shop America and come back with things that they would like in their range. So as a designer I was there in the factory and they were taking nuances from what already existed. Today everything is so now, so directly linked to your eyes, so instant. What happens to these guys at the end of our arms? *(wiggles her fingers).*

Footprints   Jimmy Choo

If someone had told me that one day I'd be a household name worldwide, I wouldn't have believed it. More than twenty years ago, I was just helping my father in our small shop in Penang, but I believe that it was destiny that took me to England to grab the opportunities that the country has to offer. It was a daunting journey to a country I hardly knew, but nothing is gained without risk and taking challenges. Cordwainers College gave me the opportunity to refine my skills, to add more to the discipline of shoemaking that I had learnt from my father.

Before I knew it, I was making shoes for celebrities and members of the royal families from around the world. And along the way I have picked up many awards and have been given much recognition – I never thought all this was within my reach.

The British Council, University of the Arts London and certainly this country have given me this opportunity to excel and in return, I am giving back to the society that has given me so much. I spend a lot of my time working to support education, as ambassador of Footwear Education at London College of Fashion and I am also a spokesperson for the British Council in their promotion of British education to foreign students.

London is a place to be if you are brave, talented, hardworking and not afraid of challenges. People are always willing to give you a chance and once you've made it, there is no looking back.

如果过去有人告诉我，总有一天我的名字会全球家喻户晓，我不会相信。20多年前我只在槟城我父亲的一个小店里帮工但是我相信命中注定我会去英国去捕捉英国赋予的机遇。到一个我几乎一无所知的国家真是一个令人畏惧的旅行。但是如果不冒风险、不接受挑战就不会有收获。是康德威那斯学院为我提供了深造技能的机会使从父亲那里学到的制鞋知识得以进一步提高。

我还没有意识到，我在为世界各地的名人和王室家族成员制鞋。这期间我荣获过很多奖项和得到更多认可－我从不认为这些就是我的最终目的。

英国文化协会、伦敦艺术大学当然也就是这个国家给了我施展的机会，相应地我也回报了给于过我这么多的社会。我花大量工作时间支持教育，是伦敦时尚大学鞋类教育的大使也是促进英国留学生教育的英国文化协会的代言人。

如果你有勇气和才能，并勤奋工作和不怕挑战，伦敦就是最适合的地方。人们总愿意给你机会，一旦你作了选择就再也不会回头。

我在时尚和设计领域的贡献在我的国家，也就是马来西亚称

My contribution in the field of fashion and design has not gone unnoticed in my own country, Malaysia. Indeed, Malaysia and Malaysians are proud that I have put the country on the fashion map of the world. And indeed they have given me many awards, the most recent being the Lifetime Achievement Award at the Malaysia International Fashion Awards 2006 in Kuala Lumpur. I am so proud to be able to stand in this fashion capital, and indeed anywhere else, and say that I am a Malaysian, an adventurous Malaysian who grabs opportunities anywhere in the world and makes good. To the younger generation, I say I hope they will do the same and not be scared of challenges if they want to get ahead in life. I took those challenges and I have never regretted it.

得上家喻户晓，马来西亚和马来西亚人以我把自己的国家推上世界时尚地图而自豪。确实他们给了我很多荣誉，最近的一次是在2006年吉隆坡的马来西亚国际时尚大奖上被授予终生成就奖。我能够站在这个时尚之都深感自豪，事实上在其它任何地方，都可以说我是一个马来西亚人，一个敢于冒险在世界的任何地方都能捕捉机会并获得成功的马来西亚人。对年轻的一代，我希望他们像我一样，如果想走在生活的列就不要惧怕挑战。我接受了这样的挑战，从不后悔。

Footprints

The Road to Cordwainers
Camilla Skovgaard

I worked professionally as a clothing designer for seven years in Dubai. A French company brought me there at the age of twenty. I only had a diploma in womenswear pattern cutting, having originally set out for Paris haute couture training. I was fast at sketching and thus got the whole ex-pat package with salary, car, flat and paid holiday flights – and at a time when Dubai was, dare I say, more authentic than it has now become.

It was the Gulf women's heinous taste in footwear during those years (the '90s) that initially set me on the footwear path, as I gradually came to recognise the crucial importance of shoes if the final look is to make any sense. Often the women would say no one could see their shoes as their dresses reached the floor, but when they danced on raised platforms, or sat down, the shoes would be revealed. I also began to pay attention to my own footwear. This was a time when the Gulf was beginning to bring luxury to the region. I clung to whatever decent shoes I could get hold of, even if a size too small. Curiously, my Dubai business partner casually remarked one day, observing me at work amongst yards of fabrics and embroidery, that while I was already successful, she felt I had not yet found my true niche. And so it has turned out – I believe I understand shoes better than clothing.

I read about Cordwainers College in London in an Arab newspaper (of all places) and was most intrigued by it – to be able to make bespoke shoes by hand and fully master the craft greatly appealed to me. There was something less 'mainstream' about it than clothing. I returned to Europe with the sole purpose of finally getting a formal university degree and the first thing I did was to contact Cordwainers in London. I decided on Cordwainers as the school has a greater focus on the craftsmanship of shoemaking. The UK and London have a long history of shoemaking – bootmaking is in fact one of the oldest industries in London, dating back 1000 years. There is a lovely story on its history at the Museum of London.

While employment in the British footwear-manufacturing industry is now virtually defunct after a steep decline over the past decades, as large-scale production has relocated to the free trade zones of South-East Asia, mainly China, there has been a slant in the general profile of the shoe industry in the UK towards retail and design. Shoe design and shoemaking at Cordwainers, whose history can be traced back more than 800 years, is now established and validated as a degree-level subject. This achievement provides the foundation for the distinctive character of British shoe design in the context that designing and making shoes has also become an 'individuated' experience of work in a world where traditional 'jobs for life' are fast disappearing, to be replaced by new kinds of jobs.

Camilla Skovgaard:
Wrap I, A/W 2006

I was in the last class at Cordwainers; our first year was in Mare Street in Hackney and in our second/third year we were moved to locations in Golden Lane, John Princes Street and Davies Street when Cordwainers merged with London College of Fashion. I remember that we strongly disliked the disruption in the beginning and found it confusing having to be at so many different locations. However, once we realised the advantages of being about town, it gave a better sense of belonging to the city and its fashion industry. Later, when I went on to do my MA degree at the Royal College of Art, I still tried to sneak into Cordwainers because of the excellent facilities for footwear students.

Cordwainers means a great deal to me. It has been one of the most positive experiences in my life. I came to the college as a mature student so it was a difficult first year of readjustment, but with the sustained challenges, support and passion of its teachers, I very quickly learnt that the college is indeed brilliant if you work hard. Respect for the craft and the work ethic I gained there are things I have taken with me into professional life. In a strange sense London has had a far greater influence on me as a person than Dubai – even if Dubai as a culture is more foreign to me compared to my native Denmark. Shoes are more than just dress; they are something complete in their own way. This is also why Cinderella loses a shoe and not a hairpin or a handbag.

The knowledge I gained at Cordwainers has impressed many a producer in Italy. Italy is a different learning curve in itself as the focus is on production and design for production, so the combination of Italian and business studies has proved very useful as it provided the platform to build from.

I am very fond of London and would like my main base to remain here – it just means I am often on a plane. It is important to me to work with others, which is why it is such a pleasure to work with Matthew Williamson with whom I have an ongoing collaboration. I treasure the stimulus and challenge various collaborations and projects bring.

In my latter years in Dubai I worked in an independent capacity, so I had some idea of what it would mean when things began to point towards my own shoe line. However, nothing could really have prepared me for the political climate that exists in Italian shoe production. It is much more difficult to produce a shoe than a shirt – there are many more subsuppliers involved and thus more to keep under wraps if things are to gel.

Sometimes I just see or feel a certain shape in front of me with no particular reference to anything; I don't know if this is what you call intuition or if it's simply a result of many impressions throughout the day. Other times it can be an advantage, as a new designer entering the market, to present a more cohesive

concept of design, to clearly communicate to first-timers who get in touch with your product what you are about. As the business grows one can expand to more basic and commercial styles that somehow borrow some of the emotional value established by the 'key' pieces.

With the fashion industry becoming ever more fragmented, turning over fast-changing disposable goods, I find it more satisfying and refreshing instead to focus on design, and shoes that will offer value and a more lasting appreciation. Cheap shoes with their poor fit and materials are, to me, the equivalent of eating candy when you are hungry. It leaves a shallow feeling of regret for not having invested in a proper meal.

I think taste is universal. Our admiration for designer goods or music, whether new insider names or Jaguar cars, seems to act as a great unifier that transcends our political, economic or religious differences – a young professional in Paris has more in common with a similar person in Seoul or São Paulo than she does with a working-class person in Nice. These differences recede in importance as the bedrock of our identities is rather formed by allegiance to common value systems, such as expressed concretely through affiliation with select designer styles. In terms of being a designer, this means that our products are more likely to find a sprawling global audience than a comprehensive home market. With the Internet, the world is truly becoming a global village. It was not my intention to start an online business, but it was a means to respond and supply to the women that contact Camilla Skovgaard for shoes while establishing a retail network, and I now find it gives me strength. It is such a pleasure to have direct contact with the end-users and it makes my day when the ladies email back to say how happy they are with the shoes they've received.

Camilla Skovgaard:
Wrap II, A/W 2006

Footprints

1997/2007 – East/West
Olivia Morris

It's weird to think that, in 1997, both Bethnal Green (where I was studying at Cordwainers) and Notting Hill (where I was living in a £30-a-week basement bedsit along with Phoebe Philo) were both considered to be up-and-coming areas. And now, a decade later, from Old Street and Spitalfields to Ladbroke Grove/ Portobello/Westbourne Grove, it's quite amazing to consider the gent-rification that's happened. What I love about both areas is that they still retain much of their original 'flavour'.

And it's also strange to observe how people who live east look at Notting Hill as being full of rich Trustafarians, and residents of the west look at those in the east as ultra-cool and alterna-tive. In a weird, exaggerated way the stereotypes aren't untrue! Essentially I think both areas are full of creative and artistic people, who just have diff-erent ways of expressing themselves.

I would spend all day, every day at college, and at the end of the day I would be straight back to West London for my social life, although Saturday nights were regularly spent at Billion Dollar Babes off Tottenham Court Road. Without a doubt I'm a West London girl at heart: raised in Richmond, school in Hammersmith, foundation course in Wimbledon.

While searching my archive it was interesting finding the picture of me and my mate Nick in the canteen at college; it made me realise how, in a 'gastronomic' way, the area that I spent time in daily has now become a hotbed of different tastes. For example, Vietnamese places like Viet Hoa. What a shame they weren't around back then, although in those days my palate and budget wouldn't have been sophisticated enough to realise it was good food! Now, whilst occasionally venturing east to eat near Brick Lane, I have an amazing and vast array of tastes on my doorstep in West London.

My journeys into college were the one true pleasure of the day. I had made my first true vintage purchase, a 1965 turquoise VW Beetle, and I have such vivid memories of listening to now-defunct long wave Radio Atlantic 252, my first introduction to old music like swing and soul, something I still love now. The Beetle was the love of my life for three years until I crashed her.

That's when my daily journeys on the Central Line from Notting Hill Gate to Bethnal Green began. The nice thing was that when I first left college and set up my label in the summer of 2000, I was making my shoes at a factory on Old Ford Road, so my connection with the area remained. My journey became only a slightly altered version of the one I had taken a few years previously.

My introduction to Atlantic 252 started a life-long love affair with soulful music. Dancing to hip hop and R & B at Rotation, which took place under the Westway at Subterrania, became a regular and

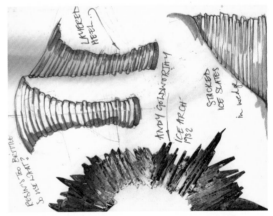

faithful Friday night for us all for many years.

Now (minus a car) I love my walk or cycle to work. It's a time to clear my head and prepare for the day before me. Whereas college was really four blank walls, the studio I work in now is full of things that inspire me: antique furniture, bought on the Goldbourne Road, photographs and prints of my previous work and current inspiration, samples, and of course the current collection. It is 'my little world'.

Looking back at my first bit of college work and at my current sketchbooks, I am utterly astounded to see that things haven't changed much at all. My brain still works in the same way though of course stylistically things have matured and become more sophisticated, but in terms of my actual ways of designing, my approach hasn't changed much at all. My process is still the same – an idea starts in my head and from the beginning, even before I put pen to paper and start researching, I often have some final ideas already decided (always a moan at college from my tutors about 'design development'!). From magazine tears, photographs etc. I start to translate ideas onto paper. Then my thumbnail doodles commence (they are as naive now as they were in 1997) – even my illustrations are still noticeably similar, although I hope a little more developed and sophisticated now than ten years ago.

So, ten years later, I can see that things have certainly moved on. I now have a growing company which is seven years old. And although the business side has the tendency to take over my head space more than I would like, I have had the chance to do exactly what I want creatively and have had opportunities to work with and be inspired by other creative people: graphic designers like Mark Thomson at Studio Thomson, up-and-coming photographers like Xanthe Greenhill, and many talented and inspiring London-based designers such as Preen, Aquascutum, Erdem and Duro Olowu.

In fact it was the strangest thing the other day when I went to meet Erdem in his studio for the first time, as he had always previously ventured west to me. I found myself standing on the doorstep of Cordwainers College, Mare Street, where he now has a studio space. I had a strong sense of déjà vu walking the very same corridors. Most weird of all was that it was almost like coming 'home'....

A montage of images of my time in West London

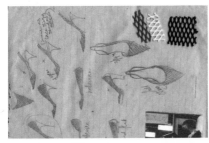

Footprints

Terry de Havilland

I can honestly say that my first memory is of shoes; platform shoes with ankle straps worn by my mother and made by my father, the house was always full of them. I guess you can say that shoes are in my psyche.

My parents had their own company, Waverley Shoes. My father was considered one of the top 'lasters' in London, and woe betide any of his staff who came up with shoddy workmanship as my mother was the most formidable quality controller in the business. By the age of five I was helping out in the workshop, hammering wooden dowels into the three-tiered wedges he was making for the black market during the Second World War. My parents had a lucrative business making quality high fashion shoes for wealthy West End ladies, supplied to them by a somewhat louche character from Maida Vale who went by the name of Curly and drove an open-topped Jaguar with a rumble seat in the boot.

I discovered the powerful effect a beautiful pair of shoes can have on a woman when my father made a pair of wedges for a wealthy publican called Goldie. Goldie had contracted polio when she was a child and was forced to wear a leg iron with a clumpy orthopaedic boot on her left leg on account of the fact that it was several inches shorter than her right leg. My father had made her a pair of his three-tiered wedges but built the left foot up with extra layers. When Goldie came over to collect them she whooped with delight at finally

owning a pair of fashionable shoes. I'll never forget how much joy those shoes gave her and how her whole demeanour changed the minute she had them on her feet.

I designed my first pair of shoes in 1958 when I was on leave from National Service. My father was, by this time, making stiletto winkle-pickers. I noticed a pattern he was working on and realised that I could do it better. By 1960 my father called me back from Rome (I had eloped there with a rich American socialite having decided I wanted to pursue a career as an actor) to help out with the business.

The winkle-pickers had taken off big time and my father needed as much help as he could get to meet the orders. People were coming from all over the country to buy them and queuing up from dawn till dusk to get their hands on a pair. We were making stiletto-heeled versions for the girls at £3 a pop and Cuban-heeled versions for the boys at £3.50. We were even supplying some of the Krays' henchmen with them.

My big break came in 1964. I was now going out with a young model. I'd made her a pair of shoes which she wore to a photo shoot. Annie Traherne, the editor of *Queen* magazine, loved the shoes so much she decided to feature them. They were an instant success and so began my career as Terry de Havilland, shoe designer.

Terry de Havilland during National Service, 1958

By 1969 London was in full swing and I was slap bang in the middle of the scene. I was digging around in my dad's attic one morning when I came across the original components from the three-tiered wedges that I knew so well from my childhood. It was a classic eureka moment. I asked my father if we could still make them and got the 'yes' answer I was hoping for. I came up with some new designs and made them up in trippy, coloured snakeskins to go with the kind of clothes that were being made by the likes of Ossie Clark. We sold them through to Rowley & Oram who had a shop in Kensington Market, the place to be at the time. The timing was perfect and soon girls were queuing up to get them, often walking out with a pair in the wrong size, they were coveted so much. Before long I had the likes of Bianca Jagger, Cher, Bette Midler and Anita Pallenberg strutting their stuff in my designs. I loved every minute of it.

My father-in-law spotted a business opportunity and took some samples to a boutique show in New York. We sold half a million dollars worth of shoes, more than we could supply but a great indication of what we could achieve.

In 1972 my father-in-law sold his part of the business on to a rich architect who decided that it was time to open a Terry de Havilland shop. He had a property on the corner of the King's Road and Beaufort Street that was the perfect location. We decked it out to look like a bordello. Peach mirror-glass walls, a purple-silk tented ceiling, an oversized crystal chandelier and velvet banquette seats with a sign outside that read 'Cobblers to the World'. The opening party was a riot of champagne, cocaine and caviar packed out with all the faces, from rock stars and groupies to fashion journalists and gangsters. I set up my design studio in the basement of the shop.

Throughout the '70s the brand thrived. I was having a ball and getting all sorts of great gigs: designing Tim Curry's shoes for *The Rocky Horror Show*, bringing back the stiletto for a Zandra Rhodes catwalk, making red silk-lined black leather thigh boots for Jackie O and all the while watching the crazy antics of Viv Westwood, Malcolm McLaren and all the larger-than-life characters that were hanging out in their boutique, Sex.

By 1979 I was getting a bit disillusioned with mainstream fashion. I had become inspired by all the lunacy that surrounded the punk movement and loved the way they styled themselves. I decided to put the Terry de Havilland name on ice and in 1980 I set up a new label called Kamikazi which made shoes for punks and goths. These were all about affordable street style. Heavily buckled winkle-pickers adorned with skulls, studs and spikes. In the space of a year we were making over 800 pairs a day and shipping them all over the world. Prophetically in 1988 Kamikazi took a nosedive and crashed.

Undeterred I then launched the label Magic Shoes in 1989. We aimed our product at goths and the newly burgeoning fetish scene. In 1990 I met my wife Liz who was designing high-tech holographic fabrics at the time. We had a huge amount of fun hanging out in all the alternative clubs for inspiration. We soon realised that if we started to make the shoes in men's sizes, we'd double our take overnight. We loved the characters we were meeting, particularly the drag queens who would demand higher and higher heels. There was no 'too over the top' for them. They christened me Mr Platform. We made the shoes as comfortable as f*ck so that our customers could club all night long and still stagger home.

By the mid-nineties the name Terry de Havilland started to crop up again. I was approached by Anna Sui to do the footwear for her New York runway show in 1997 and provided some of the footwear for Paco Rabanne's runway show in Paris the same year. I was also discovered by the costume designer Sandy Powell who commissioned me to make the footwear for the *Velvet Goldmine* movie. She had assumed I was dead until a chance meeting with a mutual acquaintance led her to my factory on the Mile End Road.

Our customers were unconventional to say the least but always intelligent and polite. The Fetish Morris Dancers are lodged firmly in my memory bank. We made them stiletto platform bondage boots. They

Terry de Havilland:
A/W 2007

attached the bells to the d-rings and gave us a demo when they came to pick them up.

One rainy Saturday afternoon when business had been unusually slow a young girl from France came into our Camden Stables shop. She had come over to buy a pair of my Transmuters. Suddenly she let out a shriek and burst into tears. Standing in the doorway was her hero Marilyn Manson with the delectable Miss Dita Von Teese. He'd come to collect the Transmuters he'd ordered. After he left there was suddenly a flurry of activity. When we cashed up that night we couldn't believe it. As the till roll printed out, the total came up as £666 ... and 50p! The number of the beast had followed in the wake of the self-proclaimed Antichrist.

Liz decided that she'd put a small display of my vintage shoes in a cabinet in the shop. Suddenly we began to get visited by stylists and costume designers (including Lindy Hemming who commissioned us to produce the boots for the *Tomb Raider* movies). We noticed that there was a buzz building around the Terry de Havilland name and I made the decision to start designing in my own name after an absence of twenty years.

We shut the shop in February 2002 and decided to concentrate solely on relaunching the Terry de Havilland brand. I had more shoes in museums than shops and I decided this needed to be redressed.

Then in October 2002 things began to get somewhat surreal. All of a sudden my vintage '70s styles were beginning to sell through at auction for huge amounts. I was then commissioned by uber-stylist Karl Plewka to design the footwear for the FrostFrench S/S 2004 collection. I came up with a range of towering wedges and suddenly my name was back on the international stage.

And so here I am now. My shoes are selling across the globe once again. I've been given the honour of Visiting Professor of the University of the Arts London. Liz and I have a design studio in London where we still make my custom-made footwear for my personal clients. I've got Jade and Lizzie Jagger doing their thing in my designs just like Bianca and Jerry used to do back in the day.

I can't ever imagine giving up designing shoes. What would I do with my time? I find London a truly inspiring city. When it comes to originality and street style there is no equal to it in the world. I have always been inspired by what goes on in the alternative scene and like nothing more than collaborating with young alternative designers. As for the future ... look out boys, I'm about to relaunch my two-inch Cuban heels. The time is right for you to learn how to strut. I'll be making them for your girlfriends too.

Terry de Havilland: seven heels for couture range, A/W 2007

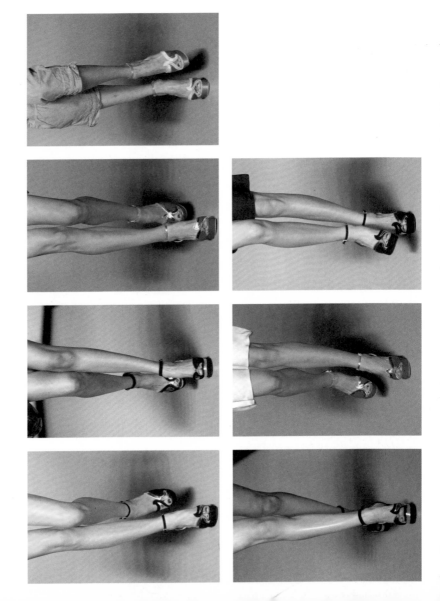

Footprints   Beatrix Ong

The chiming of bottles filled with full fat milk ... sugared
treats in the shape of tear drops and fried eggs ...
travelling around the world without leaving the country
... silence during the night ... looking up at leaves
against the sky ... cold ears ... the same language spoken
in so many different accents ...

Footprints
The Loafer
Patrick Cox

I have always wanted to design a shoe that everyone would wear regardless of age or gender. The loafer has been an enduring signature for my collection since the early 1990s and throughout my career I have continually returned to the simplicity of the moccasin as a point of inspiration.

People often ask me why my loafers are so comfortable – they don't need to know that the leather is wrapped under the foot forming a seamless base with no toe puffing or stiffening, they just need to know that it works.

When I launched my loafer in 1993, the shoe quickly established itself as the choice of footwear for the capital's cognoscenti; so much so that my first store, set just behind Peter Jones in Chelsea, required a doorman to deal with the queue.

The well-trodden paths through the streets of London down which so many of these shoes have led their owners are an endless source of fascination for me. When I see a pair of my loafers that look truly knackered, I take it as the biggest compliment.

Patrick Cox advertising campaign, 1996

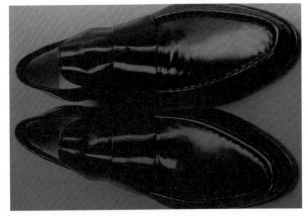

Shelf Life Alexandra Shulman

Last year British *Vogue* was ninety years old – ninety years of Ilustrations, writing and photography chronicling the fashion of our times. When we launched there was no British fashion industry, let alone one that had the reputation for great talent that we now have alongside London being regarded as one of the most innovative and creative capital cities on the planet.

To the outside world British fashion offers very particular ingredients. When people think of British fashion, it is to tweeds and plaids, hats and ball gowns, originality and tailoring that their thoughts turn. From the established couture houses of Norman Hartnell and Hardy Amies, through that mould-breaking period of the sixties when Mary Quant, Ossie Clark and Barbara Hulanicki crashed onto the scene with their young ready-to-wear and on to the extraordinary vision of designers like Vivienne Westwood and Alexander McQueen, British fashion has maintained a very distinct personality.

Accompanying the rise of fashion itself has been the rise of fashion coverage and the now overwhelmingly important and influential role of the media. When *Vogue* first launched in this country the amount of magazines and newspapers in existence was minuscule. Look now at the multiplicity of publications on any news-stand. We not only have the largest amount of daily papers per capita of anywhere, but we have

a magazine business that continues to expand even when you might have thought that we had reached breaking point. A huge number of these publications cover fashion.

Fashion sells. Much of the mainstream media is ambivalent in its approach to the subject, but they want a piece of the action – shopping pages, fashion show coverage, redcarpet style commentary, the lives and times of designers. On the one hand the fashion industry is criticised for being extravagant, irrelevant, elitist, disturbing and even corrupting; on the other, all kinds of media know that their audiences crave the glamour, beauty and aspiration that fashion coverage offers. Amazing clothes on beautiful girls sell papers, magazines, television programmes and websites.

The relationship between the media and fashion is inextricably entwined. Designers need the media; to publicise their work, the media need fashion to woo their audience. London Fashion Week, like all the international fashion weeks, exists to show designers' collections to the press and buyers, but primarily it's a publicity vehicle. The catwalk pictures taken by the pack of photographers crammed into their pen at the end of the catwalk are reproduced again and again all over the world. Similarly the videos of the shows are shown endlessly on fashion television stations – who hasn't idly turned on cable TV in some far-flung hotel room to discover a parade of models strutting

Following page: Christopher Kane: S/S 2007, *British Vogue*, February 2007

Sophia Kokosalaki: A/W 2005, *British Vogue*, December 2005

their stuff on the screen? Fashion is now an international business demanding international recognition if you are to succeed.

So here the role of fashion reportage and commentary has gained a new-found importance. The press reports of the shows are read not only by designers to hear opinions of their work but are used to broadcast their names and image. Any comment is better than no comment. To be ignored by the press is worse than to be criticised. *Women's Wear Daily* and the *Herald Tribune* are scoured by the fashion community eager to be featured in their coverage, but swiftly growing in importance and influence are the fashion news websites like *Vogue.com* and *Fashion Wire Daily.*

The role of the fashion colleges is integral to all of this. Not only is it the talented designers but also others, such as the photographers, illustrators and journalists, who emerge from the highly respected courses here. They embark on their careers startlingly better equipped than in most other countries. The education, contacts and influences they leave with are bettered by none and this means that at all levels of the industry they are regarded as the best. It is our mission for the future to ensure that it stays that way.

Shelf Life
Dan May

Having found a career that I find hugely enjoyable and rewarding, I have been lucky enough to find a magazine whose aesthetic and content I love. Working with people who share a vision and dream to keep producing images that challenge and inspire is a constant source of joy. Being able to go to the shows each season is a privilege that should never be underestimated or taken for granted, as seeing and knowing the energy and passion that constantly goes into producing the clothes that inspire us to produce images worthy of capturing, is priceless.

I do feel hugely fortunate to have 'landed' in an industry that keeps moving forward and reinventing itself, and to work with people who constantly give their all for their passion. I believe we all have something to offer in our own personal vision and what I love about magazines and *10* in particular is the range of images provided for all to enjoy and revisit time and time again. No one day is the same and we are privileged to constantly meet new people and face new challenges in what we do.

The travel and experiences we gain from being able to visit amazing destinations is also something that is both hugely rewarding and personally exhilarating, I love nothing more than visiting new places and meeting the locals, and have been fortunate to shoot in places such as Cuba, Japan, LA, Rio de Janeiro, Morocco, Mauritius and many other incredible locations, each offering a new experience and visual scrapbook to take on your journey!

I also feel very fortunate to have had the experience that London College of Fashion gave me, not only in terms of a great introduction to the industry and gaining the knowledge needed to go out there and face it, but also being based in arguably the most exciting city in the world. Something that many of us, myself included, take for granted on a daily basis is the impact that London has on us when working in this industry. There is so much to take in and see here and the array of creative people is staggering, and feels like it is constantly being updated with new talent: kids who come here to study and bring new and fresh ideas that we can all take on board and learn from. The pace of London never lets up. Having travelled extensively, I am always happy to come home and feel the energy that London gives me.

Miu Miu shoot, styled by Dan May for *10 MEN* issue 11, A/W 2007

Shelf Life

Terry Jones in conversation with William Hall

i-D, Issue 1, One Issue, August 1980

i-D, Issue 1, One Issue, August 1980

A quarter of a century has passed since Terry Jones imagined, created and first published *i-D*, a publication synonymous with nothing so prosaic and predictable as high fashion, but instead with what Jones himself has described as 'the democratisation of fashion'.

The magazine's tone was set by the 'straight-up', full-length portraits of ordinary people, often wearing extraordinary clothes, standing against a wall in the street or in a club. Each image would be accompanied by a short text listing the model's clothing provenance and their interests: 'DEREK Hair: self. Jacket: Flip, £11. Shirt: second-hand, £1. Belt: brother's. Likes: Cramps.'

i-D looked like a magazine that had been literally thrown together. Hastily trimmed photographs and typewritten texts were juxtaposed at strange angles. Headlines were distorted by a photocopier, or pasted together like a poison pen letter. But 'Instant Design', a term coined by Jones to describe the style, was a misnomer. 'Instant was always an illusion because the time spent on each layout of *i-D* was never instantaneous.' It was a colourful, urgent and irreverent look, dramatically different from that employed by Jones at his previous job, as art director of British *Vogue*. The earliest issues of *i-D* have an intense energy, which feels raw, direct and inclusive. The design reflected Jones' underlying message: Be who you want to be. Express yourself. Turn it up.

Today *i-D* fits into two big white rooms, each with wooden floorboards and tall ceilings. They are tranquil spaces, peopled by neat brunettes tapping away at their Macs. Jones himself is stylishly but forgettably dressed in a white shirt and jeans. Looking at those early editions of *i-D* with their lurid covers and cluttered, lively spreads, you might expect the magazine offices to be a disorganised jumble, but the opposite is true.

The visual style used by *i-D* was a precursor to David Carson's work for *Ray Gun* (1992–2000), a magazine that took the rule book of editorial design and shook it until the pages were on one occasion literally blank. Just as Jones had played with photostats, photocopiers and Polaroids, so Carson exploited the new and vast possibilities offered by the Apple Mac computer, creating a multi-layered, vivid, chaotic and sometimes illegible magazine. Was Carson influenced by Jones' work of a decade earlier? '*i-D* was one of the few magazines I took notice of when I first got into graphic design,' says Carson, 'especially the covers. It yelled and screamed to be picked up. It had a great attitude.'

Both Jones and Carson came to lecture when I was studying graphics at Saint Martins in the mid-nineties. Their work had a huge effect on me and I rejected it utterly, creating work exclusively in black and white, then making information-led, minimalist work. If there's nothing left to rebel against, you try to be extreme in the opposite direction.

i-D, Issue 8, The Head to Toe Issue, October 1982

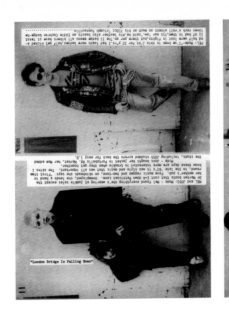

STRAIGHT UP

97

Anonymous girl with spiky hair-do.

MEL, and JOSS: Mode - Mel found everything she's wearing at jumble sales except the Dr Marten boots that cost £4 down Petticoat Lane. (though girl) she lends a hand in her mother's pub. Fave music: reggae and two-tone, on skinheads she says "First time round, in the late '60's it was style and music, that was all important. The skins I know these days are more interested in trouble when they get together. Hide - Joss bought her jacket in Portobello Rd. Market. Her Mum added the studs, including JOSS studded across the back for easy I.D.

"London Bridge Is Falling Down"

WELL Mode- "I've been in this b'l.t for 10 yr.s. I had loads more badges, half get nicked e-half were lost in fights, but there are pow by the l. badge means all bikers have it at least l2 of bad in them; to our low, said th'hts leather also boasts an Eddie Cochran badge-he loves rock n'roll almost as much as his 700cc Triumph Bonneville.................

COLIN: Mode - Colin is wearing black pleated trousers which he made himself. The cardigan is from Marks and Spencers. £9.99 and the shoes from Aston in the Kings Road, £5.99. Fave music: Siouxsie and the Banshees and David Bowie.

You will also need cups, saucers etc. and plenty of thinly cut sandwiches (devilled chive, cucumber, peanut butter, jam, whatever) sponge cakes, scones and French pastries are all welcome if there's room (checkout Corfratude, Westbourne Grove, W2, for delicious French pastries.

KAREN & KIM. Mode: KAREN aged 18, schoolgirl. Hair self. Clothes from Kensington Market. Kilt made by her mum. Likes: Throbbing Gristle & UB40 she was "overwhelmed" at being photographed. KIM: Aged 18, doing A levels. Hair by Paul in Haringay. Clothes from Ken. Mkt. Kilt by Karen's mum. She runs for Middlesex County and runs 10 miles every day. Likes gin & tonic & pink pussy cocktails. Dislikes: Adam Ant. They both go to the Beat Route on Friday nights. Photoed at the Jam Concert.

ROBERT & KEVIN. Mode: Clothes: Both get their clothes from Carnaby Cavern, Carnaby St. Shoes from Shelley's. Carn. St. also: ROBERT. Likes 60s soul and the Jam. KEVIN. Unemployed 4 mates skinheads. Photoed at the Jam concert, Lyceum, March 82.

LENE & DEREK. Mode: LENE: Hair self. Jacket Derek's £7 secondhand. Shirt hand-died (his) 2nd hand shop £2. Belt Denmark £11, boots Robot £18, earrings Spain. Comes from Denmark "I hope the Gin Club will come over to play". (American group). She plays saxophone. Real fur on hair. Getting a band together at Camp Century a place under the ice in the Arctic "they haven't got a fare fight". DEREK: Hair self. Jacket flip £11? Shirt 2nd hand hand painted '77' £1. Belt brother's. Trousers Ken. Mkt. Boots Robot £30. Derek is a paste-up artist at Better Badges. Likes: CRAMPS.

But while *Ray Gun* burnt out, *i-D* grew up. Today the magazine is as chic and sophisticated as any of the international monthlies. How does Jones explain the journey from the vibrant beginnings to today's comparatively stolid design? 'The ground rules or toolbox are there: a palette of typefaces, and style of photography. But within the palette there are variables depending on who is actually, physically in the art department. It's the same with the writing. When someone comes in to work for the magazine, they learn the process.'

Having honed the parameters, Jones learnt the confidence and prudence to allow his staff and collaborators to make the decisions: 'I choose a team, and they bring me the ingredients,' he says. 'I can do layouts if it's a deadline and we're stuck, but my job is making the mix. I see my role as being quite passive. I'm a catalyst.'

Art director Dean Langley, and his predecessor Stephen Male, who is still involved as a consultant, joined directly from college, and have both made significant contributions to the look of the current magazine. Part of its stature has come from the use of Univers, a refined and anonymous Swiss sans-serif font. Looking at early editions of *i-D* it is surprising to see the already widespread use of Univers amongst so much visual confusion. In fact Adrian Frutiger, the designer of Univers, is the strongest thread connecting over twenty-five years of *i-D*'s design. In recent years Univers has been supplemented by Avenir, another Frutiger font. 'For me Frutiger is the best typographer,' says Jones. 'Univers was a typeface that I hated as a student, but I learnt that you could do everything within the limitations of its range.'

In 1997 Frutiger was invited to redraw Univers, a substantial undertaking considering that each font includes upper and lower case, numerals and punctuation, and that Univers features over forty incrementally different versions. 'I really appreciated it when he refined the Univers cut,' says Jones with satisfaction. 'We use a mix now, the classic 45, 55, 65 (light, medium, bold), and then we'll go into some of the other weights too.'

Typography is not the only aspect of the magazine that Jones is passionate about. He is reputed to push for the best product until the last moment, stretching the deadlines and starting over on a whim. 'I have a reputation as a ball-breaker,' he cheerfully acknowledges, but he also recognises the importance of chance in his work. 'I like imperfection,' he says. 'I think the point that you reach perfection, something dies.'

Perhaps imperfection informed *i-D*'s outlook from the start. The inaugural issue announced: 'Style isn't what but how you wear clothes. Fashion is the way you walk, talk, dance and prance. Through *i-D* ideas travel very fast and free from the mainstream, so join us on the run!' It's a message which still has currency for Jones: 'I don't see that fashion is something about clothes and never did. Fashion is to do with the world we live in. About the culture we live in. Fashion is an excuse for what we do.' This notion also explains the importance and pertinence of the straight-ups as a distilled guiding principle, and suggests one aspect of what is meant by the democratisation of fashion. 'It was the idea that anybody could be a model, it was just having the confidence of your own style.' There was a playfulness and inclusivity to *i-D* not seen in its nearest rival, *The Face*. '*The Face* tended to lay down the rules, whereas with *i-D* you make up your own rules,' says Jones.

During our meeting Jones credits endless contributors. Many of them went on to have influential projects of their own: Caryn Franklin of *The Clothes Show*, journalist Kathryn Flett and *GQ* Editor Dylan Jones amongst them. 'It's like its own university,' Jones says proudly, 'the *i-D* university.' If it was a university, the photography department could be described as high achieving. Nick Knight, Juergen Teller, Wolfgang Tillmans, Terry Richardson and Ellen von Unwerth all developed their fledgling careers with *i-D*. And Jones was equally able to spot star quality amongst his cover stars; Madonna was given her first ever magazine cover with *i-D* in May 1984.

It is indicative of *i-D*'s international reputation that these contributors have had global successes of their own. 'The reach of *i-D* goes way

Clockwise from top left: *i-D* Issue 15, The Sex Sense Issue, May 1984; *i-D* Issue 94, The High Summer Issue, July 1991; *i-D* Issue 149, The Survival Issue, February 1996; *i-D* Issue 189, The Audible Issue, August 1999; *i-D* Issue 265, The Me & Mine Issue, April 2006; *i-D* Issue 276, The White Trash Issue, May 2007; *i-D* Issue 8, The Head to Toe Issue, October 1982;

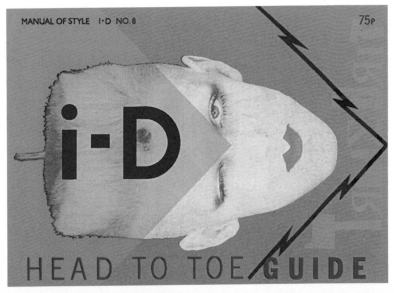

beyond the UK. We've done exhibitions in South America, the USA, China and Russia.' Despite its global reach, *i-D* remains irrevocably English. In fact three of the most influential style magazines of the last twenty-five years, *i-D, The Face* and (ten years later) *Dazed & Confused,* were all based within a mile or two of each other between London's Clerkenwell and Hoxton. Jones has a theory about what makes London special: 'The difference with London is its geographic situation. It's a gateway, so you're surrounded by a constant flow of different people. New York has similar possibilities,' he adds, 'but the essential difference is the quality of what's produced in London.'

Jones is keen that his agile, independent magazine communicates positive, sometimes political, messages. 'There is an underlying politic which I suppose is a humanitarian politic,' he says. '*i-D* is anti-racist, and democratic in principle, but more than anything it is about trying to create a magazine that keeps people's minds and eyes open.' With these lofty considerations, the 'democratisation of fashion' seems a modest ambition in comparison.

Nick Knight: *i-D*, Issue 259, The
Nationality Issue, October 2005

Naomi styled by Jonathan Kaye
T-shirt from Rellik, London, corset worn
as skirt donated by Brett Eccott, sunglasses
donated by John Galliano, necklace by
Martin Margiela.

Shelf Life

Who Needs Fashion Illustration? David Downton

In the nineteenth century, long before the advent of photography, an aspiring Lady (or Gentleman) of style relied on the exquisite engravings in magazines such as the *Journal des Dames et des Modes* to advise on fashion's latest dictates. By the turn of the twentieth century, *La Gazette du Bon Ton*, employed great artists like Drian, Barbier and Marty to enlighten readers on the ever pressing issues of 'Arts, Modes et Frivolités'. Artists held sway at *Vogue* too in the twenties and thirties when Benito and Lepape produced art deco covers of startling clarity.

During the years of the Second World War, still at *Vogue*, Carl Erickson's masterful line described a myriad of quiet but telling details from the front line and from the resource-starved fashion industry at home. After the war, Gruau's exuberant style and innate elegance signalled a return to opulence (Gruau was the poet of Dior's New Look). But by then the balance had irrevocably shifted. Photography, considered more 'modern' and 'truthful,' began to dominate and a slow but seemingly inexorable decline in the creative use of illustration took hold.

The best artists found a way through; Antonio Lopez burst onto the scene in the mid-sixties, and added the ingredient that had been missing from illustration: sex. Lopez's dexterity, energy and brilliance as a draughtsman dominated the medium until his death in 1986. In the nineties Mats Gustavsson's haunting watercolours and François Berthoud's powerful linocuts shook things up yet again, and in London, Jason Brooks and Graham Rounthwaite began producing some of the first digital fashion imagery.

Today there has never been a better, or more confusing, time to be a fashion illustrator. There is no pervading style, no prescribed way of working. Handmade and digital works are seamlessly interwoven. Inspiration has shifted from the salon to the street and illustrators now not only interpret fashion designers' ideas but, in a sense, life itself.

If the traditional high-end glossies no longer feel the need for drawing, then maybe it is their loss and just maybe the very lack of it has led to the monotonous look and feel of the publications that were once so inspiring. Diana Vreeland lamented that magazines were starting to resemble 'catalogues of available merchandise' and that was thirty or more years ago. Fortunately, the increasingly lavish, niche publications are not so faint-hearted and regularly commission some of the most innovative illustration. Of course the fact that illustrators are so much easier and cheaper to commission helps; no model, assistant, stylist, hairdresser, make-up artist or studio costs to pay. A size zero budget is the mother of invention.

Still, books and articles on the revival of the medium proliferate and all over the world, in picture libraries and in galleries, the work of a highly talented and diverse group of artists continues to shine. Perhaps we all need fashion illustration after all.

David Downton:
Dior Couture, 2006

What Makes British Fashion Great? Sarah Mower

Katherine Hamnett and Margaret
Thatcher, Downing Street, 1984

In the 1980s I was absolutely certain what made British fashion great. It was rebelliousness. It was young people kicking up against the class system. It was teenagers forced into ever more inventive extremes of creativity by the strictures of school uniform regulations. It was music. It was clubs and fanzines; punk, New Wave, New Romantics. It was Leigh Bowery and Boy George; Vivienne Westwood in a mini-crini; Katharine Hamnett facing off Margaret Thatcher in her anti-nuke T-shirt; John Galliano's girls throwing wet fish into the audience from a catwalk. It was a roar from the British streets and how it was amplified in the amazing, new, glossy style press of the Designer Decade.

Well, fond memories. They are still recycled endlessly in the fashion ether. But then came the early nineties, and everything appeared to go dead. Not true – never true – as I've learned since. Fashion in Britain never dies out, it just starts percolating some-where else. Though you do have to wait, sometimes as long as ten years, to see the froth rise again. Even when the catwalks look arid, designer bus-inesses bite the dust and emerging graduates turn intolerably timid – as they all did at that time – the truth is that talent only goes off and starts germinating somewhere you are not looking.

In this case, it was in fields, at raves and in bedsits. Even in those bleakest, most recessionary times, a generation of visually talented London

photographers, fashion, make-up and hair stylists were spawning an industry-changing look. It was shot on their skinny friends, in shredded-up, customised charity-shop clothes and then channelled through the open pages of *The Face* and *i-D*. Within a couple of years, they were propelled from penniless obscurity into the glossy professionalism of New York by Calvin Klein (ever a hawk-eye for the new) and Liz Tilberis (a fellow Brit editor with an unfailing fashion instinct) at *Harper's Bazaar.* Behind the scenes, these were the architects of the sleek, stripped-back, 'natural' look of minimalism; moving forces behind the imagery of Prada, Helmut Lang, Jil Sander and, of course, Calvin Klein. With major contracts attached, of course.

Ten years on, the roll call of fame from the early nineties is now the ruling international creative class: David Sims, Craig McDean, Juergen Teller in photography; Melanie Ward, Venetia Scott, Edward Enninful and Alex White in fashion editing and creative consultancy; Guido Palau and Eugene Souleiman in hairdressing; the revolutionary Pat McGrath in make-up.

And meanwhile, just as you thought things couldn't get more desolate on the catwalk, came another surge, mid-decade: the showmen designers Alexander McQueen and Hussein Chalayan, the Barnum & Bailey of fashion, straight out of Central Saint Martins. Their take was more high-styled, more polished, more intellec-

Leigh Bowery, Farrell House,
ca. 1983

tually passionate about the power and meaning of the image than ever before. It was the theatre of the furiously political and the flagrantly outrageous; bumsters and buried dresses, burning runways and arse-baring burkas. It was conscious, too, of playing on an international stage – even if it was in a dustbin-lorry terminal in Victoria or some blasted warehouse in Brick Lane. Rightly, because with the turbo-powered enthusiasm of stylist Isabella Blow and the intellectual force of Jane How behind it, it went all the way. To Gucci Group via Givenchy in the case of McQueen. And on to stage serially astonishing spectacles in Paris in the case of Chalayan.

But then the picture of where all this was coming from started to need readjustment. My argument for London as a unique source of street-and-club-fuelled British fashion wasn't ringing wholly true any more. This energy was different.

By the late nineties, the memorable collections shown at London Fashion Week might have been exhilaratingly unnerving, but they weren't coming out of any identifiable tribal under-ground culture any more. McQueen was from the East End, but Hussein Chalayan was a Turkish Cypriot. What they represented was something else: the growing diversity of British society, reflected upwards into the best of British art-school education. This was the fashion arm of Britart, the slightly embarrassed side of Britpop. (McQueen, indeed, was

invited to that famous Downing Street 'Cool Britannia' party, but thought Tony Blair 'a tosser'.) Their notable cohorts on the runway at the time had multicultural origins: Sophia Kokosalaki (Greek), Roland Mouret (French), Clements Ribeiro (one half Brazilian); Eley Kishimoto (half Japanese) and Blaak (half Indian, half Japanese). And what they had in common was obvious: they had studied in London.

And of course, after that flare-up, there was the next fallow time. A dreadful cull of business orders and (worse) of creative spontaneity followed the deeply pessimistic trough that set in after 9/11. As a centre of young, fledgling talent, London has always been super-vulnerable to world events, currency fluctuations and general loss of nerve in markets. Even though it had such a strong hand in commercialising the boho/girlie look (Portobello poshed up) of the mid-nineties, it was not good at the non-aggressive, unironic, ladylike cocktail dresses fashion seemed to crave in the aftermath of war. Big buyers and small boutiques turned away. We felt hopeless again, useless, in oh so many ways.

But then again fashion laughs at those who despair. Bang on a decade after the rise of 'Cool Britannia' comes the bounce-back. This time it's from a gang of optimistic, open-hearted, collaborative designers who each have a distinctive look of their own. What each of them does is narrow but specialised and

Top row from left: Sophia Kokosalaki, A/W 2006; Roland Mouret, A/W 2005; Eley Kishimoto, S/S 2005; Blaak, S/S 2003

Bottom row: Isabella Blow (1958–2007)

precociously accomplished. In their underground phase of development, they managed something previous generations had never achieved: listening and learning about quality, while also distilling the essence of their creativity. For the world's top department- and speciality-store buyers, they are the antidote to bland mass-produced 'luxury' products, making amazingly wearable clothes, full of individual verve – and delivering them on time. Perfect for a newly sophisticated generation that knows good clothes inside out but hates to be 'branded' by labels.

In the vanguard are Christopher Kane (Scottish), Marios Schwab (Greek/Austrian), Jonathan Saunders (Scottish), Roksanda Ilincic (Serbian), Richard Nicoll (Australian), Todd Lynn (Canadian), Erdem (Canadian) and Sinha-Stanic (Indian/Serbian). As it happens, there's another club explosion going on in the background – the excessive dressing up centred around Boombox and the Nu Rave scene, and something of its colour and exuberance is integral to these London designers' self-image. It is not, though, the key to their existence (and never does it distract from their hardworking focus).

What these young designers are in fact is one of the most positive reflections of Britain's vitality today – though they are not (as you see above) in any sense British per se. None of them grew up with the strictures and shared cultural references that generated the style rebellions of the eighties or the fashion boom of the nineties. Their creativity can no longer be put down to that. Why, then, are they so very good, so honed and focused, full of integrity and understanding of what they need to offer? Because, we must conclude, wherever they came from, they all passed through British fashion education. That system, in the end, for all its popularity, over-crowdedness and expense to students, is the one connecting factor behind all these successive waves of fashion high-achievers. Being a centre for educating foreign as well as home-grown fashion students has done nothing but good for the image of the UK. These multilingual graduates of British art schools, who are now contributing so much to the inter-national standing of London as a hotbed of fashion, show absolutely no inclination to leave. They stay because they love it here, find inspiration everywhere they look, and they are eternally grateful to the extraordinary academic forces who taught them. It is they who forged who these designers are. I salute them.

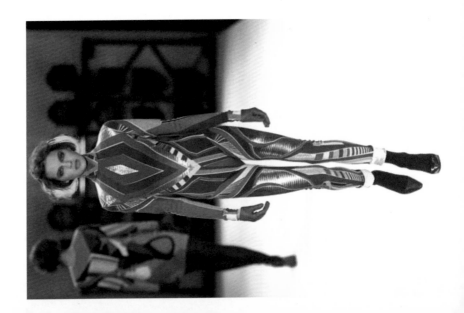

Shelf Life

Penny Martin

It is for ten seasons now that I have had the privilege of attending London Fashion Week. Equipped with the SHOWstudio picture phone, I see most of the shows and many showrooms in the interests of determining which collections, and particularly which new designers, might be interesting to work with in the ensuing months. As we are seeking *ideas* over and above technical accomplishment at SHOWstudio, it is repeatedly creatives with a 'London education' that we find ourselves eventually collaborating with. The critical studies-supported training available at the city's wealth of fine fashion colleges, combined with the rich cultural life surrounding any student living in London, consistently turns out intelligent designers who – crucially – are acutely aware of the creative world outside fashion.

The time-old criticism in the press (and complaint among the designers) is that this creativity is not matched with business acumen. What characterises London as a centre of fashion *industry* – in comparison with its international peers – is a rather cocksure commercial precociousness: designers are barely out of their BAs in London before they feel ready to assert their authorship and start up their own-name labels. Parisian designers play an end-game by comparison, assisting established designers for 5–10 years before deigning to set up on their own. Furthermore, it is commonplace for French (or US) business to invest in fashion design. In contrast, despite

Danielle Scutt: S/S 2007
(Images taken on SHOWstudio's mobile phone)

having some of the world's best paid business people in the world – and ranking fourth in the list of international cities with the highest number of millionaires – it is famously difficult to find corporate backers for London fashion talent.

Over the past two seasons there has been a perceptible shift, however. Not only is London Fashion Week markedly more thrilling and energetic: populated by a new guard of rambunctious designers such as Christopher Kane, Gareth Pugh, Richard Nicoll and Giles Deacon who have captured the attention of the global press, drawing many key journalists to London for the first time since McQueen and Galliano left to show in Paris almost a decade ago. Importantly, such press attention is also being accompanied by corporate interest at last: retail giants Westfield joining Topshop in supporting London talent through bursaries, as well as other high-street brands offering collaborative deals to young designers. Yet, cash injections of £5,000–£20,000 are but drops in the ocean to designers who require £40,000 twice per year to meet the demands of the fashion show calendar. It is inevitable that the spheres of commerce and education will have to come together to create a viable economic context in which designers can exist and the University of the Arts London will play a significant part in this.

A final word should therefore go to the many London-based designers who, despite the harsh reality of operating a business out of this expensive city, have been quietly getting on with creating beautiful, inspiring fashion collections, perhaps without receiving the press hoopla heaped upon the designers I have mentioned. What an extraordinary achievement: bravo!

Giles Deacon: A/W 2006
(Images taken on SHOWstudios's mobile phone)

Marios Schwab: A/W 2006
(Images taken on SHOWstudio's mobile phone)

Shelf Life
Shona Heath

Dazed & Confused, 2007

Although Dalston is not the most glamorous place in London, it is my home and home to most of my ideas. Inspiration is often in the things that at first glance I find depressing. Plastic items for overzealous consumers, bin bags, cheap clothes, they contrast with my ideology of a life lived amongst nature. Random objects and buildings and materials spark three-dimensional ideas, colours jump from one-pound packets of erasers, patterns jump out from every other window in African prints – the most random selection of information on fabric you will ever see. These are true genius and show no fear. Stacks of plastic ribbons boast colours suitable for funerals, Rastafarian parties and Prada's next season colour palette.

The cultural diversity and amount of weird 'stuff' going on in Dalston sparks my imagination off at a tangent. I am always relieved something does not have to be beautiful to trigger inspiration – it is more a state of mind to receive, filter and respond.

I love being taken to back rooms to look at sun-faded old stock, or begging to buy damaged goods from proud shopkeepers who can't bear to sell – all are part of London and make up a huge part of my job. Trying at all costs not to explain what you are going to do with a yellow plastic buoy for fear of being rejected a sale from diehard sailing shops (I wanted to make an S&M-style swinging seat). Putting the sale and demand off-kilter in small shops by having one-

off jobs for which I need 400 metal colanders and 200 radio aerials. I like to spend big budgets locally; it feels like it is doing something. The small shops are still here. The stationery shop loves me, even if it is for the wrong reasons.

Phases of short-lived obsessions mean I am not precious about my work and move on quickly to new sources and directions. The chaos of the city defiantly heightens the speed that I work at. Sometimes the effort behind something that ends up in a skip, never to be seen in its moment of glory, is lamentable. I suppose I am lucky to have this private view, so exclusive no one is invited! I feel vaguely responsible for not archiving or recording moments, stages – often the frantic nature of shooting means I am careless and irresponsible with the work I produce. These images are the offcuts, the backstage, the failures. To me these are my reality.

At the moment I find the most interesting part of my work is different from the finished, glossy, glamorous images you see in magazines. When there are no people, I love the way sets become scaleless. These places could be huge or they could be minuscule, 3D or flat illustrations or paintings. Where to go from here ... backwards.

Although I travel a lot, a lot of my ideas normally start in England, depending where I go ... Paris ... mmmmmmm ... is not chic! Milan ... eeeeeee ... is too trash! New York ... it needs to be super-slick! The grit

All images taken behind the scenes: Unfinished set for Emporio Armani, 2006

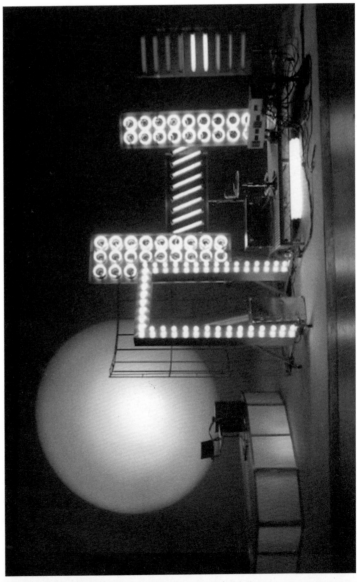

Clockwise from top left: SHOWStudio, 2004; Animals in corridor, 2004; Unused set for *Numero*, 2006; British *Vogue*, 2005; Backstage, 2006; Serge Leblon, 2006; Mixte, Rose for Italian *Vogue*, 2006

Italian *Vogue*, 2005

Numero, 2006

is often removed and the edges smoothed off. I think this edge exists because I live in London. I like that. Sometimes commercial experience compromises raw creativity and spontaneity, but its boundaries only make me push harder. The higher profile the job, the more restraints, the more at stake – the bigger the challenge to bring the creativity through. I actually enjoy the sharp embarrassment when somebody thinks my idea is way off brief and I am clearly mad – it makes me feel real.

I think my success is due to the fact that I am unafraid of making mistakes and never doubt my own or other people's capabilities. The worst thing that could happen could happen anyway without your say-so ... so you may as well take risks. Failures are often the way forward, tight budgets often have the most genuinely creative solutions.

It is the by-products and happy mistakes and complete disasters that make the most memorable moments. Burning something I have worked on for weeks, smashing it up or squashing it into a bin bag so it fits in the minicab after a shoot. The back of the hired Boleyn van rammed with sticky, painted coloured tyres that are risking my deposit (and will never dry ... even after six months and thirty tubs of Johnson's baby powder, which make them look like giant travel sweets). Me and my team are some fantasy removals section from your dreams.

Studios – vacuous, impersonal places – are a challenge for the soul. They are also a tough opponent to impress a convincing environment on. To give them a sense of place, something authentic, this is my challenge. Once the daylight has gone, New York, London, Paris, Milan, they are all the same – a playground for me.

Often it is the process of the work that is believable. We are a team, working to a goal. This is authentic, somehow images of this process are more acceptable to me. I have to believe in what I am creating, in its abstraction or realism. I am not fooled by the perfection in the finished pictures. When the model walks on set, it is a reality check – the photographer, hairdressers, make-up artists all bustle in – the world I have just created becomes a blank canvas once again. Oops, I forgot it wasn't about me!

The thing I miss in London is a horizon, infinity. Drive-by glimpses of a skyline are precious. Over bridges I turn my head quickly to look both ways, to give each view the same attention; if there is a sunrise I am speechless. At an equally depressing and liberating point on the A40 towards Oxford the road rises up above the buildings like a helter-skelter, the sun comes through the ugly office blocks on the left, but it's enough. This is also the way to my home, where my family are and the way to the prop houses in lovely Acton.

Mixte, 2006

Alison Tanner, 2005

AON I want to start with an observation about your practice. There was a television programme screened in 2001 called *Year One: A Snapshot of Britain* that you featured in. You were shown working on the *War* series of images that you created with the stylist Simon Foxton, and one of the things that I found particularly illuminating about this clip was that it showed you working on-screen digitally and then turning around and working with cut-out elements over a light box in a very hands-on way. I just wanted to use that as a starting point really to ask you how important that kind of hands-on approach to creativity is to your practice?

NK I think they're all different parts of an overall equation. I don't make any difference really between any part of the process and I don't place any more emphasis on one part of the process rather than another part. I feel the process of making an image from the moment it's conceived in your head to the moment that it's published; the moment it is on billboards or on screens – all that is all one continual process.

Throughout that process there are different media that you use, that you choose to work with and there are different forms that you express it with. To me, there's no difference between the moment that you start photocopying things and cutting them up, to the moment the model stands in front of the camera, between the moment that you're sitting in your room thinking 'What would

it be like if we mixed that with that?' You know, to the moment you're referencing to the moment that you're talking to the people on set. It's all part of the continual process of which I don't see a sort of helpful way of dividing it up. What I'm trying to say is that a lot of people view that, the moment you take the photograph, as a paramount moment in the whole of the equation…

AON Yes, the decisive moment.

NK …and I don't think that's true. I think it is an important moment but I think there are a lot of other important moments, and so I don't make any difference and therefore I don't have any problem with swapping from things cut up on a light box to then moving them around in Photoshop; any more than I have a problem moving from one lens to another and changing film, or asking the models to stand, sit, pose, move, etc.

They're all little parts of an overall creation, or an overall equation where you end up being one step further on. In an even broader sense I don't see my work in terms of pictures that are hung on the wall which are admired or critiqued – I don't see that as the final point, as I don't like the arrogance of that way of presenting work. I just see them as an ongoing interest in life, an ongoing quest and an ongoing conversation. So, I see the whole thing as very transient and very fluid; as once you've learnt or understood something, you don't want to then go back and try and

reunderstand it; once you've opened that door you don't feel that you want to go back and reopen that door to discover what's in the room again, because you know what's in that room.

AON But just to return to that moment at the beginning of the twenty-first century, it seems that the *War* series was very much caught up with the publication of *The Impossible Image* too, and it seemed at that point in time that the notion of digital imaging and the digital age was very much at the forefront of the discussion about creativity and possibility, and it seems to me now that that's somewhat modified since that point in time.

NK Well, it was a new toy in the same way that when people moved on to a handheld 35mm camera and stopped having a huge great big tripod and a single sheet 10x8, when Martin Munkácsi revolutionised the fashion world by suddenly grabbing hold of a camera and running with it. Or when people like Robert Capa used it for war reportage or David Bailey kind of famously injected life into a posed sketch just as Beaton had been doing – these are all moments where the technical side of things becomes very, very important, and people talk a lot about those moments when they're happening and they discuss them widely. Even the advent of photography was discussed in similar sorts of terms, and actually I don't really make those differences: as there is no difference between Photoshop and the new wide-angle lens.

They are just toys if you want, or less glibly, tools that you use to express your point of view, and some are more profound as you can do more with them and some are less profound. If you're moving from holding a 35mm camera to having a camera on a tripod that doesn't essentially move, you've got quite a different way of working.

In the same way, you can now have your camera plugged into a bank of computers at the back of the room with somebody getting the images and viewing them on the screen; that engenders a different way of working, and quite a good way of working I'd add; and then more people can join in and the discussion of the image is more open. I think that is a very beneficial thing for the image-maker and all those concerned in the image.

After all, we tend not to make images just for ourselves, just for our own viewing pleasure; we tend to make them for a reason: for other people, with other people. So I think opening up that process is very important. There are several things that the digital age has done in terms of the technicality of making the picture, but there's a much broader change that has happened which is fundamental and is probably bigger than anything we've talked about, which is the advent of the Internet.

AON Of course.

NK The Internet as a communication device is revolutionary, as much as paper was when it was first invented. I think we now have a completely new way of communicating as a species and I think that's never really happened before. The fact that I can take my mobile phone, take an image and have it published within a split second to a global audience without anybody saying to me, 'Well, is that going to make me any money?' – that's a revolution.

Before, if I wanted to do a set of photographs I would have to convince the magazine publisher, a music company, or whoever it would be – some client – to allow me to publish that series of photographs. And it would be to some degree to, you know, nearly always, to make somebody money, whether it's a gallery owner or your dealer, your gallery dealer, or whether it's the head of Warner Brothers or the head of Condé Nast. Somebody in the end is making some money from you. Now that relationship between the artist and the audience has fundamentally been changed by the advent of the Internet. Now I can publish a set of pictures, not for anybody else's financial benefit, and other people can see them, and if they're good, people like them and want to see more of them, then they're not going to be ignored. It's a simplification of the situation, but it does mean that not only can we communicate in a totally global and unfettered way, but it also means that the sort of work that we do now is much more free; because I can take a series of images and have those downloaded with some sound, I can

put bits of film in there, I can use mobile phones, I can still use 10x8 cameras – it just opens the whole thing up. It's a completely, completely different way of communicating to anything we've ever had before.

AON Yes, and I think that SHOWstudio as a project demonstrates that interface between digital imaging and a digital community interested in that form of creativity. One of the things that I think SHOWstudio has been brilliant at illustrating is process …

NK Yes.

AON … and secondly, an understanding of fashion in motion and I just wondered if you could reflect on that?

NK I think they're very good observations. I think that's almost the core value of SHOWstudio. One was to show the whole process of creating a piece of work, and the other was to show that actually now we have the medium that can support this, that in fact is very good for this.

We can now show fashion moving, whereas for the last fifty or so years it has, to some degree, been only shown as a still image; and one could argue that that stillness is a compromise to the understanding of that piece of clothing. I think that now you can show a piece of clothing in movement it's quite a different medium and I think that's very exciting.

AON Well, there is another sense of movement which I've observed, looking at SHOWstudio, and that's your personal movement when you're creating things. It's very easy to see you pacing around when you're shooting and it seems to me that this sense of movement is quite important to your creative process. There are other precedents: Alexey Brodovitch comes to mind, and the idea of him doing a kind of dance around his layouts at *Harper's Bazaar* when they were laid out on the floor …

NK You're being very astute, Alistair. The show was originally going to be called performance.com because there were certain things that I believed in when we started SHOWstudio. One was process, the second was performance and the third was moving fashion.

AON Right.

NK Performance is something that I've noticed is an important part of what I do. It's an instantaneous moment of creation when I'm taking a photograph; and that performance is very charged. It is a performance you do in front of a small audience, normally of between ten to twenty people, and you give a physical performance in the same way that the model is giving a performance. I've become much more aware of my physical presence on a shoot and I've taken certain photographs in some ways to try to explore that. One always thinks that the model is actually doing all of the physical work, but actually the photographer or the image-maker is doing an awful lot of physical performance. The whole thing taken together with all the attendants, stylists, art directors and everyone else on the shoot is a piece of theatre – it's a piece of contemporary, live, creative, ongoing theatre and I think that's fascinating.

And the actual physical performance of pacing is how you deal with your own physicality. I pace, and I tend not to do it so much now as I'm much more aware. It's been mentioned in interviews too many times that I pace up and down and I find myself becoming a caricature of myself, but I've noticed there are physical things one does. I've always videoed my shoots, so there is always a video recorder on the tripod left recording, which has allowed me to go back and look through some of those shoots now for different projects. I should make a film about it, and I do realise now that there are a whole series of gestures and body shapes that you throw to encourage the models to do the same thing, even though I have a completely different physicality to the model, so the physical performance is enormously important.

When I photographed Naomi Campbell for Yohji Yamamoto in 1986 when she was just starting out, Yohji had done his take on the early collections of the original Christian Dior and he had done these fantastic inspired coats but they were just in colours, either bright green or bright red. Naomi put on one of the red coats and did a performance on a piece of beautiful perspex which was laid down on the floor of the

walkway, and she put on a tape that Prince had just given her and started doing this sort of series of walks up and down.

Just standing there watching Naomi in the red coat with the flash going off in the background created a latent image of her frozen in the back of your retina. It was quite a performance; as a piece of contemporary fashion theatre it was quite stunning. And it's from those days really, back in 1986, that I thought – well, there's something here that nobody else is seeing because they are only seeing the end image, of course, and they're not witness to this, as it's only a very fraction of what I'm experiencing. A performance that happens in a studio is exceedingly interesting, and one of the things we try to do in SHOWstudio (and coincidently we are doing Naomi again on Monday and Tuesday) is allowing people to witness that performance as a live broadcast.

AON A very rich area of SHOWstudio's archive is the rediscovered films of fashion shoots, I'm thinking particularly of those by Guy Bourdin and Erwin Blumenfeld. It seems to me that you are suggesting that there is a much broader history to this kind of film-making that needs to be preserved and needs to be better understood?

NK Well, we have a series of artists and photographers that we gain things from. Most image-makers tend to dabble around in different mediums that they are connected to, so I know that Bob Richardson, Terry's dad, videoed everything. I know that Helmut Newton produced lots of films, as did Serge Lutens and Jean Paul Goude. We are securing these to show at SHOWstudio at the moment because they show another version of the understanding of that person's world; and what they are trying to express through still photography often opened up through moving image in quite an interesting way. And the images that came through on Bourdin and the images that came through on Blumenfeld were just as powerful or as beautiful or as surreal or as menacing as their still images.

AON I quite agree with you on that.

NK And I found that fascinating. It's an ongoing project and we are talking to the estates of those photographers, and we are also talking to the ones that are still alive and trying to secure the footage.

AON I can certainly see it as offering a completely different dimension to the understanding of a creative. We were lucky enough to have Jean Paul Goude give a talk at our university and he screened a film that he had made about his work, and it gave a completely different reading to it as it was contextualised through the traditions of American dance …

NK Right.

AON … rather than American fashion or American photography; it was just so illuminating and I think that a lot more work needs to be explored in this way.

NK Well I would happily if someone gives me some more money …

AON Ha-ha.

NK … that would make it better, but that's what we are currently working on. It's one of those things isn't it – there are so many things to try and do.

AON Well, we've spoken about the kind of difference between still image and moving image and I want to talk about another kind of divide or a way of understanding your work. Your work is collected by museums internationally and in this country the most obvious site for it is the Victoria and Albert Museum, our National Museum of Art and Design. Yet people are perhaps not so aware of the fact that you also have a relationship with those museums that exist on the other side of Exhibition Road, that articulate that division between the arts and sciences, and I'm referring to the *Plant Power* display for the Natural History Museum but also *Flora*, your publication of photographs from 1997. How do you situate yourself across that nineteenth-century dividing span?

NK Well, I started my studies as a scientist as I came from a family of scientists. My brother was a Doctor of Chemistry, my father was a psychologist and my mother was a psychotherapist, so I was destined to

Nick Knight:
Design Download, Alexander
McQueen, SHOWstudio,
March 2004

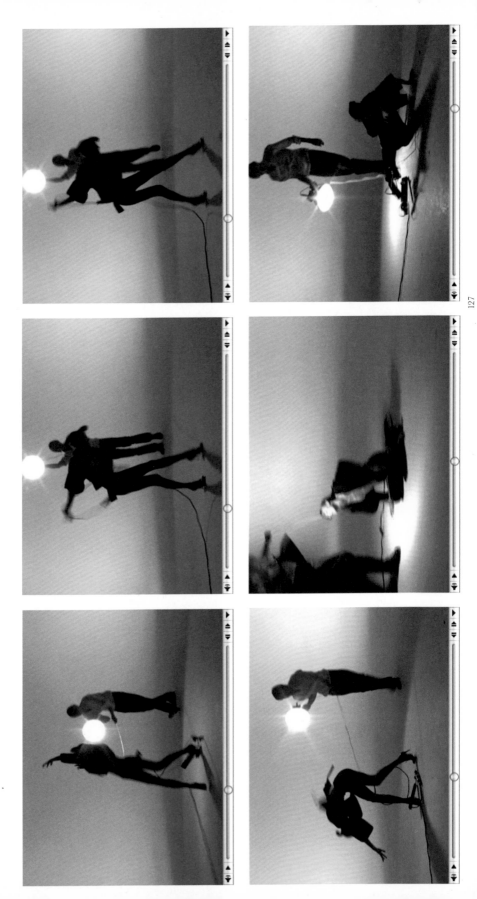

go toward science. I studied Human Biology at London University in 1978 and I hated it, I absolutely hated it. I couldn't see any reason to study at university as the plan was to go into medicine, but I just couldn't see any relevance to the emotional desires that I had at that point of my life. Just sitting there bored, watching massive equations going across the blackboard and thinking, I just can't be bothered to concentrate, I'm not interested; I don't want to be here, this isn't for me.

So I backed out of it. I left after a year and went to Bournemouth and Poole College of Art and took up photography against my family's advice; but they knew nothing about the arts: all they probably thought was, 'Our son is going to be poor and starving and we are all going to end up supporting him.' So they were supportive of me in an emotional sense, but just worried that I would never be able to make a living from this because they only had experience of making money through science, through that side of life. So I found throughout my photography career that I have approached the problem-solving of imagery in a scientific manner.

AON How interesting.

NK   There was a lot of trying to do a scientific experiment: accepting the fact that something doesn't work is as important as the fact that something does work. It just proves or disproves what you believe and helps you get further towards a better understanding of your topic. Now, failure is an important part of what I do and so in a pragmatic way, when I stand in front of whoever it is – whether it's Robert de Niro, or whether it's Kate Moss – to some degree I have to produce an image of them.

The first one that comes out of the camera is usually going to be, you could term it as a failure; and facing up to the emotional factor of that failure, in a very public way, is a very healthy growth of the overall process. In science this would be quite normal, but in the arts there is a sort of desire to hide away the fact that you actually don't know how to do it straight away – it's usually a lot of trial and error.

There is also an understanding of trying to see things as they actually are in science and I think that's useful

Nick Knight: *Flora*, 2001

in terms of image-making: to actually try to work out what it is you're trying to say and what's actually there. I think there's an analytical approach applied throughout scientific research, which I've applied again and again through my image-making. And despite of myself in my early, formative years science has informed – or if you like shaped – my approach to image-making. I'm interested in an inquisitive way in how an image functions. I'm interested in how a latent image records on the back of the retina. I'm interested in how memories affect our work. On SHOWstudio we've had the chance to develop things like synaesthesia. Those sorts of projects are created through a love or questing for knowledge which is a similar situation that might find yourself in as a research scientist, and so in that way I think I'm actually probably pretty much on the same sort of course I would have been; I just have gone about it in a very different way.

AON Well, that's a very interesting response to my question because it confirms an observation that I've had about your body of work, *Flora*. They are undeniably beautiful modern images of flowers, but they are also very reminiscent of William Henry Fox Talbot's photograms of floral forms; and it seems that this idea of quest that you've just raised is very much in keeping with the techniques that the early pioneers of photography were dealing with. So I suppose that leads me on to ask you how you situate yourself in relation to that very broad trajectory of photographic history?

NK I've always felt that I've come in at the end of photography the end of its existence as a medium as a predominant image-making medium. Ever since I started it in the late seventies, I've felt that I wasn't really at the beginning of something; I felt I was more at the end of something and the beginning of something else. So I've never felt anything other than a sort of love for the future and a love of what's happening next, so I don't have any sort of emotional ties to photography. I'm not sure if I'm answering your question…

AON No no, you certainly are.

NK … but I think there is a new

medium happening and almost from the beginning of my career I've been waiting for the Internet to allow this to get through. I think that there is a very exciting thing happening and I think that photography really is holding us back in a lot of ways. There is a lot of discussion about manipulation being a negative thing and I think photography has been saddled, quite wrongly in my opinion, as the bringer of truth, as the witness to the unwitnessable event. So now I feel I'm actually in my real medium, whereas photography was a way into that. Just as those early pioneers of photography, must have also felt that they were doing something different from painting, I feel a sort of kinship in that way. So if there is any link to be made between myself and the early pioneers of photography it's simply being at the beginning of a new medium – but I'm not at the beginning of photography. I'm at the beginning of a new medium which is defined by the Internet, digital technology, mobile phones, even 3D scanning. 3D scanning is a very exciting and new part of what I do, allowing me to produce 3D objects, which we could call sculptures if we wanted to, using the same skill set as I would use to produce a 2D image. So how I approach the person in front of the scanner or the person in front of the camera is very similar.

AON Well I think 3D body-scanning technology is an interesting example in that it was developed as a measuring tool rather than a creative tool. It was primarily for body metrics and it seems to me that how one goes about galvanising this technology is very important in the sense of changing the technology's intention.

NK I've always been delighted in a computer going wrong.

AON Ha-ha.

NK And I did my first 3D scanning with a company based in the former Ealing Film Studios site who were creating, who were trying to reanimate old dead actors, and they had a 3D scanner rig which had been developed in Edinburgh, I think, or one of the other Scottish universities. The technique applied a photographic image over a sort of contour map of the body, but of course what the computer couldn't decide when

putting this together was if something that reflected was a solid object or not and whether that solid object was receding from the lens or advancing towards it.

So the computer would have to make it up and it produced wonderful and beautiful patterns of geometric forms, which seemed to go on as if the computer didn't know how to stop it. And I loved the fact that the preciseness of the technical age was quite quickly being shown a random set of badly worked out equations it couldn't work out. It gave it a human side, which I thought was rather intriguing. So I've always liked the fact that when these things are set up to do something, you try to use them upside down or the wrong way round etc. – it exposes parts which are very interesting.

AON Quite. I do think that that notion of imperfection is something that you chart through the different bodies of work that you have produced across your career…

NK I am sorry to interrupt you but it's something that in my mind is linked to failure and I think that's a very helpful thing

AON …yes, a very human thing.

NK Yes.

Nick Knight: *Flora*, 2001

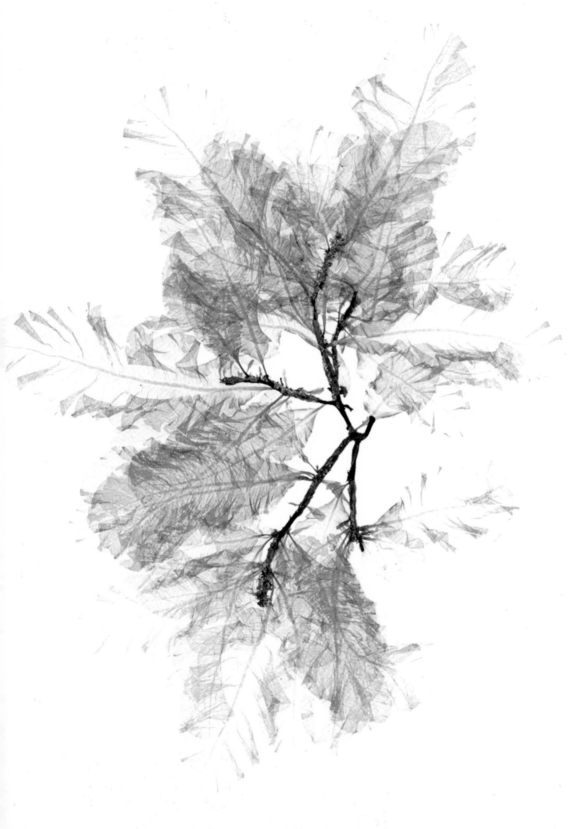

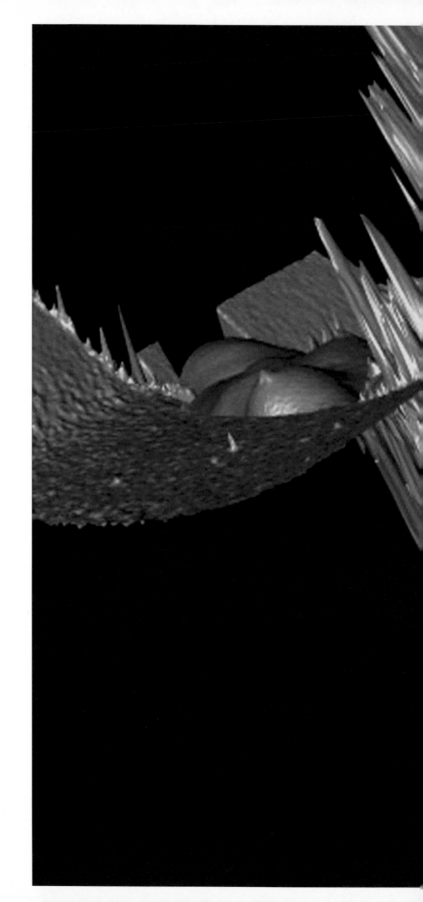

Nick Knight: Naomi Campbell, 3D
scanning Kev Stenning Rapido3D,
SHOWstudio, 2006

Freeze Frame
Sean and Seng

'living in london really excites us, so
much style, so much hair! everyday'

Sean and Seng; Vivienne
Westwood A/W 2006

Freeze Frame

Gavin Fernandes
by Val Williams

Gavin Fernandes' most recent series of photographs, *Monarchs of the East End* and *Empire Line*, represent a new order within British photography. Emerging from the hybrid and multi-layered research culture of London College of Fashion, Fernandes' work breaks both with the strictures of documentary portraiture and the demands of fashion photography. His series employ, in their complex construction, historical narrative, costume detail and political discourse. The complexity of Fernandes' photographs lies in their ability to combine these disparate elements in visual constructions which combine notions of visual glamour and theoretical argument. As Fernandes himself has written of the series *Monarchs of the East End*: 'The project was complex and definitive, motivated by a profess-ional commission that enabled the practice to be located in the public domain within the context of current critical and cultural debates.'

Gavin Fernandes' work is under-pinned by comprehensive research; while making *Monarchs of the East End*, Fernandes adopted regality as his central theme. Transposing ideas about the costume and character of the Pearly Kings and Queens, the quintessential show people of the 'other' Royal Family traditionally located in working class areas of Lon-don, Fernandes has mused upon the changing culture of the East End, where costume continues to play such a significant role in signalling class, aspiration and pride. As Niki Gomez of the East London cultural

Gavin Fernandes:
Empire Line, 2005

foundation, Rich Mix, has remarked: 'It links past and present and global and local. It investigates the regal aspirations of Pearly Kings and Queens and Afro-Caribbean immigrants, both minority groups, and links their styles to that of local people in East London today, from different races – black, white and Asian.'

When preparing the project for the eventual shoot, Fernandes became highly aware of the importance of the location of the commission, identifying Bethnal Green and the East End of London as an important site of immigration, including the early Huguenot refugees who established the silk-weaving industry in Spitalfields, to Jewish migrants from Eastern Europe during much of the first half of the twentieth century, newcomers from Bangladesh in the 1970s and '80s, through to the most recent wave of immigrants from the former Eastern bloc states. In his research, Fernandes has identified the markets of the East End as the conduit of style and aspiration for a wide variety of residents, including a 'media middle class who revel in the modernity of the new millennia', plus 'those who aspire to the traditions of British subculture both past and present'.

Like all those who become involved (and sometimes complicit) with the mythology of the East End, Fernandes sees *Monarchs of the East End* as both reinforcement of and challenge to familiar legends and new colonisers: 'Figures such as Jack the Ripper, the Pearly Kings and

Gavin Fernandes: *Empire Line*, 2005

Queens, the Krays, the Windrush immigrants, the music-hall tradition, the costermongers, the Oswald Mosley fascists of Cable Street, skinhead protests on Brick Lane, the Queen Mother's visit to Bethnal Green, the Repton Boys' Boxing Club, the posturing and pretension of neo-beatnik nightclubbers in Hoxton and Shoreditch.' By using the styles and methodologies of fashion photography, which in itself is adept at freely utilising histories for its own purposes, Fernandes was able to construct a series which both subverts and celebrates narratives of style.

One photograph in *Monarchs of the East End* shows two young Asian men dressed in branded sports clothing, their shirts customised by the stylist Judy Blame with an assemblage of buttons and chains. The image interrogates the notion of masculinity and race, inviting us to decode the symbols that Fernandes has used, of the branded laurel wreath and the equally logoistic arrangements of buttons and ribbons. There is a suggestion of medals, of inscription, of the wearing of both the signs of global capitalism and the everyday objects of dressmaking as a source of pride.

In making this series, Fernandes has tellingly noted his referencing of the work of the African studio photographers Seydou Keïta and Malik Sidibé, whose work is now well known in British art-photography circles and both of whom have come to represent a kind of 'authenticity'. In the works of Keïta and Sidibé, costume and ornamentation have come to be seen as central in the description of both the naive and the 'other', at least in the Western imagination. Fernandes takes our fascination with exotic 'otherness' and subverts it by using the customised and reinterpreted regalia of the Pearly Kings and Queens to interrogate the ways in which we read photographs, each other and the world around us.

In another photograph, in which Fernandes explores and parodies the character of the Jewish East-End artisan, a young man is festooned with cards of buttons, watchmaker's tools, a tape measure, a Catherine wheel of pins and a jewelled Star of David. It is a riotous assemblage of implements and objects, all determinedly workaday, yet emerging from this portrait as an extravagant array of jewellery. His subject looks affronted, almost abject, burdened with these scraps of history. Yet another photograph examines the idea of the dandy aristocracy; a boy-woman, hair coiffed in forties' roll, is dressed in a satin ruff, her earrings are miniature royal crowns and a portrait of a horse is enclosed in a brooch ringed with pearls. This regal figure, posed as a dubious heroine from a latter-day Bohemia, is perhaps the central character in this highly wrought series of four photographs; she is difficult to locate through the familiar codes of race, gender and period which Fernandes has used throughout this project. She could be now, or yesterday, or a hundred years ago. Fernandes' photographs are elusive, their meanings disguised with the pyrotechnics of style.

Monarchs of the East End, like Fernandes' earlier series, *Empire Line*, examines our multi-intersecting identities and histories using a methodology which is more commonly used to clarify rather than interrogate. The uses of fashion photography are more commonly to make simple what is complicated. Fernandes has refuted this simplicity and made complex, many-layered narratives around ideas of race, culture, history and society, persuading us to look more closely at ourselves as creatures, rather than masters, of our histories. That his work is open, available to interpretation and constantly aware of its own fictionality, proves beyond a doubt that photographers have broken the boundaries of 'issue-based' photography in the 1970s and '80s, and are now able to use the medium, in all its multiplicity and complexity, to explore beyond the bounds of genre.

Freeze Frame
Chris Moore

The overworked phrase 'London is a melting pot' applies equally well to style as anything else. Fashion has morphed its way through the twentieth century mirroring the culture, politics, art and music of pre- and post-war generations for this last one hundred years. The debate over originality manifesting in design rebounds across these decades, but London like nowhere else would suggest that style and design is a collective ideal, its fabric resting on the frame of contemporary culture.

Style-hunters hawkishly swoop over London's buzz, and a customised jacket in Camden can inspire an entire collection in Tokyo or Paris, be bought and worn by pop idols in New York and then in turn influence school kids in Fulham. This carrousel of inspiration continues to be the driving force of fashion and is why over time utility became chic, why military turned mainstream, and why big business still keeps as much of an eye on the street as it does on the drawing board.

London too has a uniquely diverse news and media culture, sharing a symbiotic existence with fashion. Both industries, like many others, are undergoing the fastest change they have possibly ever experienced, thanks to new technologies, and in turn, as a photographer servicing both, my business has changed with them. Ironically at first glance the bottom line remains the same, a garment, a visual and the printed page, but the processes behind them have come through as complex an

evolution as the Wright brothers and the aeroplane in roughly the same window of time.

As a photographer based in London with work and clients across the world I have seen the digital revolution march with differing pace from country to country. The UK media concentrated in London with its huge public appetite for news, pressured its photographers for faster and faster deadlines, which meant that by the time manufacturers like Canon and Nikon piloted their first still somewhat inadequate digital cameras, photographers like myself were already champing at the bit, and London put itself at the cutting edge of the digital revolution.

The birth of digital photography happened at exactly the same time that business was realising the potential of the Internet to enhance its presence in crowded world markets and suddenly the race was on. Everyone it seemed wanted to embrace this new technology, everyone that is except the fashion business.

There was and is a festering suspicion that originality is coming under threat, new ideas and designs are being published at uncontrollable rates and the growth of the luxury goods market means there is more to lose from counterfeiting or so the argument goes, despite the vastly differing nature of their point of sale, price and appeal, meaning that the target customer can rarely be the same animal.

Chris Moore:
Julien MacDonald, A/W 1998

Every good fairytale needs an ugly sister or a wicked witch and fashion has pinned its woes on news photography and the Internet. This is unfortunate for an industry at the mercy of changing tastes and reliant on harnessing and even creating trends; the Web is now driving both to a great degree.

Fortunately in less than a decade the new generation of designers and businesses not burdened with the baggage of tradition and established practices are now using the Web as their preferred marketing tool. This relatively affordable medium has given much-needed oxygen to young talent, which in the past has prematurely expired, unable to compete with the fat promotional budgets of fashion giants.

London designers particularly have suffered from lack of exposure and its Fashion Week depleted from brands seeking audiences in better-attended cities. To squash publication on the Web is to stamp all over the new shoots of talent wherever it is, putting even bigger businesses than mine at risk.

The concept of 'originality' has been a useful one in structuring patents, but in this modern world of cyber chat, the natural web of inspiration means the that the true relationship between design and its references is more complex. Beauty is in the eye of the beholder but, like it or loathe it, the Web is here and it is here to stay. Big business can learn to master it to its huge advantage or sit like King Canute on the shoreline.

Chris Moore:
Alexander McQueen,
10th Anniversary Celebration
at Earls Court, July 2004

Freeze Frame
Wendy Bevan

Having grown up in the countryside, I constantly have a love-hate relationship with the city. However, London stirs a restlessness within me and I am attracted to every source of inspiration the city can offer. You can never stop searching here; there is always something new to do and try: what a fantastic place to be associated with!

I love how London allows you to pick and choose from its endless options to create an infinite number of new combinations for how you live your life; everybody has a different routine. You can do anything here if you look hard enough, and that eclecticism is what I thrive on. I have never stopped exploring.

It seems that the only way to find harmony when you live here is to find your personal space. It is enormously satisfying when you finally piece things together and start to get a feel for what your London is.

As a London-based photographer many of the locations I shoot in are here in the city. I have spent countless days exploring and location-hunting, watching and being a part of the city.

I love sitting in cafés and watching the passers-by: how they dress, how they walk, are they happy or sad? It's funny how you can take in so much about a person in so little time, and how those very rare physical moments that are shared between Londoners dissolve almost immediately into the fast pace of the day. Photography and voyeurism go hand in hand, watching from a distance but understanding intimately when taking the photograph.

Witnessing any moment is a precious thing, and recording that moment is the core reason I am a photographer. I love catching a moment that existed in real life, then recontextualising it.

Moments that are true to life remind you of the past; we take pictures so as not to forget. Memories dissolve too quickly, but photography allows us to remember them vividly.

Sometimes you can become so familiar with someone or something that you forget the details that made them so interesting and beautiful in the first place. Fashion imagery typically dramatises perfection and often there is a hidden implication that imperfection is somehow undesirable.

Our magazines are filled with page after page of perfection and making it seem inspirational and attainable. But do we really want this unattainable perfection that fashion imagery thrusts at us?

Why would we want to record only perfect moments? Isn't awkwardness or sheer heightened emotion, a sense of reality, honesty more interesting to view – where true inspiration is sourced from?

I aim to produce a sense of timelessness in my photographs that crosses over the threshold of fashion and art.

Wendy Bevan: O Magazine, Hampstead Heath, 2006

Wendy Bevan: *Lula*,
Hyde Park, 2006

I enjoy playing with the emotive connotations my images give to the viewer. Subtle links that tap into their subconscious, allowing them to reminisce and feel a sense of nostalgia.

I love theatre and film and this also transposes itself directly into my work. Often on a shoot I feel as if I am making a short film. I enjoy the process of building a character and adding depth by creating a scenario/ concept for them to interact with – characters with identities that often never have to be justified or explained.

Although the clothes in my images are secondary in the initial character development, they do add another layer of intrigue, offering clues that entice us, raising questions without answers.

I think many people choose to express their identity through the way they dress, something which fascinates me. London allows you to do this because it is an anonymous place that will equally hide and expose you. For this reason I love dressing up and the idea that every day I could embrace the silhouette of a different character.

Yet London becomes overwhelming at times. For all its creative freedoms and opportunities, it is equally an unforgiving and unloving place. Your identity is not always noticed and this leads to a loneliness that is often recognised within my images; a sense of searching, haunted by nostalgia. I don't like everything to seem perfect in my images; they are certainly not glossy sweeping statements of false perfection that make the viewer idolise the impossible.

All the images in this book are examples of photographs I have taken in London. Like London, my work is as surreal as it is real.

Wendy Bevan: Unpublished,
Baglionis Hotel, 2006

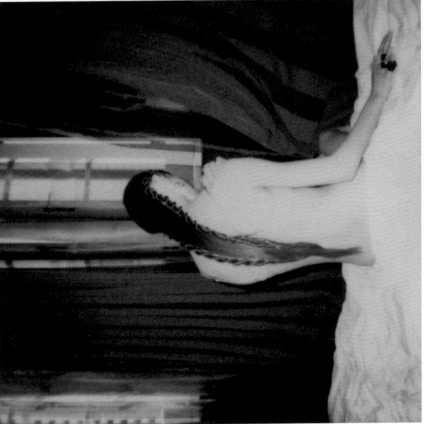

Tim Gutt: *London*, 2005

London

In contrast to the regulated, manicured streets I was used to as a child in Holland, London in the mid-eighties and early nineties could, if I squinted hard enough, resemble seventies films, and its grey concrete office buildings had the allure of the modernist lifestyle of the sixties. It's this nonsensical cocktail of associations, a childish longing for what you cannot grab hold of, a foreignness, that I am still pursuing with my photography today.

Hype

Part of the attraction of London is based on its hyped reputation of being an edgy hotbed of energy and style. It's the promise of glossy magazines and clever people wearing clever clothes. Hard-nosed, hard-working, hard-playing creatives. It's an expensive cocktail served on credit. It's also highly inspiring.

Inspiration

My practice is inspired by documentary photography and cinema. I find it on the streets of Manhattan where I spend months roaming public spaces. I pick up on scenes of everyday encounters and experiment with the notion of reality that is inherent in documentary photography: manufacturing a suggestion from snippets of information; unrelated events taken and put into context. Simultaneous action provides tension between people and implies a relationship. It all comes down to provoking an interest in a person, the curiosity to understand their motivation. New York informs the imagery with a collective memory of movie scenes.

Location

The setting for these events has to be a blank canvas, to provide a simplified, recognisable yet nondescript backdrop.

Obstacles

London has posed an obstacle for me in this respect. I often find myself at the beginning of a project looking for something that exists as a feeling but actually does not exist; a preconceived idea of how something should look. I end up either shooting it further afield or setting it up in the studio.

Identity/Culture/Foreignness

Not being English in a city that is marked by an extravagant mix of nationalities, it seems like an opportunity to seek 'the other' and to examine and embrace being from a different place by looking at other cultures and relating them to my own rather than adopting an English sensibility. It has made me want to go to places where the culture is yet more remote from my own like Korea or India, but instead I end up recreating a notion of these places here in London.

Fashion

To me fashion means to go much further than a visual style. It's the messages that clothing holds about its bearers that are a source of interest and inspiration. It tells you who people are, as in cultural connotations on a broad level, but more

Tim Gutt: *Off) course*, 1996

interestingly it tells you what people stand for and what they care about.

Important

I like images that have relevance beyond the clothes that are on show. I was never inspired by the notion of luxury, a beautiful girl in a beautiful dress. I like images that haven't got a date mark on them. This makes my relationship with the fashion industry rather complicated, seeing as fashion and particularly fashion styling are intrinsically connected to a season, a 'look'. The challenge that this poses has been a strong motivation to develop a number of co-operations with like-minded people from within the fashion arena.

Collaboration

Shona Heath, art director and set designer extraordinaire, has been a key collaborator in the last few years. Working with Shona has been very liberating for me in the way that it has allowed me to loosen up and think in new ways about photography, and fashion in particular. Being so obsessed with the right location, it was a very refreshing thing to go into the studio and create from nothing. Equally for Heath, this has meant a step outside her usual terrain of set design, in the sense that the collab-oration is not so much about sets or big interventions but more that of an art director/photographer.

The initial clash of our respective visual styles, my aesthetic being more minimalist, hers more expressive and romantic, has opened new ways to explore the domain between reality and the surreal and cinematic. Heath's contribution has been essential both in the conceptual sense and in the actual styling aspect for the projects described below.

'Case Study', a project instigated by fashion curator Louise Clarke, led to a series of images entitled 'Between The Lines' that investigated inter-personal space by means of 3D photography. This has been an opportunity to reconnect with those childhood memories of Viewmaster bliss. Rather than choosing the archi-tectural, space this was an exploration of the dynamics between two people and the space they shared in a stereo-scopic photo shoot. Peter Jensen contributed the fashion.

Above: Tim Gutt: *The Boy,
Kilimanjaro,* 2006

Below: Tim Gutt: *The Continued
Gaze,* 2007

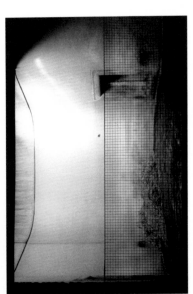

Michael Olu Odukoya, publisher of *Kilimanjaro* magazine in London, is a source of inspiration and a fellow outsider, whose shared interests in art and fashion have been the basis of a number of projects. 'The Boy' was an exploration of a different kind of black identity: to see someone black in a different light from the familiar urban angry young man. It drew from the experience and the excitement of an African adolescent growing up in a distinctly European culture.

Storytelling
Jigsaw of making a reality / Interaction between people is the focal point / You have to believe in it for it to work / Not to be able to see your own hand as a photographer / A crucial part in this process is casting.

Casting
Who you choose to carry the story, it's the single most important thing in drawing in your viewers. Where did you find her? Whatever the outlandish idea/concept it needs a coherent believable reality to portray it. There's a stringent set of rules to warrant this. I spend a lot of time on casting the right person. There is nothing more boring than a beautiful young girl with an empty gaze repeated over ten pages. It often means I prefer working with older people or amateurs or both.

Fashion + Art =
Art embraces fashion / Fashion feels underdog to art / Fashion is often not backed up, written about until it has become an era / Art is an excuse for fashion / Fashion is a sexy bed companion.

Freeze Frame
Mario Testino

I am, above all, a fashion photographer and I became a fashion photographer because I love clothes. I didn't have a plan about what I'd do or how I'd do it, but I did have determination and I did have luck. I found wonderful teachers and I was always open. I kept learning; I keep learning. Some of my best teachers have been fashion editors, and right from the beginning of my career I've been lucky enough to have worked with some of the best editors and stylists in the world. What do good editors do? They hold the photographer's hand. They guide him or her, teach him, excite him, change him. You simply can't take a good fashion picture without a good editor. I've always been mad about English editors, and three in particular have been crucial to my development as a photographer: Amanda Harlech, Hamish Bowles and Lucinda Chambers. Their take on clothes is always quirky and interesting, informed and inventive. You never quite know what they will do, and yet they are subtle with their ideas rather than heavy-handed. That precision combined with such originality is magic to me, and as a fashion photographer I rely on it.

I grew up in Peru, but when I was a teenager I used to go to New York with my father, a businessman, who went there for work. I was his translator, but I had time to shop, and my father was generous and gave me plenty of money so I could buy clothes. I used to construct whole looks, not only for myself, but for my sisters too. I read *Vogue*, and in New York of course I could wear anything, however crazy. But back in Lima the same looks – bell-bottoms and platforms – especially on a young teenage boy, did not go down well. I spent a lot of money on taxis, because travelling on public transport only meant getting a lot of verbal abuse.

I came to London in 1976 to study – I had to have an official place in a school in order to get a visa. I wanted to study communications but was told I'd have to wait a year to begin the course because I had enrolled so late. Instead, through a friend, I joined a photography school run solely by the theatrical photographer John Vickers. He couldn't have been further removed from fashion, but still, it was working with him that provided me with my beginning in photography. Sadly, John Vickers died of cancer four months after he began teaching me, which meant the school closed down.

This did not deter me, and soon after I met the student John Vickers had taught before me. She was called Zoya Al Ahdab, and she'd started her own photographic studio with her then boyfriend, Paul Nugent, who now teaches at art school. When I went to meet Zoya, she offered me a job as her assistant but said that instead of paying me, she would teach me about photography. In order to earn money I took a job as a waiter.

Mario Testino:
Harper's Bazaar, 1989

At that time one of my close friends in London was called Waldo Roeg, the son of director Nicholas Roeg – who also became one of my teachers. I used to ring him up and say, 'I'm sorry I'm interrupting you while you are making a film, but please can you tell me about focusing?' It was his other son Nico who said to me one day, 'What are you doing being a waiter? Is that what you want to do with your life?' I quit immediately. I said, 'No, I'm not a waiter. I'm going to be a photographer.' The first photographs I took were of the waiters I had been working with, all of whom were artists, dancers, singers and actors.

I began working with Amanda Harlech in 1981. Vanessa de Lisle was the fashion editor of *Harper's & Queen* at that time, and she was one of the first editors to give me work, along with Nadia Marks at *Company*, Liz Connell at *Over 21* (Liz was the first editor to allow me a free hand in my work), and Sara Jane Hoare. Sara Jane and I worked together on my first ever paid assignment, which was for *Miss London*. I couldn't believe it when we were given the cover!

Amanda was *Harper's & Queen's* teen editor, and she was pretty wild. I remember going to her house and seeing clothes everywhere – hung over lampshades, used as curtains, draped across furniture. I had never seen such irreverence. To me clothes were precious things, but Amanda played around with them. She was decadent, but not haphazard, and she was talented, which meant her quirkiness worked.

London was an exciting time for fashion then. Amanda and I first saw the work of John Galliano and Stephen Linard when they were students at Saint Martins and we used their clothes for our shoots. It was the time of Bodymap, the New Romantics, of make-up and dressing up.

It wasn't all about being wild though. Working with Amanda at *Harper's & Queen* in the early '80s was when I learnt that being a fashion photographer was not about simply dealing with fashion, but about adapting looks. How do you create a story about evening wear? Or about life in the country? Maybe you have to do something classic or something

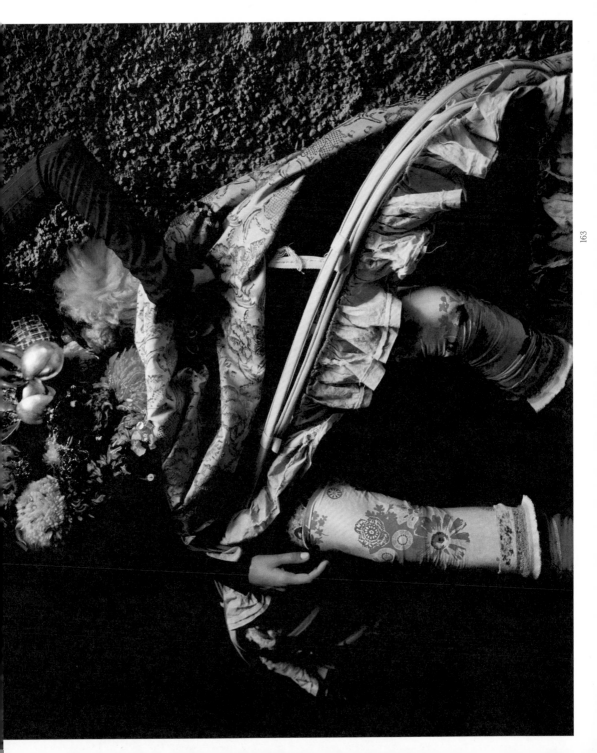

funky. How do you put all the pieces of the puzzle and all the ideas you have gathered together? I learnt more than anything that to be a fashion photographer means you have to be a problem solver.

Every five years *Harper's & Queen* produced an issue edited by teenagers and in 1985 a teenage Hamish Bowles won the competition to edit a fashion story. That was the beginning of my long and enduring relationship with Hamish. I learnt very different lessons from him. While Amanda was mad and eccentric, Hamish was all about formality and chic. He was interested in society and quoting from history – not in tearing it apart. As a result, my work became referential. I was so impressed by what I was discovering – the work of Cecil Beaton and Norman Parkinson – that I began to imitate them, and so my photographs were not that successful.

But it was an interesting and important period for me, because as a photographer you have to know what has gone before you. Imagery is a language: if you learn it, even by imitation at first, you become more confident. You understand what works. You become aware of clichés, and eventually you become able to express your own vision and ideas. Quoting so much at that time helped free me later to create original images.

I met Lucinda Chambers soon after I arrived in London. One of my first jobs was taking photographs of a hair salon's new hairstyles, and Lucinda was one of the first people I photographed for them. Back then she was a punk with bleached blonde hair who worked as the assistant to Beatrix Miller, the editor-in-chief of British *Vogue*. We soon began working together, though not yet for *Vogue*. Not for years for *Vogue*!

I was also doing test shots of models for their portfolios. Models I would pay me £25 for three photographs of each girl they sent me – and so of course for each picture Lucinda and I would create a different look.

At this time I lived with five friends in a set of rooms in the Charing Cross Hospital, which was a dosshouse for alcoholics. That didn't put off Lucinda, and she would come over for the shoots with an array of clothes.

She was always a total original. She didn't just dress girls: she completed visions around them. I used to say to her, 'How many pieces of fabric are you going to wrap around that girl?'

Lucinda came up with weird ideas, but they worked. I think that's a particularly English thing: to have such innate style, to know your history, to understand references, and then to create something new out of all of that. To abandon convention, yet create something that makes sense takes intelligence, confidence, wit and knowledge. Lucinda has always had all those qualities. Now, over twenty-five years later, we still frequently work together. I am still learning from her.

I work all over the world, and have spent a great deal of time working with editors in France, Italy and America. They have taught me much too. In particular I must mention Franca Sozzani, who helped me a great deal in the late '80s, as well as Carinne Roitfeld and Anna Wintour, both of whom have taught me so much and who continue always to inspire me.

Although most of my work takes place away from London, it is the place to which I always return. You go for a walk in London and on one street you'll see every single idea in fashion. My love for clothes has been a constant theme in my life. So too has my love for London. It is a city that constantly feeds and inspires me.

Mario Testino: *Harper's Bazaar*, 1984

Freeze Frame
Craig McDean in conversation with Glenn O'Brien

GOB This is about British fashion photographers. Are you one of those?

CMD I guess somehow I'm grouped with those photographers who all shoot in London and talk about how cool it is to be there. I left London. I'm not even from London. I'm from Manchester. I escaped from London. I don't want to be there any more.

GOB I like London, but it's so spread out you spend all your time getting from one place to another. It's like LA that way. And I think it takes about a lifetime to fit in. Here it takes a week or so.

CMD Right. I haven't lived there for thirteen years and people still ask me what's going on there. I really don't know. I don't know what's going on at White Cube, I don't know if Amy Winehouse is trying to kill herself.

GOB It seems like fashion photography is all about New York now. Most of the photographers are here. The models are here. You pick up European *Vogues* and it seems like it was all people from New York, sometimes in New York.

CMD Or we all get packed off to Paris to shoot. A lot of the clients are European – Milan and Paris. It's partly an economic thing. Is it cheaper to bring everything here or ship it all there? I go to the shows in Paris and then I stay to shoot Dior, Max Mara, Chloé …maybe something else, and I'm there for a month.

GOB What made you want to be a photographer?

CMD I don't know. You kind of drift into things. I was interested in the arts. It took me a while to figure out what I wanted to do. Then when you find it you kind of carry on doing it. If you do something long enough, you end up kind of good at it. I never thought the technical side, the cameras and stuff, was very important. I thought the ideas were important and you use the camera as a tool. I was racing motorbikes as a kid, doing motocross. I loved doing that. My family moved away and I was working in this crappy garage and I thought, 'I've got to do something, go to college or something.' So I went to art college and started taking pictures. I went to a great college – Mid-Cheshire College, run by Barry Hansett. I was this punk with bright orange hair and I walked in there and said, 'Take me on; I want to take pictures.' I had no qualifications. It was just 'trust me'. He let me in and I studied art and I started to take pictures. Then I moved on to Blackpool and hated it. Living in Blackpool was pretty damn depressing in the first place: a lot of Scottish people getting drunk at the weekend and fighting. It was freezing cold and I was always trying to figure out how to rig the electricity on to the landlord's to keep the heat. It was depressing but kind of interesting.

GOB Blackpool is an art college?

CMD Yeah. Meant to be one of the

top ones there. But I kind of fell out with the teachers and lecturers and I'd never take the cameras back. I was always banned from having cameras, which kind of defeated the purpose of being there in the first place.

GOB I went to a very good film school that couldn't afford film. We never shot. We got very good at loading the cameras, however. Thank god for video.

CMD Yeah, here's a roll of film. Let's see what you can do. One roll of film a month? That's ridiculous. Use a motor-wind and there goes your quota for the year. I was shooting loads of rubbish to buy film and equipment. I'd go to Manchester and shoot lingerie catalogues or model head cards. I'd phone up agencies – send your girls up here and I'll do all your cards for you. All my friends were working in bars and I was doing headsheets; far more interesting and lucrative. I did portraits too, but I always had a love affair with fashion. Growing up I loved David Bowie and Marc Bolan and Bryan Ferry; I loved their dress sense. There were all those great clubs like the Hacienda. At seventeen it was an excuse to go out and get dressed up and check out the music.

GOB I went on a junket to London where they took a bunch of American writers to see Bowie at the beginning of his career. We saw him play a gig at Aylesbury and then we saw Iggy and Lou Reed at the Roundhouse. Bowie's clothes were amazing then. He had bright orange hair.

CMD That knitted one-armed thing, and the kabuki stuff.

GOB Yeah, it was that period.

CMD I used to be so into Bowie and Iggy and Bolan. Unfortunately Bolan died way too early.

GOB He was great. I thought he would be bigger than Bowie because T-Rex's music was so danceable.

CMD But he hit a tree. I used to go out every night and I'd get my clothes made for me. People knitted jumpers for me that I designed. There was a great nightclub in Manchester called Pip's. They had the Gary Numan floor, the David Bowie floor, the

Bolan floor, the New Romantics floor and you'd go between them. You'd find the most outrageous thing to wear and have a great night out. When I was taking pictures in college, I'd hook up with designers and get them to make things for me in exchange for pictures. Everyone else was attending classes on how to make money as a photographer and I was working.

GOB I had that experience. Teachers don't understand people actually working because chances are they've failed themselves.

CMD Actually I always questioned them. What have you done since you graduated Blackpool College and now you're teaching there? Show me your work. They were evasive. But if someone is teaching, they should have at least done something. It was time to get out of there. It's hard, college, isn't it?

GOB I still have nightmares where the exam is tomorrow and I haven't studied. But I was basically working full-time in college and I didn't go to a lot of classes. I didn't graduate with my class because I failed Art History as a senior. And I'm sure I'm the only graduate in the history of my college to work as an art writer. I knew I could pass. I didn't know they were taking attendance.

CMD It's all time and experience. I never went to class either. I wanted to take pictures and I thought that's why I was there. I wanted to use their equipment, take pictures and figure out what I wanted to shoot. Not take business classes! And all that useless information. They wanted you to be able to name the fourteen layers of a Polaroid.

GOB That'll come in handy!

CMD Are you sure about that? I had my own darkroom, but the only time I could print was at night, so I'd wake up at four in the morning to do it. I couldn't go to class in the afternoon.

GOB Was assisting Nick Knight your first job?

CMD I went on a couple of excursions before that. I think I lasted about two hours. I was photographing food for a few minutes. Still life wasn't for me.

I had to leave. There were a few people I liked. I liked Nick Knight so I phoned him up for work. He was working for Yohji Yamamoto, doing these amazing catalogues. I was obsessed by what was going on … *The Face* and *i-D*. I'd go by the newsstands every day to see what new fashion magazine had come out. I was blown away by what Nick was doing. I'd been thrown out of college. I didn't know what else to do, so I got the job. Actually I ended up living with him. I told him I had nowhere to go and so he said okay, you can stay here. He was living in a great David Chipperfield house at the time. From a grotto in Blackpool to living in this amazing house in London. It was genius!

GOB He did a great campaign for Barneys when I was doing their ads.

CMD The week that he went to New York to do Barneys was the week that I joined him. Vanessa Duvet was the model. He said to me, 'You've only been here a week so you can't come. You're not experienced enough.'

GOB The pictures were amazing. I remember one of the models running away in tears. She couldn't handle it. That wasn't that long ago, but models were different then. They'd go off the deep end.

CMD They're not so like that now. There's so much money involved now that the girls have got to get it right. Now it's about utter professionalism. Today the girls understand the implications for their career and how much money they can make. They're very professional. They don't come late and hung-over any more. They don't come in at twelve with a bottle of champagne.

I had a lot of fun in the beginning because there was more freedom. I just remember going out on editorials and having a great time with the models. It was more relaxed. If you went out the night before, you could start at twelve. Now that's unheard of. Everything is so much tighter. You have one day to shoot something instead of three days. There's less time in the year to work. And with digital the work is non-stop because it's immediate. You see it right there. They're doing the layouts right there in the studio. I mean it's good in a

way, but before you'd have a break after shooting because you'd go to the printers. Now you're right on to the next shoot. You used to have chill time; now it's back to back to back. There's a lot more pressure and less time to focus on creativity.

GOB Have the clients changed?

CMD They never used to come on shoots. Now you can't get away from them.

GOB I think they want to get out of the office.

CMD I'm always amazed when they come from Paris or Milan and bring a posse of twenty people. You're trying to figure out what exactly is the job of each one, but they just want to get away from the office and hang out in New York for a while. There's no creative input from those people. I'll look around and there are fifty people there. I don't know half the people at the shoot now. I have no idea who they are.

GOB People think it's just the most glamorous thing, to be on a fashion shoot. Antonioni's film *Blow-Up* made everybody in my generation want to be a fashion director.

CMD I watched that the other day. It doesn't really stand up as a film, does it? I hadn't seen it in twenty years.

GOB It's Swinging London. I think it was made to be watched while you're stoned. It was an art movie and you're intended to be thinking, 'What does that mean?' What does the billboard behind the trees mean? Why is the grass so green? Who are the mimes? Now we take things at face value. So I think what does hold up are the shoot scenes with Veruschka and Peggy Moffit and Jane Birkin. It says a lot about the fantasy of the time. They're still sexy anyway. Do you think all these new alternative fashion magazines have had an impact?

CMD Do you mean like *AnOther?*

GOB Yeah, and *Purple Fashion, Ten, Self-Service* ...

CMD Photographers need a vehicle, to start with. For us it was *The Face, i-D,* and *Blitz.*

GOB Did you start out with *The Face?*

CMD I did work for *The Face* a lot. And *i-D.* I'd say *i-D* more. It was more of a springboard for my career. Nick had become the photo editor for them so he could set me on things. If you haven't got a vehicle, it's really hard. I talk to my assistants about this. They get very worried because they don't know who to work for in America.

GOB It seems as if there are a lot more vehicles now than there used to be. There are all these little glossies that keep popping up.

CMD But the problem is that it's the same people working for all the magazines. They want a high-quality standard. In those days *The Face* could be experimental with Corrine Day, David Sims, Glen Luchford and that group. Now what are the vehicles in America? So it gets harder and harder.

GOB It seems like there's a new magazine every month. I don't know if anyone looks at them.

CMD That's what I tell my assistants. Go to the newsstand, get all the magazines and if you like one, just phone them up. But in America there's an obsession about being paid for things. In England there wasn't. You just did it to have your work out there. You'd go and sign on the dole. You'd figure out another way to get money. I don't think I ever got paid for five years. But here it's a whole different thing. How can we make money? That's why people are more driven here in New York. They want to get paid straight away.

GOB Have you had assistants who went on to be successful?

CMD You always want to say yes, because it means you're doing something right with them, you've taught them something. I've never had an American assistant until now. I've had Brazilians and Australians and French. Now I have Chris, an American. But maybe they're doing well and I don't know it because they go back to their countries and I don't see the work. But you can only teach them so much. It's funny when you talk to them about ideas. I'll want to do a project for a magazine that's

Craig McDean: Kate Moss, *i-D,* June 2002

Craig McDean: Kate Moss, *i-D,* June 2002

art-related and they'll want to do Victoria's Secret. They'll think that's exciting. It's a generational thing. I just did a project for *AnOther* that's forty pages long – it's kind of carte blanche, do what you want. We took photographs and video and mixed all these formats together. It was basically creative chaos. It was fun, but you can only do that sort of thing for *AnOther* or *Pop* or a magazine like that. I find *W* to be a good magazine. Dennis Friedman lets you be creative and experimental. He loves photography and art.

GOB Do you work with the same stylists all the time?

CMD No, not at all. But I must admit I do a lot of work with Alex White at *W*. We've had a collaboration since we were kids in London. And I work with Edward Enninful. We've been working together since our London days as well. And I work with my wife Tabitha sometimes.

GOB So why did you leave London?

CMD Actually I went to Japan. I had a Japanese girlfriend and I went with her. It was perfect for me. Just the right change at the right time. So different from London. I used to go to temples and shrines, and then I'd be off to this huge department store called Tokyu Hands just to look around because it was so amazing. It's massive, filled with all this crap, just layers and layers of it. It's like a maze, filled with layers and layers of the most absurd things: electronic

technological things flashing, accessories for your poodle. I would go there every day and take pictures because it was so bonkers. You couldn't make up something like that. They used to throw me out of there for taking pictures.

I felt very at home in Japan and it was really good for my creativity. But then after a while I went through withdrawal from the English language. If you're isolated somewhere where you don't speak the language, you can get too much in your own head. I think it was good preparation for being a New Yorker.

I'm a Brit but I'm a New Yorker. I work for American *Vogue*, but I still work for the English magazines. Everyone asks me, do you miss London? I don't. You can't get a drink after eleven. What's that about? Work is hard enough.

Craig McDean: Kate Moss, *i-D*, June 2002

East End Boys and West End Girls

Vivienne Westwood in conversation with Brenda Polan

This is an extract from a conversation staged in November 2006 as part of the symposium The Death of Taste, at the Institute of Contemporary Arts, London, and organised by London College of Fashion and University of Applied Arts Vienna.

The fashion designer Dame Vivienne Westwood was first interviewed by fashion journalist Brenda Polan at the ICA in 1993, so the possibility of bringing them back together to reflect on that first interview and on more than a decade was a rare and insightful opportunity.

BP   In 1993 Vivienne and I did an interview here at the ICA. What we have done is extract a tiny bit from that interview that we are going to play now:

VW   *Art is never popular and in fact popular culture, that phrase is a contradiction in terms – if it's popular it's not culture and in fact art survives because in the past there was an avant-garde who cultivated their taste so that when they saw something original (art is always original), they were able to appreciate it. These days we don't have any art and we don't have any judges, we don't have people who have cultivated their taste to the extent that they can recognise originality and we all know that art has become a marketing hype. I'll just say one thing that has got nothing to do with the point, but I am responsible for what it means.*

BP   For you what has changed in the last thirteen years? Is there anything throughout those years that you found quite significant?

VW   Well I do, I was surprised that I do agree with what I was saying there. I have not changed my opinions essentially about that. I am really intellectually inclined. I always read, I make time to read, but I can't read unless I have a block. It's so difficult because I am always thinking.

The best thing about my job, and the worst thing is that it's really non-stop, and you never, never can stop. Some of my best thoughts occur at night, just because I'm reading and I'm hatching ideas. Everybody must have that experience where the ideas are sort of there and then you develop them, and you think you mustn't forget that, and sometimes you even get up and write it down. And then I must just say, because it's an incredible, fantastic tip to give to people, I always write thirty quotations, quite a few of them in French; I do try to read in French when I can, because it's so brilliant, the body of literature in France, it's amazing. I'll write thirty quotations, poetry and all kinds of things. For example, Rousseau – if you read some, it's so concentrated, you can just go over that quotation and you can find answers for all sorts of things that are in your mind at that particular time. The quick tip is that if you want to go back to sleep, go over a familiar quotation and you'll fall asleep halfway through it. And you will find the more you memorise things, the easier it is to remember them. It's such a fantastic thing to do.

And culture is connected with human rights. If you want to be able to lock people in jail and never tell them why, then you can't have civilisation. I mean, you have to have corpus, you have to have justice before the law. And I've recently incorporated this into my fashion. And it interests me much more to be able to do that because I'm very literal and I really like to work out my ideas. The other thing that is important for my work is stamina: I always have stamina and I've got fantastic health. It's incredible. I'm so fortunate.

I believe in doing my best at all times. The clothes I produce are always my best work, I couldn't do it better. Even if I'm in a rush trying to get something done for a show. So I know I'm doing something special and if I didn't have those standards, the clothes would not exist. It's incredibly exciting, and it's very important to keep going.

BP   The theme of this conference is taste. If established standards of taste are regularly overthrown, then is what you end up with is a kind of stagnation of spirit? Do you have a culture which is going nowhere? And essentially you are back to a kind of mania, which is looking at subversion of expression. You seem to be at the heart of these ideas. That appears to be your method of work through which British fashion has been defined.

So, what I really want to ask is, if it is a conscious way of working?

VW   Well, you ask a question about subversion and what it means. It's like rebellion in this context. I would acquiesce in certain things; I will rebel at certain things. Subversion means to undermine the status quo. If the status quo is totally crap, then one doesn't want to undermine it in the sense that one wants to make it even worse. If we make the hole underneath it even bigger, then one can fall even further. One wants to try to do something to re-establish something, and so I certainly am not trying to subvert taste at all. I would like us to have a bit more of it.

BP   Would you say that you are revolutionary, that you are a catalyst for change?

Vivienne Westwood:
Russian Fashion Week, A/W 2007

VW   I am a thinker. And I don't think many people do think. And I am in the process of hatching a manifesto about culture. So yes, I think I am a catalyst for change and a revolutionary. I do think that I constantly challenge the status quo, and there is only one way in which one can do that and that is by having perspective so that one can criticise. You have to compare things in order to create new perspectives. That is what intelligence is about. That is what ideas are about. Is something better than something else? For example, when I used to teach in Berlin, I used to send the students to the art gallery and I said, imagine the fire bell would go, and you've got to save something. After six months, you would not choose that picture, you would choose something else, because you are comparing things, and that is what intelligence and taste is about.

You see, regarding this manifesto, what I'm trying to say is that the worst thing that happens today is non-stop distraction; people cannot think, nobody's questioning anything; we live in a consumer society. And of course there have been consumer societies before but this is on an incredible low level, mass consumption of lots and lots of things that we don't really need, none of it doing us any good. Totally disposable, non-necessary, horrible things. It's not enough just to read all the newspapers and follow politics; you have to go deep if you want a perspective. Three hundred years ago people had an entirely different ethic than the one we have today. Everything that people think is so great today we would have been ostracised for, it wouldn't have happened.

I'll just tell you an Irish joke, and it has to be Irish because it has to have some sort of bottle and the Irishman was right anyway. So, there were two people lost in the middle of Ireland. They were so lost and they couldn't find a signpost. They stopped their car and to their great relief they saw someone coming up the road, and they said to him, 'Excuse me, can you please tell us the way to Tipperary?' and he said, 'I can, but I wouldn't start from here.' And I wouldn't start from here either. Nobody questions the status quo, nobody, that's what I'm trying to say.

And I don't think we have culture, and that is the whole problem. And to have a better world, the questions that need asking are: Could I change anything? Would it matter? Could it be better?

BP   But the call to arms I read was where you raised your hand to something which you were calling a civilised age. And can you tell us what that meant to you?

VW   Well it's something that I took from Huxley who said we don't want a crusade, we want a civilised age, and I agree with that. If we want to change anything then it's only through culture that that can happen, because culture involves human beings: it shows what human beings are potentially.

BP   So what exactly do you mean by the cultural high? Because you have said before that popular culture is not culture.

VW   I found something embedded in one of Aristotle's poems. He didn't need to spell it out because in those days it was more or less a truism, people knew it. But we have gone so opposite from what is true culture I don't think people know what it is; in fact I know they don't know what it is. On Question Time with Jonathan Dimbleby some young woman asked the panel, 'What is culture and how do you get it?' None of the panel could answer it at all and Jonathan had to ask what is in the back of the question because nobody could understand what she was actually asking. I went to a symposium in Paris two weeks before and the symposium was all about Europe, what the point of Europe is: does it have something cultural to hang on to? The point of it was to make sure that somehow, though it can't produce necessary cheap goods, they must still have something that is tradable, which is worth something. And it completely disintegrated because nobody knew what culture was. Nobody tried to defend it; we were all supposed to know what it was.

Anyway I think culture is the key to the universe and it is representative of human nature. And what the artist should be thinking about and concentrating on, it's not 'me, me, me, can I

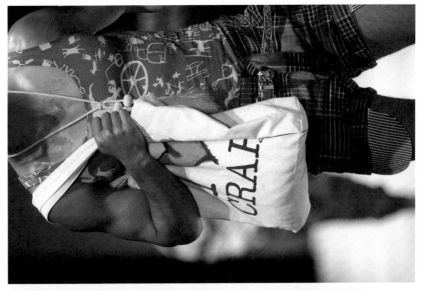

be different, can I say something that nobody else has thought of before?' Of course you can't anyway, somebody would have thought about it seventy years before you. It's like Chaucer, it's got to be something that people would recognise but it also has to be human nature as it ought to be, and so this is a creative factor; Aristotle was correct.

BP   It kind of sounds like in some sort of way it needs to reflect human nature.

VW   Well first of all I think you have to accept that there is such a thing as normal experience that people can relate to. If one was to expect that one was not trying to be extreme, one was trying to be representative as it ought to be, then this is a creative act and it's a sort of mirror to life and it's something that everybody can relate to. And the thing about this is it's a centralising idea. We are moving to the centre. You will never have the truth because the truth is undiscoverable, but you will feel like you are moving towards something, saying something that is more truthful than anything else. But it's like a hole in the centre, it goes on to infinity. You can never find out what the truth is and I think there are a lot of other things that could be bought into this argument, but the point is, what is so great about this is it does depend on the individuals, it depends on everybody. It depends on the artist who is creating something and it depends on the judges deciding if they think it is good or not, and it depends very much on something that the Greeks, or at least the classicalists, would have called decorum. And that means when an artist creates something they have to think: Is this right? Is this my vision? Am I really being true to my vision?

And the point is not about self-indulgence; it's about self-discipline. It has even been called the ethical imagination because when using your imagination, you have to be really strict with yourself. You will talk to people and you will communicate your idea. This person is real, I have invented them but I've used my own experiences and my vision of life and this is how life could be. And the thing about tragedy is it's a microcosm about being alive, and this is why we are so attracted to art because it is

something that seems to have a beginning, a middle and an end; it's a whole thing. Not like a life where you have cause and effect or part of a flux of things that you can never grasp properly. And that's why we love the theatre. I think it's terribly, terribly important and I think that all art forms are important because they hold a mirror to life and they are aspirational. But I also want to say that in the end it's really about the individual. What I aim to do with this manifesto is to offer it as a practice not a theory.

Vivienne Westwood: A/W 2007

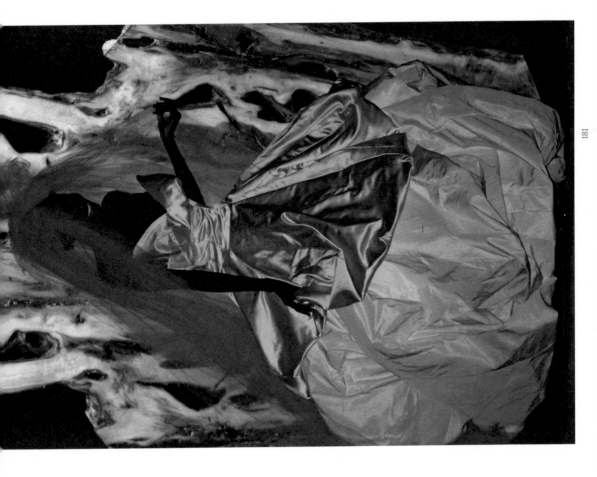

East End Boys and West End Girls

Judy Blame

Judy Blame: Collage, 2007

John Moore found the building off Kingsland Road, before Dalston Junction. It was a lovely old studio and shop. At first he was only going to use upstairs, but the shop just called out to be used.

We knew so many creative people who didn't really have regular outlets. So I helped John collect the collective. Richard Torry's glorious knitwear and leather, Christopher Nemeth's genius clothes from recycled fabrics, Dave Baby T-shirts and of course my jewellery and John's fabulous shoes. Fric and Frac made furniture and helped with the interior. Other people came and went but this was the core. John and I ended up living and working above the shop. You could ring the studio bell during the week and we opened the shop on Saturdays, staffed by the lovely Scarlett.

The whole area was full of different designers (Bernstock and Spiers, Leigh Bowery, Jimmy Choo, Slim Barrett etc.) so it was hard work and play. Very social and supportive.

We were really a bit amateur but super creative. Everything came from the heart.

The house of beauty and culture became our home, studio and shop. The perfect place to showcase our work and lives.

John Moore Advertisement,
Blitz Magazine Fashion Supplement,
April 1988

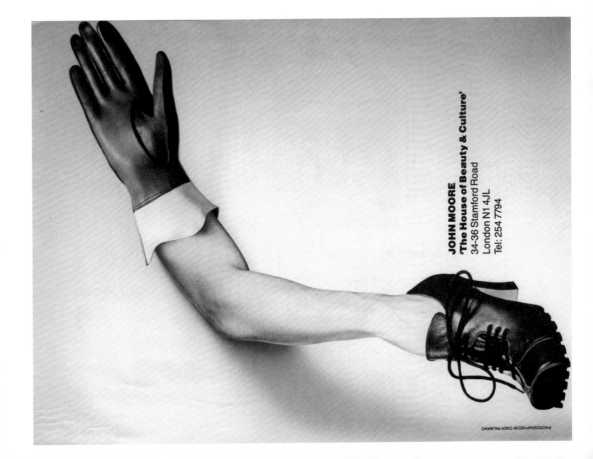

JOHN MOORE
'The House of Beauty & Culture'
34-36 Stamford Road
London N1 4JL
Tel: 254 7794

PHOTOGRAPHED BY CINDY PALMANO

East End Boys and West End Girls

Joan Burstein in conversation with Louise Clarke

LC   Your reputation in the fashion world precedes you. Was fashion a love of yours from an early age?

JB   I have always loved clothes. My mother was a tailor who sadly died when I was very young. My aunts were court dressmakers and I would often watch them at their work. I remember they used the front room as the showroom and the back room was their workroom. I can see it so vividly: I used to sit on the large cutting table when I came home from school, swinging my legs. I often looked through the books on fashion which they had and which I never liked. They were old books at a time when all the models were long and thin and I thought it looked very unnatural. But that was my introduction to fashion.

My family was not well off so it was a very special treat for me when I was given anything new. I remember I used to love playing with dolls, making clothes for dolls, things like that, so I think my interest in fashion must have always been in me.

LC   How did these formative years lead you into the fashion business?

JB   Sidney, my husband, had a stall in the market during the war. We met in 1944 and the war finished in 1946. He was a wonderful merchant. After the war he and his brother had made enough money to be able to buy a little shop in Kingston Apple Market where I helped him. I had been a pharmacist's apprentice,

mainly to keep me out of going into a munitions factory or having to go into the forces because nobody knew how long the war was going to last.

I helped them to decorate the shop and I remember painting the boxes and painting the floor. It was an instant success. We started off with underwear, then moved on to clothing. We managed to find people who could supply us and it was a great success, enabling us to go further afield and add another shop in Maidenhead.

We then had a very big business called Neatawear with shops on every high street in London. We had prime positions all over the place: two shops in Oxford Street, one in Regent Street, Knightsbridge and Kingston. We never manufactured; we were always buyers and Sidney did the buying then. I only became a buyer later on because before then I was raising our children. It was Sidney and his brother's business really.

Sidney's philosophy of buying was that you should buy a certain way and you should buy in depth. It's the right concept really; you define it by being very selective in what you buy and you always have the depth so you have something there for the customer: whatever size or colour she wants, you've got it.

LC   So if there was a fantastic dress, you would get it in all the sizes and all the colours?

David Bailey: Patty Boyd modelling Neatawear, *British Vogue*, September 1964

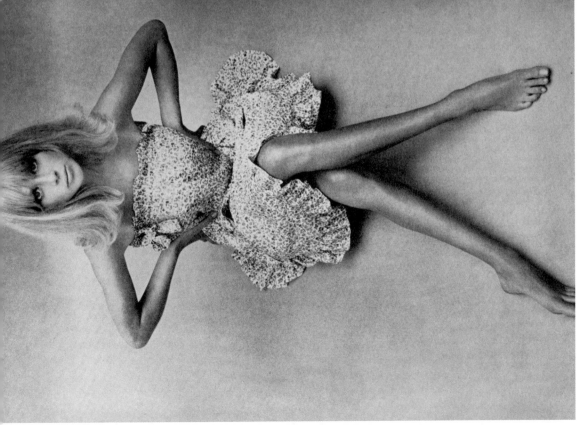

JB   All the good colours, yes. We only went into dresses when Stirling Cooper started. It was really separates and knitwear and skirts and pants and it was very successful. Unfortunately Sidney's brother had invested in shops in Belgium, against Sidney's wishes, which it turned out we didn't need and didn't want and the business went into receivership, which was devastating: devastating for Sidney because he had pledged our home as a guarantee. So we lost everything.

We had to take our children out of school because they were at the Lycée Français, a private school. Caroline and Simon were in their teens. We had to sell our house and its contents. It was very traumatic. So when people say to me 'what made you start Browns?', it was truthfully a matter of survival. But we had a lot of luck. Our friends helped us with the children and finding a place to live.

At this stage we had no business at all, but Sidney had an older brother who had a haberdashery shop in Church Street, Edgware Road, which we started to transform into a trendy boutique. People who we knew in fashion, such as Ronnie Stirling and Geff Cooper, helped us by giving us merchandise to sell on a sale-or-return basis. This put us on the map. We had £5,000 worth of merchandise and we sold it on the first Saturday, which gave us such a boost. Some time before we had transformed the lower ground floor of one of the Neatawear shops in Oxford Street, helped by my daughter Caroline, into a boutique along the lines of Biba and Bus Stop, with music playing, and it was that shop that gave us our inspiration.

Then in 1968 we found ourselves a property on Kensington High Street. The shop was right next to Antiquarius, which was a wonderful position. We called the shop Feathers. We didn't have the money to fit it out, but there again we were very lucky. A friend of mine had a nephew who was at RIBA and as he was on a sabbatical, he and four of his friends came to do the shop for us. I told them I didn't want it to look like a shop, so they came up with a concept where, instead of rails, everything was done in bamboo.

The shop had a high ceiling and they lined it with bamboo on the inside going all the way up to the top, so it looked almost like a church as you came in. We had armoires on the ground floor to put everything in and we had the clothing spilling out of the drawers, with wonderful pine tables that they had found in flea markets. On the lower ground floor we had a large communal fitting room and that's where the New Man jeans were sold. Manolo Blahnik was in charge of the New Man jeans, which was very funny because he could never get things right and Sidney would say, 'this is how you fold them' and 'they have to be stacked in the cupboard'. Manolo was charming and he has always been grateful to us because we helped him get his visa.

We went to buy clothes in France. When my children, Caroline and Simon, had been at the Lycée, the pupils there had so much style. At that time the fashion was for short kilts, Shetland sweaters in lots of different colours, with knee-high socks worn with a navy trench coat which came from Marks & Spencer. The trench-coat belt was always tied at the back. It wasn't the school uniform, but that's what all the fashionable children there were wearing.

And that's how we opened up, with that sort of image, and I was always determined that we would aim to attract a particular woman that I had in my mind. I have always said I cannot sell to everyone.

LC   Who was that person you had in mind?

JB   The same person that I have in mind now. It has to be someone who has an image they are aiming for, someone who wants to achieve if they haven't achieved already. Somebody who is aware of fashion, has colour sensitivity, has clothes sensitivity. It has got to be a woman with an open mind; I cannot bear people who are nasty or unkind because I find that distorts everything. It is very important for me to see that clothes give my customers confidence and that they wear the clothes and the clothes don't dominate them, rather than somebody who has no idea and just thinks they must have it because it's the fashion of the moment.

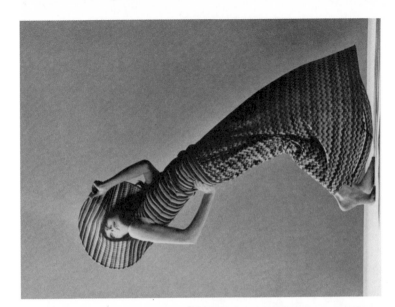

Years ago when we had Feathers I went on a buying trip to Paris and when I came back to London, there was a gold crochet dress in our shop window and I thought, 'I didn't buy that. That's not what my shop is about.' Even though we could have sold a hundred of those dresses I didn't want it, as it was not right for the customer that I wanted to attract.

Then we had another piece of luck – Vidal Sassoon, who always did my hair at that time, phoned Sidney. He had a shop on Sloane Street called The Shop and wondered if we would like it. So we did a deal with him where we took the shop at the front and Vidal's hairdressing salon was at the back.

At this point we realised we were ready to start something new. Sidney's brother took over Feathers and it is now owned by his son.

The way we found Browns was that my son, Simon, had got a Saturday job in a shop called Browns, owned at the time by Sir William Piggott-Brown, in South Molton Street. He loved what they had in there and after a few months they asked Simon if he thought his father might be interested in buying the business. It was a gorgeous shop. Very eclectic. Word got around and it was a great success from the very beginning.

LC   So you kept your philosophy of who you were buying for?

JB   Oh yes. It's bigger now, but I still want everything to be a must-have. It has got to be the best and that's why when we go and buy from designers, the editing we do is enormous. To me 'minimums' mean markdowns, so we have to buy that which we feel we can sell, otherwise it's not going to do us any good whatsoever.

LC   You must have to train your buyers very closely to understand your concept?

JB   Oh yes, absolutely. I have to let them go away on their own now which has really upset me, but when they come back they show me all the photographs. It's not the same, and I have to accept that they make mistakes now and again, because that is the only way you learn. I made mistakes. I can't say everything was

a success but I was lucky. I was one of the first buyers to go to Italy to buy, which is how we first brought Missoni to the UK.

LC   And the result was that you carried forward this idea of focus in your approach to buying and used it as the name for your most recent shop?

JB   Focus is quite different, Focus must be six years old now. We found that Browns was becoming rather elitist and we were always in magazines or newspapers as being the most expensive. We wanted to buy clothes with a younger image for a younger customer who might be too frightened or intimidated to come into Browns. We felt that in order to attract her, we had to open a new shop and then one became available immediately opposite. I have a marvellous buyer, Yasmin Sewell, who I asked to come over from Australia to work for me. She has a great image and great vision and I knew she would be a success, which she continues to be.

LC   What does the future hold?

JB   Well I'm always dreaming. The future is the website in my opinion. We have people who order Australian brands who live in Australia and we have customers who live here in the area but because they are career women, they don't have time to shop so they order online. It's a fascinating and potentially huge business.

The future also became the Browns Bride shop because Comme des Garçons moved to larger premises which they wanted us to go into with them, but Sidney said no as he felt we had enough. Sidney is not a greedy man. Thirty-two years ago he wrote his 'Philosophy of Life' which is based on: how much do you really need? As Gandhi said, there is enough in this world for everybody's need but not for everybody's greed. You know you cannot take it with you.

Gavin Fernandes: David Szeto shoot for Browns, 2007

East End Boys and West End Girls

Matthew Murphy

When we first started b Store, six years ago, we immediately realised that the only place we could make the concept of the store work was London. One of the reasons for opening the store was to act as a platform to showcase new, young, design talent, particularly in fashion. We wanted to offer them as much support as possible, for them to achieve their visions as designers. Other than the Fashion Academy in Antwerp, at that period in time, the most interesting and innovative work was coming from the London fashion schools. We also felt there was an audience in London, hungry for something new, individuals with the confidence not to be sucked into the ideals of big brands and high street culture. London is a city that has a history of encouraging and showcasing edgy, young designers with something new to say.

As a store, we gained a reputation for finding new talent who could become important international designers of the future. We were lucky enough to gain the support of the British press, who felt we were brave to offer a mixture of unknown designers and artists in the heart of central London, with no security of stocking established luxury brands. The response was far greater than we ever envisioned, which gave us the confidence to push things further. Our customer, in turn, encouraged us to take more risks; it became more and more important for us to find a new crop of graduate talent each season.

b Store installation, 2007

A way for us to do this is to keep
adding to our roster of young talent
that we support, our b Store family.
This was not difficult as the colleges
in London seem to produce a
fresh new group each year. This
constant introduction of new
designers brought interest from
the international press, resulting
in London being seen as a more
important destination for shopping
and culture. We found that the store
was creating a reputation in other
cities and when people visited
London, b Store was on their list
of destinations to visit.

After four and a half years, we had
outgrown our original space and,
needing more room to showcase the
talented collective that we worked
with, we looked for a new site for the
store but felt it necessary to stay in
close vicinity to the original site. We
were again lucky to find a space,
literally around the corner, on one
of the oldest, most recognised streets
in London, Savile Row. Many
thought this was a strange move, for
an experimental fashion store to
move to a very traditional, English
street, but for us it seemed a natural
progression. It feels right that a store
that supports young creative stars
of the future should sit alongside
heritage and tradition. Only in a city
such as London can two extremes sit
next to each and both thrive.

East End Boys and West End Girls

Pippa Brooks

My relationship with London probably started to form when a teenager. I read *i-D* or stayed up late with the portable black and white telly watching Andrew Logan's *Alternative Miss World* with Divine compèring; or when I discovered Michael Clark and his dance company who collaborated with The Fall, Bodymap, Leigh Bowery, all the people I'd read about in *i-D* and *The Face*. Going to one of his shows was a perfect amalgamation of all the creative forces setting London ablaze at that time and I decided it was where I needed to be.

Day trips to London became like a search for the Holy Grail, dragging my mum to PX, Hyper Hyper (where I later ended up working), Kensington Market and the King's Road, hoping to absorb some of London's underground glamour. Snippets were glimpsed and obsessed over, like 'Newsnight' doing a special report on Westwood's 'crazy' Nostalgia of Mud collection or the Buffalo Girls on 'Top of the Pops'. In Gosport, where I grew up, there was only one punk and one soul boy, so I felt it important to broaden my horizons.

Unfortunately I ended up at college in Coventry, not Camberwell (my first choice), to study fine art. But I used to take regular trips to the Big Smoke, sometimes to stay at my dad's London digs, when we'd go to art exhibitions, drink at the Dive Bar at the edge of Chinatown or go to Wendy May's Locomotion in Camden. At that time my hair was

cropped and bleached, I only wore Doc Martens shoes and a lot of Pam Hogg stretch Lycra. In my tiny mind I was a dead ringer for Jenny Howarth, but when I look back at photos I look like a bloke!

One of the best things about going to college in Coventry was meeting my friend Lucy who shared my fascination with London and the fabulous who inhabited it. We had begun going out in Coventry dressed up like a dog's dinner in Divine-inspired wigs, plastic miniskirts, false eyelashes and the highest platforms we could find in second-hand shops. Our London debut was at Bang on Charing Cross Road as the Phantom Pregnancies in a Halloween-night special, which of course Leigh Bowery won as Leigh Monster. Winning wasn't the point though, and we knew our thrift store lurex dresses with cushions stuffed up the front weren't going to set London's avant-garde on fire; the point was that we were taking part; sniffing poppers and dancing next to the people we'd been reading about. David Cabaret said something snippy to us in the toilets: he said something about us wishing we were drag queens: but instead of being offended, we were secretly thrilled ... drag queens were our biggest inspiration!

This was the time I started hanging out in Soho, and met the people who I would be collaborating with creatively in the future. I was on the dole, living in Kentish Town and sleeping late, going out late. This was

Pippa Brooks and fellow bandmember James Dearlove (after Eve Babitz playing chess with Marcel Duchamp) ca. 2007

the time I started making music with another art college friend, Bradley Tuck, and it was basically my ticket to getting up on stage to perform at clubs like Ciao Baby at The Fridge in Brixton or my first ever performance at Kinky Gerlinky.

Kinky was an incredible club run by Michael and Gerlinde Kostiff, which grew from a small night at Legends to an extravaganza at the Empire Leicester Square, with a revolving stage, laser light shows and one of the most dressed-up crowds London had ever seen. There was always a theme, for example Rio Carnival where they flew actual Brazilian performers in with their gravity-defying feather headdresses and the whistle-blowing could probably be heard south of the river! Amanda Lear, Naomi Campbell and Sinéad O'Connor all performed or strutted down the catwalk at Kinky Gerlinky, but the real stars were the crowd. There was always a chance to show off your finery in an over-long cat-walk competition, and many of the regulars became Kinky celebrities; the Pleased Wimmin, Stella Stein, Sheila Tequila, Darina and Tasty Tim were the scene's shiniest stars.

Fred's was a member's club in Soho where we could ring up for a guest list on Saturday nights and rub shoulders with the well-heeled, but with five pounds in my bra, I would try to cadge as many free drinks as I could, while dancing in the basement where Max Karie was DJ'ing. We first spoke one night when I was lying across the bar singing for Cathy Jordan's birthday and Max said I should be wearing Azzedine Alaïa – to which I replied shouldn't we all but there's only so much you can stretch to on forty pounds a week! But from there a firm friendship flowered, and later grew into us going into business together.

I've always hated it when people have the attitude that clubs are very shallow places where friendships are on the surface, because I've met some of the most creative, inspiring and important people in my life through my years of going to clubs. It's amazing the confidence of youth … I can remember striding into the press offices of Vivienne Westwood or Katharine Hamnett and managing to borrow pieces for PAs

or photo shoots; or maybe it was easier then, but there was definitely a sense of going out and grabbing what you wanted.

Smashing was another club which was important and intriguing in that the gay, dressed-up, freaky side of London would mix with the straight, interesting, slightly less dressed-up side. It moved venue a lot, sometimes a clip joint behind Piccadilly, sometimes Maximus, the old Taboo venue, and finally Eve Club on Regent Street. Hosted by Matthew Glamorre, music by Michael Murphy and Martin Green and door Rott-weiler Adrian Webb, its pinnacle was in the mid-nineties when Britpop was huge. Pulp filmed a video there starring Smashing Kids, Adrian managed his band Menswear, and later my band Posh, formed on a night out in Smashing with James Dearlove when Courtney Love was crowned May Queen.

Max and I opened our first shop, Shop, in the same year as I started my first band Posh. With typical bravado we asked Papa Nino, who owns Bar Italia, if we could rent a couple of rails at the front of the Lavandaria they had a couple of doors up on Frith Street (now Little Italy restaurant). This was to be an incredible six months when we stocked Judy Blame, Sofia Coppola's Milk Fed from LA (she actually walked in one night with her dad Francis Ford Coppola as they were staying at Hazlitt's up the road and needed their laundry done! It wasn't quite the boutique she'd imagined as we'd sweet-talked her in her suite at the Sherry-Netherland in New York!), Anna Sui (she had wandered in one day with Marianne Faithfull – sorry to name-drop but we were gagging!) and Anita Pallenberg's degree show collection.

That first six months crystallised the desire to do a proper shop. Max found a basement store on Brewer Street which had been empty for ages and we set about convincing the landlords that we were a good bet, despite the fact that we had no security to offer them. We persuaded everyone we knew with a business in Soho to call the landlords to appeal to their better nature and give us a chance, and miraculously they did. There was only one place to open a

197

shop as far as we were concerned and that was Soho. At the time there were no boutiques, just sex shops, but this was our stomping ground and we wanted to claim our part in its history.

Shop was all about Fiorucci, especially in its heyday: the neon, the pin-ups, the pop-art brashness, mixed with the East Village in New York, where Max and I had been so inspired by the strange little shops you would find up a flight of stairs or somewhere unexpected. Over the years we sold Hysteric Glamour, X Girl, Milk Fed, Dead in England, Tocca, Fiorucci, Marc by Marc Jacobs and on and on.

One of the other venues in Soho where we had plotted our takeover of the fashion/music business on many occasions was Maison Bertaux on Greek Street in Soho. In leaner times, if my mum would send me ten pounds, I'd settle myself in there with a café au lait and a copy of Italian *Vogue* and be content for a couple of hours (she'd be horrified that I frittered her cash on such frivolities!). There was always an interesting crowd in there, very arty, very gay, plenty of students, and quite often some kind of drama or on occasion even a play upstairs. There's no-where else like it, and the layers of decoration which have built up from Valentine's to wedding celebrations, births, Christmas, one on top of another, only adds to the sense that you're entering a little world which almost exists in another time or at least in its own bubble.

Michelle and Tania Wade have become friends of ours over the years and when Michelle decided to take over the dilapidated shop the next year, to extend her seating and create a *chambre à côté de* Maison Bertaux, and found there was a funny little basement downstairs, she immedia-tely thought of Max and myself – 'they love a basement!'

Within three months we had opened Shop at Maison Bertaux! Collab-orating with Eley Kishimoto on the interior (we basically slapped up some wallpaper and made doors and shelves out of old catwalks of theirs), we set up home under the cake shop. The combination has proved to be spectacular, restoring my faith in the shopper who seeks something off the

beaten track, a bit of eccentricity and a sense of fun or ritual in their shopping experience. You basically have to fight your way through the café down some stairs to find us, but more and more people are discov-ering us through word of mouth and 'Madame's' mail-outs. APC, Eley Kishimoto, Sonia Rykiel are the mainstays with guest appearances by Obey, Princess Tina, Marimekko and Westwood jewellery. Purchases are wrapped in candy-coloured cake boxes and shopping is all about the personal touch, with the gentle hum of the cake shop filtering down the stairs – the temptation to partake of a cream-filled confection is part of the appeal.

This is a million miles away from a department store or Topshop and thank god there's still an audience for our taste. I've got a family now and my sons love the fact they're within a hand's grab of an éclair when they visit me at work. I still make music with my band, All About Eve Babitz; we rehearse and record around the corner at Tin Pan Alley on Denmark Street, or in the shop if it's fully booked! We even took the photo for the CD cover in there, which shows what a home from home it is.

East End Boys and West End Girls

Joshua Galvin in conversation with Louise Clarke

Students at Barratt Street Technical College with Joshua Galvin: Micheal Nelkin, Mary Kushner, Martin Rudash, Ann Weinstock, Anthony Frieda, Joshua Galvin

LC   Can you tell me what initially led you into the world of hairdressing?

JG   I didn't have any privileged education, but back then you had chance of going to technical college where you could then learn a skill. The Regent Street Polytechnic was the place for boys to go to learn hairdressing. I come from a dynasty of hairdressers going back to my grandfather in the early 1870s and it was my father who wanted me to continue this heritage. He was a master barber, and he wanted me to learn everything about hairdressing, so he directed me to the Barrett Street Technical College.

I was this young lad of fifteen in amongst a whole class of girls. They made a lot of fuss of me. In those days we had general education, everything appertaining to hair-dressing: maths, stocktaking, book-keeping and things that helped you in a business sense; general science, history, drawing, sketching, French and English. To become a master hairdresser you had to study all subjects, also wigmaking and period hair. It was five days a week, full-time.

I also used to do full-time Saturdays down at my dad's barber shop and Sunday mornings as well, so I only used to have Sunday afternoons off. That's the only way that I could make money and when you're that age, you want to look the business. So we'd spark up camaraderie with the tailoring department and they'd run us up a nice pair of trousers, and in return you'd cut their hair. I was very fashionable in those days, quite flamboyant waistcoats and silk brocades. We looked really sharp in these things and bespoke made, that's the great thing about it.

We were taught by a tough old cookie called Mr Tyler. He looked like he had a board up his back, a real military man with a moustache. He wasn't a very tall man but by God he was on the ball. He kept an eye on us, like when we were practising shaving. We shaved people with open razors in those days, the old cut-throats, we had to look after the cut-throat razors and practicing on each other and all that sort of thing. And then the face massages and the throat massages.

When I finished the training, then it was National Service. So you've been working away, learning your skills, pass your final examination and the next thing is you're being pushed into the army, the air force or the navy. Instead I joined a company called Ocean Trading. They had shops and salons on-board the ships and liners. You could carry on doing what you'd been trained to do. You wouldn't necessarily have been able to continue your trade if you did two years' national service in the general forces. I ended up doing that for four years.

So that was a further four years' fabulous education because I was travelling the world and seeing other nations and geography. Hong Kong

Joshua Galvin: Merchant Navy Hairdresser, 1958

was just magical, and Singapore, Cambodia. I had all that privilege of those times and I got to do lots of different types of hair. I was on a banana boat for a time and I got to do some black hair. And then the Maoris in New Zealand, unbelievable hair: thick and really really curly. It gave me a great education in dealing with all kinds of people; building on my skills so I could deal with other kinds of hair.

When national service was abolished four years later, I came back to Mayfair. I went to French of London in Curtain Place – it was one of the top hairdressers. My flat in Fulham cost me £1.50 a week but I wanted to be back in the West End again. The top places, that's what we had been groomed for at college. Back in those days class distinction was still very much evident. Vidal Sassoon even went to elocution lessons to get into the West End of London with Raymond. Now it doesn't make a difference. I joined old Freddie French for a fiver a week and worked my way up, for there and then I was allowed to go on the floor.

You see our business is a service business; it's creative but hairdressing is 100% service as well as skill, and that's what people come for: to be respected, pampered and to get good quality work at the end of the day. In those days barbers operated as mini-chemists for men's needs. Many men went to get their shaves in the barbershop; it wasn't unusual to go for a daily shave. Or certainly on a Saturday ready for the weekend having let the whiskers grow a bit over the week.

But in the sixties, the quick in-out hairdressing of the old barber style changed as the fashions for men's hairstyles changed. They couldn't get their cut in that way; they had to go to a ladies' hairdressers and that's where the very first unisex started. So the girlfriend or whatever said come with me to my hairdresser and then men started getting colour in their hair.

That really started about '62, '63. I can remember Michael Caine coming into Bond Street at Sassoon's and he had his hair all bleached up for *Lawrence of Arabia*. You never got these things back in the fifties. Men

Following page: *The Bell, Vogue*, 1974

Preparation of a model for *Playboy Magazine*, 1963

Joshua Galvin in a Vidal Sassoon Suit, 1968

looked like men and women looked like women, but that sixties thing began to change all of that. It was a time of change in fashion much as it was back between the two World Wars, in the twenties: the music changed, the way you danced changed, the places you danced changed. The classes began to intermingle a bit. Your upper-class gent could be there out of his mind alongside Harry the lad who has a stall down the lane; because he is earning some decent money, he can afford to be there.

LC   And I suppose film and television created a new sort of social class, a period defined by the advent of celebrity, by people like Mick Jagger and Michael Caine who were the new aristocracy.

JG   Yes it did, it did. It was a success/money thing that brought people through; so your successful actor, or David Bailey as a photographer, or 'The Shrimp' as a model, Sassoon as a hairdresser, they all mingled together in this swinging set and that's what it was, the Swinging Sixties, and it was all happening. So there was all that type of inter-mingling and from that the fashions of make-up, hair, the places you would go to, the holidays you had, and the whole scene was changing in a big way.

When I talk to young people I teach down at the academy I run in the East End of London, I say: 'One thing that's different between us is that my birth certificate is much older than yours is, but other than that there is not that much difference between us.' And I tell you why: because I keep in touch with what the young people are doing. Because I teach them and I'm listening to their music, I'm watching the way they dance, I'm seeing what they wear. I have to do that because my business is all about fashion.

I then explain to them what went on in the sixties, that it was the first time that young people were independent and they had their own money. They would be taking their parents to where they got their hair done, whereas before it was always the other way round. I tell them about the excitement of the times. And many of them have said they would

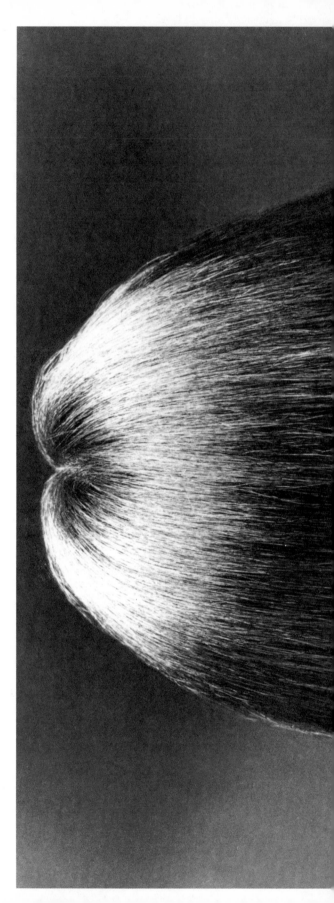

like to have been around then.

I don't think 'I wish I were younger'
or ' those were the days'. I don't have
any regrets. I've lived my life the way
I've lived it and I'm happy with it in
every sense. But if you're coming
into this business, what you have to
have is a love for it.

LC   So training young people for the
future of hairdressing must be very
important to you.

JG   Very much – it always has been.
I started off the Vidal Sassoon School
which is now one of the greatest
schools in the world and I based it all
on the original curriculum that I had
learnt at Barrett Street, all those old
techniques. Because I believe that if
you learn all those strong basics, they
will give you the foundation for anything that changes in the fashions of
hair as the years move on. Whether
pin curls come back or rollers come
back or working with lines in a certain
way, having a good training will
equip you with all the skills you need.

It's the old thing with fashion that
what goes around comes around,
and I teach all those old basics that I
learnt at London College of Fashion
as a youngster. It gives me the
confidence to know I am a master
hairdresser and I can master
anything that is put in front of me.

Joshua Galvin with model showing
latest cut and colour, Austria, 1975

Elan Magazine, 1973: Back Row:
Dorcas Adedrian, Ann Humphreys,
Giles Nadraga, Vidal Sassoon,
Sonya Lugowska, Sally Phillips,
Robert Edele, and Roy Gerrard.
Middle Row: Katie Jones, Susie
Scott, Joshua Galvin, and
Marianne Hewitt. Front Row
Nuaka Flynn, Jan Hart, and Mary
Ann Leslie

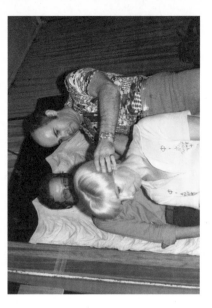

East End Boys and West End Girls

Serena Rees in conversation with Carla Yarish

CY Do you consider Agent Provocateur to be British or anti-British?

SR I think we are British: Joe and I are British in the sense that we were born here, but I think our view of the world and what we do is much more open than just being British. We have a global vision, is the idea of crossing many boundaries and borders. On the business side we are now global. I would say there is a British element to it purely because of our heritage, but I think our outlook is much broader than that.

There is this British prudery going back to Victorian times, and it still remains to this day, where people think it's absolutely disgusting and terrible to buy sexy lingerie. But there is nothing wrong with it, and when we started the business we wanted to change people's attitude. And we have done that. Not only have we done that here in the UK, but we have done it worldwide and we have completely turned the lingerie market on its head. Thirteen years ago there wasn't anything like Agent Provocateur and we have managed to influence the whole market, even down to the high street where once upon a time you could only buy black, white and ivory. AP was a revolution in lingerie.

CY And therefore a revolution in attitudes towards lingerie?

SR Yes, and the true meaning of the phrase, Agent Provocateur.

CY So you would say that the public's attitude has changed, since 1994?

SR Well I don't think we have managed to change everybody's opinion, but we have done a damn good job.

CY I think you have done a damn good job! What have been the challenges in creating and maintaining a brand that is so closely related to the system, to a system of values and morals?

SR The wonderful thing with Agent Provocateur, and with what Joe and I have done, is that is comes from within us, a deep-rooted passion within us – a belief. We have followed that, and kept true to those beliefs. We haven't followed trends and we haven't always gone down the most commercial route. We are a business and we have to make commercial decisions, but the creative decision is key to us. We will only make things that we think are really great. We would never have something in our store that we didn't think was fabulous; we wouldn't have it in there purely for commercial reasons just so we could sell tons of it. That is not the way we work. Everything has to be special; it has to be personalised; it has to have the quality and the luxury, the design, the colour, the fabric – every little detail. And I think that's how we stay true and that's how we maintain the brand. We have to keep moving. We can't just rest on our laurels and churn out the same thing. Because we are truly creative and

that's how we maintain the standards. Maybe what happens is that other people try and see a gap in the market and say, 'Hey, obviously there is a gap in the market, and there is only Agent Provocateur in that gap. Come on – we can do it. We have some money for designers, and we have all the magazines that feature lingerie, and we know what people are wearing and what all the trends are. Let's put it all together and that formula should work.' But of course it doesn't because they are just taking little bits from everybody. There's no reason, there's no passion.

CY   In terms of your location in Soho obviously you have become a big part of the history of London. Has the area changed or affected your company's image?

SR   The history of Soho is fascinating. Soho was effectively green land used for hunting.

CY   Hard to imagine now.

SR   Yes, hard to imagine. But it's kind of ironic and amusing that the hunting community still exists in Soho around Old Compton Street, amongst the gay community. Also in the seventeenth century the area was mostly cottages and land, and during this period the area was developed because there was lots of overcrowding. And then a lot of immigrants arrived, so there were French, Italians, Greeks, Russians, Poles and Germans and most of them were craftsmen such as tailors and furniture makers and painters. After that Soho established itself as a cosmopolitan area of London, and it had a very creative energy because of all the people who came there as poets or whatever. And it had a very hedonistic atmosphere to it.

Then the sex industry was established in the late eighteenth century. Initially there were brothels where they offered rooms and provided an alternative to the street prostitutes. One of these was on Soho. It was from these beginnings that the sex industry grew until the very late '50s, early '60s when the government decided things needed cleaning up. There was a large number of corrupt policemen working in the area at this time. Even in the fifties it was also famous for musicians and poets and writers, home

for so many creative people. It was known as the artist's corner and all of the really important jazz musicians were living there.

So it's always had this really creative energy. I think that's why a lot of advertisers and media companies moved in. And we changed that area because it wasn't a shopping area when we arrived. It was an old-fashioned shopping area, but it kind of gave what we were doing a bit of irony. And even though there were lots of sleazy sex shops, we did something that was really glamorous and upmarket and luxurious; we said, 'Look, this is sexy and it's ok to be sexy – come on in!'

CY   Was it quite slow to start? Or were people saying, this is what we need?

SR   It was amazing. We opened the doors and people did truly, honestly run in. And it was like 'Oh my god, this is what I've been waiting for all my life!' It is what Joe and I always imagined existed somewhere and we could never find it. We looked for it in Paris and New York, LA, Rome, Berlin. You know, we believed there was this beautiful place that had beautiful sexy lingerie, a beautiful environment, and we created it. Of course it didn't exist apart from in our minds, like a sort of fantasy. But it existed in other people's minds and it was their fantasy too. So when it was put in front of them, they were like – wow! Anyway it's here now and growing in lots of different countries, so everyone can enjoy it.

CY   Are future developments of the company influenced by your past in London and where do you see your company in the next twenty to thirty years?

SR   Our aim at the moment is to have a store in every major city of the world. In twenty years time or fifty years time your view of what is going to happen can change.

CY   And it seems like the company has grown very organically anyway.

SR   We haven't rushed; we have been very careful with our growth. We have done it all by ourselves. It has grown very organically: very carefully but quite smart.

CY   Collaborations have played a key role in your development. Can you tell me how this has benefitted your company and how it has been to work with other people – working with other artists to produce campaigns, like Damien Hirst for the windows?

SR   Oh, it's been great. First of all it's working with people who have a similar vision to you, and working with people who are really creative and want to do something special and maybe push the boundaries a little bit. People who are not scared and really enjoy working with us because we have that same outlook and that same view. And also in terms of us being allowed to publish anything – we can publish whatever we want to.

CY   You're not worried about alienating or offending your customers?

SR   We never want to offend anyone and I don't really think we do anything offensive. We don't want to shock anybody for the sake of it; we want to show people something great, exciting and fun. Some of the people are confined by the type of clients they have to work with, and it's frustrating because they are never allowed to do what they want or because they are too scared to rock the boat. We are not scared – we have something to say, and we're happy to say it.

CY   I was going to ask about your ad campaign in 2003 for fifteen real women to become the deadly agents. What was the significance there of using real women?

SR   It was great. We thought, why not use real women – they are fabulous people – because Agent Provocateur is for real women. We have women of different shapes and sizes and different ages, which is fantastic. We always say it's quite democratic in our stores because where we have the line in the store to the till, you could see a pop star next to the check-out girl next to the banker next to the taxi driver, – whoever. It's like everyone comes to that store regardless of age, background, social background, with their cash ready.

It's something that everyone loves and can afford it. Some can afford loads of it; some can only afford one pair

of knickers. But they are all there, they love it and they all have one common interest: they want to feel sexy, they want to feel fantastic, they want to feel feminine and glamorous, and men want their women to feel and look that way. So it's male and female, young and old, rich and not so well-off and everyone in-between. And I think that is exciting, I like that. We are excited that we offer a huge range of choice. We are fashion, we are a fashion retailer. We are probably the most fashionable luxury lingerie brand, out there at the high end, yet we are not fashion retailers like Prada whose underwear will come in small, medium and large because it's a fashion lingerie. Or their skirts come in 8, 10, 12. Our bras come in twenty-four different sizes and might have two different styles, so that's forty-eight different bras. So you can imagine the investment is very, very specialised.

CY In terms of videos, they have been a very successful medium in your marketing campaign. What do videos do for the company that other mediums don't? Have you found that it can give more of an idea about the brand?

SR Well, there is more interaction. They work well. It's like saying what's the difference between a book and a film. But it's fantastic, especially online. Before we had a really big presence online we did make some short films which we used as cinema commercials. You don't get a big audience, but it's really exciting to me that you can be anywhere in the world and watch a five-minute film, like our recent film starring Kate Moss directed by Mike Figgis. You can watch that anywhere in the world, you can click on something, buy it and have it through your door two days later. To me that's exciting.

CY I agree. It's the future

SR Plus it's interesting, plus it's sexy, plus there might be some suspense and will leave you wanting more. It's exciting. But then you get things like the most watched whatever on YouTube and it's like Star Wars boy or something, which is good – you need humour and you have to make people laugh. Normally we do. That was the first campaign without humour. It was darker. We haven't

ever made the films as part of the campaign; they have always been different and separate entities, like the one we did with Kylie Minogue. That was the most successful ad campaign ever. It got leaked, which kind of ruined it for us because we wanted people to go to our site to watch it. But now, in the end, five or six years later, it's still way up there.

CY You draw inspiration from a plethora of sources for your designs. What inspires you the most?

SR Everybody has a different idea of what they think is sexy or sensual or erotic or feminine. So for some people white lace is weirdly sexy and for others it's black see-through mesh or cutesy girlie. And some people think that red patent is super sexy while some people might think that floral is really beautiful and romantic, or that classic chic and down to the ground is elegant. There are lots of different ideas about what is sexy and we try and provide that at any one time in the store. So it's about a real choice of lingerie. And when I say a real choice, I don't mean lots of the same thing, which tends to happen in the marketplace. If you go to high street shops, you have a choice of the same thing. When you come into our stores you have real choice: different styles, different looks, different choices. There is floaty, pretty nightwear and there is really full-on sexy nightwear, and then there is chic nightwear – we try and provide every-thing. And you might think that all of those things are sexy on different days of the week. On Monday morning you might not want to wear that red PVC thing, but you might want to wear it on Friday. So it's about different fantasy stories and they are there and they are available all the time.

CY So one other thing. I guess this fits into you working outside of trends.

SR Yes. Our designs fit into a celebration of femininity, if you like. So what kind of woman do you want to be? That's what we provide, hope-fully. For example fashion designers will work on two seasons, spring and summer and they might say my inspiration this year is Eskimo meets Japanese girl or something – some mad theme. And you watch the show

and think, 'Oh I can see all of those references; look at all those fluffy bits', whatever. I don't know. Whereas we don't work like that: our seasons are quite different and we try and find a newness and a freshness.

And as I have said, the other thing that is really impor-tant is the sense of humour. It is a serious business, it is a good business and we are really proud of what we have done, and our product is seriously glamorous, luxurious, sexy and high quality. But there is also an element of fun. It's about having fun as well as looking good.

Backwards/Forwards

Suzy Menkes

The Internet is a giddy success. The iPod is the ultimate cool accessory. Shopping online or on eBay can help you find your heart's desire. So why is it that the words 'global' and 'fashion' are always twinned with a grimace, if not a snarl? Ever since designer labels went corporate, worldwide concepts and techno wizardry are regarded with suspicion.

Here are some of the moans: Who wants the same cookie-cutter shop windows from London to Tokyo? Why can't we go back to hand-spun luxury and forget about the logos? Creative designers are getting out of the big houses where they are being crushed by the demands of soulless, hard-nosed bosses. Shopping online is a weak virtual version of visiting a boutique.

But why treat globalism and cyberspace as negative when both are bringing so much to fashion?

Perhaps the most heartening part of my job is to talk to fashion people in Shanghai or Mumbai and to realise how connected they are to the current scene. That can mean a far-flung designer logging on to *Style.com* and finding that he/she, although miles away from Paris, shares the same Lanvin aesthetic; or that a local co-operative is able to sell, via the Internet, handwoven fabrics that only five years ago might have remained in a dusty village.

Then there is the creative power of new technology. Already the ability to change the scale of patterns by computer and to choose shades out of a range of forty-seven different blues has revolutionised colour and print. Now the techies have produced fabrics that change colour according to body heat. Invented as a hazard warning against hypothermia or too much exposure to sun, designers are just beginning to explore the aesthetic possibilities of a dress that is sober grey in an air-conditioned office, but flushes red when bodies are crushed together in a club.

If it is the perfect-fitting suit you are after, some stores are already using biometrics to make a digital image of the body and thus adjusting the pattern to individual needs. In theory, a Hong Kong tailor could now scan a client in London, send the form through cyberspace and hey presto, send back the bespoke suit. On the futurist agenda is a garment that can be reduced to fabric pulp and then be reconstructed as a brand new outfit, as a space-age form of recycling.

In a world where both clothes and shops look much as they always have, these inventions might seem to belong in a parallel universe, but the speed with which laser cutting was absorbed into the fashion industry proves that the future soon becomes now.

Many of these modern miracles are about connecting – and that applies as much to the exploration of ideas as it does to marketing. The 'greening' of fashion is working because people are becoming more ecologically

conscious and 'green' websites enable the creators to link up with each other and with consumers. If you are working for a pittance under the African sun, 'going global' can mean being able to sell 'fair trade' cotton and make an acceptable livelihood.

The history of fashion over the last 150 years has traced the rise and fall of hemlines and the ins-and-outs of bosoms. It has seen fashion holding up a mirror to its times; as Edwardian women dressed to show status, then morphed into independent-minded flappers, post-war ladies returned to hearth and home and feminists asserted their equality with men.

But what about the thread of invention that has been sewn into changing fashion? There is the development of uplifting underwear; of the zip fastener; stiletto heels, stretch fabrics; and the weightless warmth of microfibre. Their names may not have the clout of Coco Chanel or Karl Lagerfeld, but they deserve a place in fashion's forward march.

Of course, not all advances are equally welcome. The downside of the cyber revolution is the speed with which an idea becomes general currency. It takes less than thirty seconds for the key pieces from a runway show to be sent round the world. And if designers now feel exposed to the global winds of change, just wait until new-generation, high-definition screens allow every fabric weave, leather embossing, belt buckle and button to be seen in minute detail.

They don't call the current trend 'fast fashion' for nothing. But you can see it either as the biggest threat to creativity since the sewing machine turned seamstresses into robots or as a fresh opportunity to bring fashion to the masses. As with downloading music, it seems smarter to join them than to beat them – and thus to see fast fashion as an opportunity for creative designers to join quick-thinking teams.

Whatever happens in fashion – even its total banning in Chairman Mao's China or the struggle to dress during the deprivations of war – the human spirit remains indomitable. Those hand-embroidered blouses that peeped out from the Mao collars

have now been replaced by colourful, factory-made clothes. The 1940s hide-your-hair turbans have been revived by Prada. But the fashion energy behind the original creations could not be suppressed.

So it is today, now that the Iron Curtain of communism has lifted and the world is opening up far beyond Paris, London, Milan and New York. In Central Europe, as well as in Asia and across a cyber-connected world, fashion aficionados are joining the worldwide club. Design schools, like museums, are mushrooming in the Gulf States and in China. International contests are drawing applicants from places we cannot yet pronounce, nor even place on a map.

Weaving a web is a traditional concept in fashion. It is the fabric of fashion history. And now that a worldwide version has appeared in cyberspace, we should do what smart people in our industry have always done: grab it with open arms – and tailor it to our needs.

Alexander McQueen: A/W 1999

Backwards/Forwards

Revival
Celia Birtwell

When you are close to your work, you don't think in terms of revival; you just keep on trying to produce what pleases you, and hopefully others too. I have been doing this for more years than I sometimes care to remember, but now it seems that I have undergone this modern phenomenon known as revival; I suppose I am beginning to have a sense of what it is and to fully appreciate that old adage: 'what goes around comes around'.

The type of revival I am experiencing now is nothing really that new; fashion revives itself on a regular basis – it's just slightly different each time. When you have a huge high-street fashion store, with outlets throughout the country driving the machinery, as I have experienced recently, you suddenly see girls wearing your prints, which is very new and exciting for me. But making the dresses affordable for everyone has been the real joy of my revival.

I suppose to look at what revival is gives me a chance for some retrospection and allows me to look back on my career – artists get retrospectives, but designers, and certainly textile designers like me, rarely get this sort of moment of reflection in their lifetime – they just keep on going forward with little time for backward glances.

I started working in fashion in 1964 – that itself was a moment of revival. At that time, I was very influenced by Léon Bakst and the Ballets Russes from 1912; the sense of romance and sheer exultation that I felt seeing his creations certainly inspired some of my early work. Even before then I had briefly flirted with op art, but certainly in the '60s I was reworking themes from the turn of the century.

As a designer, I have always looked at the world around me for inspiration; from fresh flowers in the garden and whatever I see as beautiful and interesting, but also historical sources in painting and textiles: the work of Raoul Duffy, Picasso and Matisse – all these have had their own different role in my work. Flowers have always been a dominant theme in my textiles, but also a sense of painterliness and a tender use of colour combinations; all of this is no doubt shaped by the things that I love to look at.

By 1965 I suppose the look that Ossie and I became known for was starting to become popular. The hippy thing was becoming more influential in lifestyle and music and susbsequently the clothing that people wanted to wear. Soft floating fabrics like chiffon and silk crêpe de Chine took over from the stiffness that had come before. The stuffiness forced on people by post-war austerity gave way to a romance inspired by the likes of Botticelli. I was lucky as I was working with a genius, who let me experiment with the types of textiles and prints I was creating. I could do what I wanted with colour and Ossie would cut the most beautiful creations that made the body look so pretty.

Illustration for Topshop: *Little Rock*, S/S 2006

Illustration for Topshop: *Mystic Daisy*, S/S 2006

Celia Birtwell   31st III 2006~

30th III 2006   Celia Birtwell

Celia Birtwell

The dresses suited the time, but then, as is the way with fashion, everything changed and punk appeared. The hard edges were in opposition to everything we had been doing in the years before. Now designers wanted to show the inner workings of the clothes. This more brutal look was a look back at different influences like workwear and architecture, again a revival of certain themes in itself.

As a textile designer, you see certain themes that are always being reworked; they *never* go away because they are classics. Gingham had been around since time immemorial, yet Brigitte Bardot was able to revive it for her wedding dress. Stripes, polka dots, and so on – they are like fashion's version of the the the Golden Mean in classical architecture: you always come back to what naturally pleases the eye.

In the 1980s I started looking at new areas, both personally and professionally. Having always had a passion for decorating rooms in homes that I've lived in, I felt a natural progression would be to move towards developing ideas for textile prints in the home. The V&A has always been a source of inspiration for me, and by browsing around there, I realised I could move into the home textile world. I was able to let my imagination wander, and eventually the *Little Animals* came to me from sixteenth – and seventeenth – century prints and embroideries I saw. This developed into the work I did for my new shop, where the shelf life of a design was

now much longer, and I found I didn't need to come up with a new look each season; rather I could develop thoughts and ideas as the mood and commercial demands determined.

I have spent my life looking at textiles from all periods. For example, Bess of Hardwick, Countess of Shrewsbury, was a great collector of embroideries of the sixteenth century at Hardwick Hall, and it could be said that I have been inspired to revive some of the themes that I see in these pieces. They have a closeness to nature that amuses and delights me. I see them as innocent and charming and they provide the inspiration for my home furnishing fabrics that I see as providing a little piece of sanctuary in the home. The shop has given me direct contact with my customers; in the days before PR seemed to be the way that one gauged the public's response to you and your work.

When people ask about the Topshop experience, I have to say it has been very enjoyable revisiting my archives for a new audience. I have many sketchbooks that Caren Downie and the team have used in the new pieces and they have done a very good job of interpreting my style. It sent a shiver down my spine when I first saw the rails of clothes from the original collection last year. They looked fresh and new with delightful colours in soft crêpe de Chine dresses, and it was a very co-ordinated collection. I have worked with other brands before, so I think there is certainly something to be said about being in

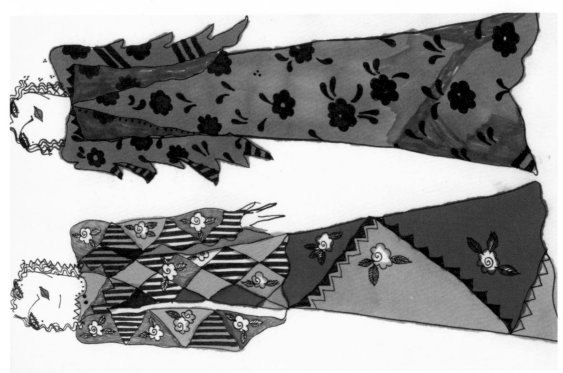

the right time and the right place and that a sense of zeitgeist comes into things. My fashion agent Vanessa Denza got it right and I am very lucky that Jane Shepherdson at Topshop also saw the point of it, and wanted to tap into what we had been doing all those years ago.

When I look at the way girls wear the clothes today, there are some that look as though my past has just walked into the room, but what's great is seeing something with its roots in another era being styled for a modern look, teamed with jeans for instance, which is very now. The next collection is my favourite so far; very glamorous but also slightly more feminine and softer, with lots of romantic chiffons and satins – it looks great!

I think these textiles work as well now as they did thirty years ago because I work with the body's proportions when I design, by working on a drawing of a person, rather than a flat design. My friend Brian Harris, a constant and reliable source of advice, said that I was one of the few textile designers he knew that designed by using a figure drawing, which seems odd to me if you are designing for fashion. It's the same with the home; the basic dimensions are pretty constant: walls and windows or arms and legs. You need to design in context I think, so that the scale works and sits properly when it comes off the page or computer screen. This comes back to the idea of classical proportions – the ethereal thing that makes the heart sing.

Advancement in fabric and textile manufacture is great, as with art or architecture – whatever creative pursuit you may follow – but I think the important thing that revival always teaches us is that whether it's romantic or brutal, hard or soft, whimsical or practical, there are constants that run through life and art, and will return again and again. Being a textile designer, and a well known textile designer at that, is a very lucky position to be in, as many of us don't get a mention in the fashion hierarchy. I was blessed to be able to work with a master craftsman, and we were able to break the mould. This summer the readers of *Elle* magazine are going to be wearing my prints on their bikinis and beach bags; I have created a design for a dishwasher manufacturer for a charity and I am going to be creating other collections for more home and fashion brands. I am incredibly fortunate that revival has also meant new doors opening, and I am enjoying being able to continue creative work!

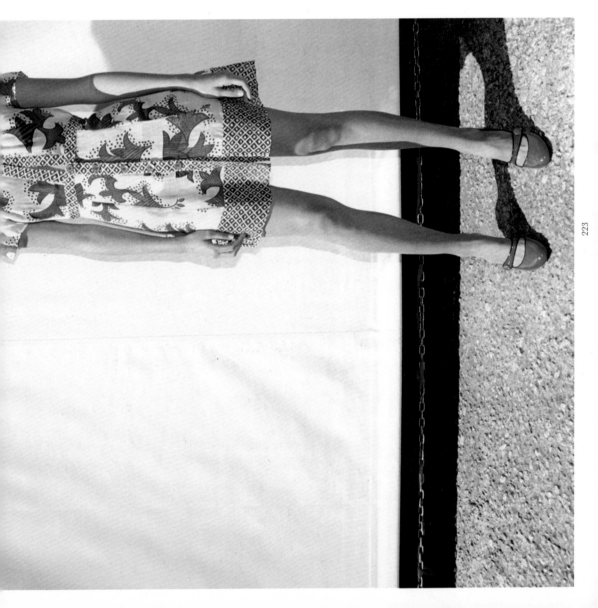

Backwards/Forwards
Venice Yu Xiao

I was not able to imagine my journey to London before I first arrived there in the fall of 2005. I had a general impression of the city from the materials I had read, which were quite obscure, and yet my true experience of London was a kind of voyage on a spiritual level.

From the trip to Kew Gardens to the visit to the British Museum, from the passing of tiny old streets, to wandering around the fancy and fashionable shopping districts…those experiences have become part of my daily life. All the details, be they shades of colours, sounds and smells of the environment, or my vivid impression of the people in this culture, have changed into a series of interesting elements which attract me very much.

The beginning of my research was a bit difficult. It raised many questions and yet I got a lot of encouragement and support from my friends, tutors and even strangers I met. Through the baldness of repetition and complication, many experiments were carried out in my work which improved the results and eventually I got the method and experiences I wanted. Roadblocks disappeared after much communication with others and all the elements linked and mingled together.

An artwork full of the imagination always impresses people most and artistic creation has no limitation in terms of specialisation. In London, musicians, artisans and photographers all inspired me. I

2005年秋，我刚到伦敦时还无法想象即将开始的旅程。虽然有很多资料已经给了我关于这个城市的模糊的一般印象，但我在伦敦真正的体验却是在精神层面的。

从在Kew Gardens中的小栖，到对British Museum的参观；从穿过年代久远的街道，到光顾时尚的商业区，这些经验都已成为我日常生活中的部分。那些细节，无论是环境中的色彩、声音、味道，或是我对那种文化中人们的印象，都成为十分吸引我的有趣的元素。

开始，总是有些困难。这里给了我质疑，但更多的是支持，他们来自朋友，导师甚至陌生人. 在枯燥的繁复中，进行了很多的改进与尝试，它们产生了好的效果。我得到了经验与方法，它们也许就来自于一次次的沟通当中，屏障消失了，一切都联系在了一起。

充满想象力的艺术作品总能给人以深刻的印象，艺术创作也没有专业的界限。在这里，无论音乐家，手工艺者，还是摄影师的工作都给了我很多启发我总是让自己安静下来去观察与思考。研究与创作的过程最终应该反映的是一种态度。我认识到的也许不止是一些经验与方法、而是一种想象的状态

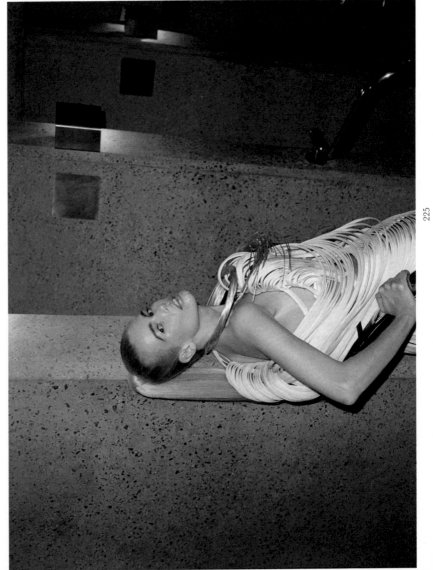

always allowed myself a chance to enjoy solitude and to observe my surroundings. I realised that the process of research or creation should end up by expressing an attitude. What I found might not be some experiences or methods but rather a state of imagination or a sense of awakening.

My project 'Time' has finally been completed; what it aims to transmit is the idea of the discontinuity of time. It is an emotional mark and expression of my past year and a half living in London.

一种醒悟的感觉。

我的设计系列"时光"终于已完成，作品表现传达的就是这个"时间 的变化"。我想这个作品的本身就是对我过去一年多在伦敦生活的记录与表达。

Venice Yu Xiao: London College of Fashion, MA 2007

Backwards/Forwards

Nostalgia Mode
Elizabeth Wilson

Whenever I watch one of those old British post-war black-and-white, films it is as if I step into the past. There it is once more, as if in a dream: the shabby, bomb-site, weary streets of London in the forties and fifties. In memory that London remains a monochrome cityscape, in which both buildings and trudging armies of workers and housewives inhabit a world of crumbling walls, rainswept alleyways and broken dreams.

It took at least ten years for that mood to shift. Certainly by the time I reached university a brighter, newer, more modern world was on offer and I plunged into the shiny freedoms, the Mary Quant dresses and the opening-up world of pop design.

Yet now the sub-noir frames pull me down the infinite regress of the corridor of memory into a world whose melancholy constitutes its promise. In the London of half a century ago you could cross an invisible frontier beyond which the safe, middle-class world of West London bled into something vaguer, more uncertain and ambiguous. To wander about the streets was to penetrate what Iris Murdoch called the interstices of existence, labyrinths, on the edge of which, as described by Claude Lévi-Strauss in 1940s Manhattan, 'the web of the urban tissue was astonishingly slack'.

In Paddington or indeed in West Kensington you could find yourself suddenly passing the leprous façades of once grand stucco terraces, on whose steps Afro-Caribbean children tumbled up and down and adults sat watching and waiting, as if beyond the grey streets their gaze caught sight of the tropical island they had left behind. They may not have been remembering the Caribbean at all, but the fact is that the consciousness of streets stretching endlessly away in all directions magnified the sense of nameless potential in a city whose recovery from war had scarcely begun to take the shape of bombastic office blocks and towering council estates. Things seemed more provisional. London was barely in recovery, supine like the mangy old lions who lay in torpid resignation behind the bars of their narrow cages at the zoo.

Yet it was just this negative capability that created a sense of potential, the expectation of finding, if not an island paradise at least a secret garden at the end of an alley, the Tailor of Gloucester behind an ancient façade or a Dickensian scavenger along the neglected banks of the Thames at Rotherhithe. True, there was a poverty of surface: the strangers treading the pavements wore class uniforms. Men in hats, for men wore hats in those days; bowler hats, homburg hats, trilby hats, the latter when worn with suede shoes suggesting something a little more daring, a refugee from the racecourse, an ex-RAF officer, a con man perhaps. Women in headscarves and shapeless coats shuffled along the street markets in worn-out shoes to buy vegetables from costermongers

Engraving by Gustave Doré, 1875

in flat caps and white scarves. The younger women were still wearing strict wartime suit jackets, often over printed frocks, with bare legs and socks set off precociously with platform or wedge shoes. Fashions lasted much longer then. Elsewhere, women in fur coats swam among the glass counters of Harrods, then a store utterly different from what it is today. The morning after the 1955 election my father took me there to watch the results, winking blue and red on an electric board set up in what was then the Harrods bank, where discreet cheers greeted each Tory gain.

There too I caught a shocking glimpse of Una, Lady Troubridge, 'widow' of the lesbian writer Radclyffe Hall, as she sped through the glove department accompanied by an Italian couple, both clad in de luxe camel coats. After her lover's death, Lady Troubridge, always the femme in the couple (which became a triangle, but that's another story), took to wearing her deceased part-ner's butch outfits and so on that morning in Harrods she was unmistakeable in a kind of formal black morning coat and masculine hat above a papery pale face adorn-ed with a monocle. Heads turned at this arresting sight, but at the same time she was so small and slight that there was a wraithlike quality to her appearance, as though she were a ghost from another era, which indeed she was.

I am sure I was far too young to know about Radclyffe Hall and Una, Lady Troubridge, but I had inveigled an assistant at the local library to let me have the copy of *The Well of Loneliness* that was kept with other forbidden books under the counter. And although Harrods hardly seemed the most likely place in which to encounter that louche other world beneath the stoic surface of post-war London, for which I was already precociously searching, the passing of this famous lesbian through Harrods' stately halls suggested that, as Lévi-Strauss had found in New York a decade earlier, the surface of the city was porous, or melting, like Alice's looking glass, so that you could slip into another dimension and find yourself, surreally, in a different world.

When styles so closely conformed to class distinctions, the task of trans-forming oneself sartorially so as to signal some form of as yet only vaguely conceived dissidence was rather baffling. The acres of carpeted space in Harrods' dress floors offered only humiliating encounters with sales assistants who would insist on accompanying me and my mother into the enormous fitting rooms to offer a running commentary on everything tried on. There was a department allegedly catering for young(er) women, but it offered only modified versions of the post-New Look fashions of the period, which were stiffly middle class and middle-aged. Blue jeans existed, but where to buy them was a puzzle.

In any case, blue jeans hardly repre-sented the kind of appearance to which I aspired. Instead I appropri-ated my grandmother's black lisle stockings, having heard of existen-tialists and the Left Bank, and wore Black Watch tartan trousers of the kind made fashionable by Juliet Greco, existentialist chanteuse (later taken up by Edward Dmytryk, the film producer, who transported her to Hollywood, where she had a nose job that ruined her appearance).

The jazz clubs held promise as a scene in which one could shine, dressed in an 'arty' fashion, for 'arty' seemed to be the only word to indicate some alternative mode of dressing, some variation from the matronly coat and skirt ensembles and wool dresses; a black polo-necked sweater, perhaps, possibly a dirndl skirt. The dirndl skirt, along with embroidered Magyar blouses, may have harked back to some idea of 'peasant dress' as indicating alternative or progressive views, left over from the immediate post-war period when the Soviet Union was still an ally, before the Cold War was declared.

En route through Soho to hear Humphrey Lyttleton's trad jazz band at the 100 Club in Oxford Street, it was noticeable that the tarts who stood on every corner still wore the fashions of a decade earlier: platform shoes with ankle straps and suits with military shoulder pads, and I used to wonder why this was, whether they were too poor to afford new clothes or whether it was an informal

prostitutes' uniform, to show off legs
at a time when most women's pins
were muffled in voluminous skirts,
dirndl or otherwise.

The streetwalkers offered a reminder
that other worlds through the looking
glass might be dangerous as well as
alluring. But that was part of London's strangeness, or perhaps it is the
strangeness of any big city, that every
pedestrian could be an incognito
refugee from any of the hidden social
worlds that lay beneath the uncom-
promising façades and dour
panorama of passers-by.

When the noise of traffic faded as
one found oneself in some backwater,
some road or square that became un-
canny simply by being uninhabited,
the consciousness of hidden lives
intensified, and perhaps this sense
of hidden worlds was stronger in
London when there were so few
cafés or public spaces, when life was
lived beyond closed doors, in private
places, as was not the case in Paris or
Athens, not that I had visited these
cities then.

Because London was, or seemed to
me, a secretive place, dress played an
important role. It gave off signals of
adherence to those imagined worlds,
it played an essential part in the
panorama. But sometimes the signals
themselves were so covert as to be
invisible to all but the already initiated. A gay friend – he'd been a
queer in those days of course – asked
about the signifiers of his sexual
identity back then was hard put to
think of anything. Eventually he
offered, doubtfully, 'perhaps a green
corduroy jacket?': the uniforms of
those who were then beyond the pale
had to be almost as hidden as the
circles to which they gestured.

To be young is to be of the future. It
may be that, aged thirteen, fourteen,
fifteen, sixteen, I was searching for a
hidden world that didn't exist, that
was really nothing more than my own
future adulthood, when simply by
growing older I would get to be given
the key to the door, even if it was not
the door my mother would have
wanted me to open (was it even the
one I wanted to open myself?). By
contrast, perhaps nostalgia is an old
person's game. Yet new millennium
culture seems saturated with nostalgia: pastiche film noir, endless Jane

Austen, forward to the past, retro eclectic interiors, even the contradictory recycling of sixties futuristic styles, all in a kind of phantasmagoria of repetition.

Everyone sneers at nostalgia. Richard Hoggart suggested it was memory gone sticky, sickly sweet, a sentimental reworking of the past. At the same time it is ubiquitous and powerful and must, therefore, mean something more complex and awkward than rosy visions of a vanished yesteryear. I sometimes feel frustrated when absorbed in one of those ancient films – *The Fallen Idol, Hue and Cry,* or one of Robert Hamer's masterpieces of cynicism, thwarted passion and lost hopes – at the impossibility of penetrating the screen, of actually *being there* again, not just to remember, but actually to experience what it was like. Tired of excess, I want to know again the poverty of that time, the visual austerity, above all the unfinished, untidy London of my childhood.

In the new millennium the future is fast fashion with styles in such quick succession that one can get caught in a hamster wheel of change spinning so fast that it seems to be stationary, while the coming horror of the Olympic village threatens to destroy all those unfinished, disregarded, interstitial wildernesses, the spaces between, indeterminate spaces with no name, which are to be concreted over with sanitised municipal arrangements that exclude all deviance from a managerial norm.

In the light of this, the gaze backwards into the past is less a sentimental longing than the appalled stare of Walter Benjamin's angel of history; the backward gaze of the subject being blasted forward by the winds of history: 'This storm irresistibly propels him into the future to which his back is turned, while the pile of debris before him grows skyward. This storm is what we call progress.' Human beings are poised forever on a tightrope between past and future; the present is a knife edge.

Not sickly sentimentality then, but the horror of nostalgia in the recognition that we have been whirled away far ahead of ourselves into a landscape of estrangement. At the same time, though, beware. The familiar past we recreate so lovingly in memory lacked, when it was real, the certainty we retrospectively endow it with. If nostalgia were sentimental, it would be a lie or at best a gross distortion of the past. But nostalgia is, rather, an act of mourning. Just as, eventually, the pain that accompanies the loss of a loved person at least partly fades into loving memory, so nostalgia dissolves the pain of the past in a memory of its beauty. But if I were to enter the celluloid dream and find myself back in the grey streets of the fifties, I would only long, of course, to get away.

Hue and Cry directed by Charles Crighton, 1946

Backwards/Forwards
Carmen dell'Orefice

'I love London, enough to get married there anyway (in 1952). I started coming over professionally in the late fifties, usually for shoots with Parkinson. In the eighties, when I began doing catwalk shows, Sir Hardy Amies used me to represent his vision of his older customer. I do the same thing today for Ian Garlant who took over from Sir Hardy. London is the only city (aside from New York) that I would consider living in.'

David Downton:
Carmen dell'Orefice,
in Hardy Amies, 2003

Backwards/Forwards

The Background to the Zandra Rhodes Vision

Like London College of Fashion I celebrate being a product of London and its influences on my work. I am a textile designer who could not find a job and went into fashion by accident as a vehicle to use my prints.

My designs begin with observations of the world around me. It is a very personal view, beginning in the pages of my ever-present sketchbook where I draw whatever catches my eye: knitting stitches, banana leaves, high-rise buildings catching the sun or Chinese fretwork. These inspirations become the basis of a textile design. Even my childhood memories appear, whether it is the zigzag, the wiggly line, the Z in Zandra or the repetition of a string of words that become a visual dialogue for me to evolve into a pattern, suggesting a colour or inspiring a texture. These are reworked on to full-size large sheets of paper, defining and redefining the motifs and their placement. It is the print that will become the dominant force in the final garment.

Vital to the next stage is the relationship of the paper design to the human body. By pinning the paper design on to my own body and observing the ways in which the pattern moves with or against the form beneath it, I begin to manipulate and reposition the motifs until the desired effect is achieved. The next stage is to produce the colour separations, then make the screens and print the fabric.

As a textile designer, I enjoy the discipline of the printed fabric that

Zandra Rhodes, ca. 1977

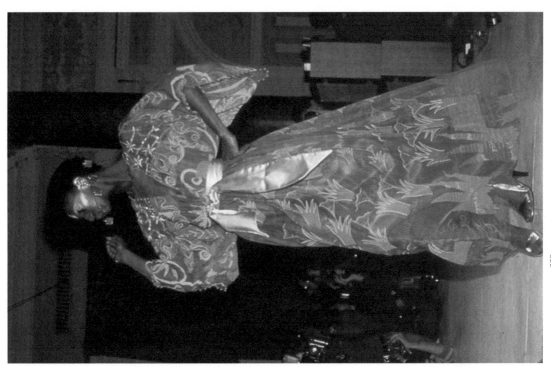

has to be cut and used economically and in a very special way. I have to consider measurements and repeats of both the design and of the spaces in between the main design. It is both technical and artistic and dictates the end product. I am proud to be a textile designer. It is my métier first and foremost.

The printed sample length of fabric is sometimes draped on a stand to create a garment or sometimes laid out flat. The printed fabric is cut out or around so the print becomes the shape that controls and influences the final silhouette of the garment. This is done by means of printing paper with the textile print and the pattern is drawn on the paper in heavy lines, grading included. The sheer fabric which I mainly work in is then overlaid on to this printed paper and the print on the chiffon fabric is matched with the pattern on the printed paper beneath it. The cutter can then cut out by following the lines underneath the sheer fabric.

The Zandra Rhodes vision extends beyond the garment to the accessories, hair and make-up, which are integral to the theme for every collection and an essential element. Even my own look is part of this world that I create. The final effect is a design that comes alive on the human body, my unique artistic expression and interpretation of the world I see around me.

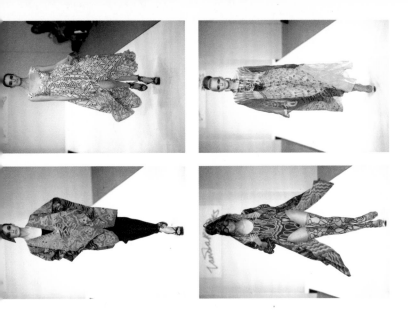

241

Backward/Fowards

The Travelling Circus
Belle & Bunty

It sounds funny when we are asked about the 'London fashion scene' – as designers we seem to lead the least glamorous life of all the 'fashion people'. We work all hours, we pay ourselves last and of course when 'It' hits the fan, as it inevitably does, the buck stops with us. Why do we do it? Not only because we love it – we're addicted to it – and London is what feeds our habit.

It was incredibly hard finding jobs after graduating as London is packed with talented, young, hungry designers. However, as the rent had to be paid we both took on freelance jobs and unpaid work experience, eventually finding ourselves designing for the high street – not the illustrious job at Chloé that we'd hankered after whilst at London College of Fashion!

Hannah and I started up our own label, Belle & Bunty, after a couple of years working in the industry. We spent a great deal of time together on weekends trawling round London's markets, vintage fairs and galleries. Inspiration was all around us and it was only a matter of time before this evolved into a business concept.

Belle & Bunty derives from names we were both given as children and subsequently we take a lot of inspiration from those times. But as we grow up and London becomes the foundation on which we live, work and raise our children, so inevitably does Belle & Bunty evolve, through a London-centric lens.

There is also common ground with the London designers that we are growing up with. If we stick together, if we trade secrets, we will survive. We come out to play twice a year during the selling seasons, presenting our new collection at the London Fashion Week tents. It's almost a relief to see the same faces reappearing a season on; we discuss business, buyers, press and of course the dramas that have been suffered or diverted to get there. Then, after far too many coffees and expensive sandwiches, we pack up our collections and off we go to the cries of 'see you in Paris'.

The misconception that we are backstabbing, creative lunatics seems an all too easy brush to tarnish us with. The reality is that we are members of a travelling circus – another exhibition, another city and so it goes on. Resting safe in the knowledge that six months on London will pitch its tents and kickstart the circus all over again.

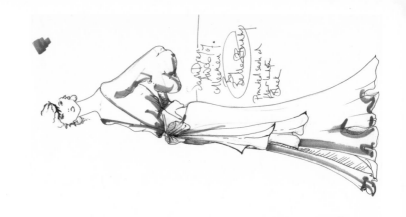

Backwards/Forwards

Future Dreams in Sound, Fashion and Space
Phillip Neil Martin

Fashion or art, music or noise, movement or stasis, sound or silence... synergised art forms within broken space... new forms of presentation.

My recent work has been concerned with the magnetism between fashion and music in areas that perhaps reside outside the standardised forms of fashion presentation. It is a performance and collaborative space which is growing rapidly, but in comparison to other collaborations with music, like film and theatre, is still relatively young.

My explorations both on and off the catwalk have sought to engage audiences with fashion through music, live performance, space, architecture, fractured environments, sensors and light with an interest in creating both engaging 'spectacles' that bind the audience to the fashion, music and space in a way that highlights the aesthetics of a collection; at the same time elucidating the symbiotic relationship between them and the emotions/energy of a collection. I'm extremely excited about breaking down the barriers between fashion and performance, between music and theatre, working with concepts and forms of presentation that hopefully begin to challenge the way that audiences view music and fashion by creating 3D sensory environments that look forward into the new century. The union of music and image is really exciting... the way music can illustrate the shape and movement of fabric and form, the speed and movement of models and the way the space of the music can interact with the architecture of both fabricated and natural catwalks.

When sound is allied with image people unwittingly relinquish themselves to the subjective emotional content of the music. In the modern world of escalating sensory stimulation we as consumers and audiences are demanding more. When coupled with image, music and sound become the primary sensory triggers for emotive response; as Robert Cresson said, 'the ear goes more toward the within, the eye toward the outer'. Studies related to customer behaviour in retail stores show that music (music, sound or silence) directly influences the shopping choices of consumers, though most customers are unaware of any effects and deny the influence of the music.

Other examples of research indicate the speed of music determining the time spent in one location or the amount of information processed when in the space. The combination of the aforementioned processes can elevate the sound from a supporting role, or from background wallpaper, to personifying the image so that the music and fashion environment becomes inseparable. Yet if the music/sound is placed in the wrong psychological or physical space in relation to the audience, this alone can disengage viewers from interfacing with the image, collection or performance space.

Fabrice Lachant: *Necropolis*, April 2007

The writer Jacques Attali said, 'societal philosophies of time typify a cultural methodology because time is the medium through which we pass through being. Music, being a time-based art, reflects the crucial philosophy of a culture through its treatment of rhythm.'

Recent technological developments point to numerous collaborative possibilities between sound and fashion in the coming years. Complete sound/fabric environments, contained worlds of sound in garments, and thus the new and future technologies (like slimline speakers that can be inserted into garments and intelligent fabrics containing MP3 players) suggest that the multiple sensory environments enclosed within personal spaces, and not just on the catwalk, are within touching distance. The recent Viktor & Rolf show was conceived from the premise that each model should be a self-contained fashion show. Each model carried individual metal cages rigged with spotlights and speakers so they were in the midst of their own musical world, 'to incorporate the show and the performance of the show into the actual garments, so that the show becomes the clothes and the clothes become the show'.

This aesthetic connects directly to philosophies relating to the experience of the virtual and the real, or technology as the creative stimuli (like the recent Alexander McQueen show with the Kate Moss hologram finale), to the customised aural world inhe-

rent in iPods or any of the bespoke personalisation processes in digital media and the Internet. The iPod, for example, has radically transformed the way we approach music, listen to music, and dispense music; turning all of us into DJs and curators, adding both layers of immersion and functionality to the experience.

The acute awareness of the effect of music can not only place greater control in the hands of the creators, but perhaps personify collections by giving the illusion of placing the garments in a position of power over their sound environment or by creating an interplay with the other sensory stimuli. The codes of everyday music are constantly developing and have grown over centuries of changing tastes and artistic.developments. We have subconsciously learnt many of these essentially arbitrary codes (based on the environment we as individuals have engaged with) and formed our subjective responses around these codes just as we have with language and metaphor. Numerous musical codes have risen directly out of the fusion of image and music, for example the clichéd stab in horror films or the childlike or haunting music that does not represent the evil or horror on screen but seeks to represent by symbolic inversion the ramifications beyond the moment, namely death and the unknown.

The symbolic dimension of music is gravely important. The subjective symbolic value can completely

Fabrice Lachant: *Necropolis*, April 2007

change the context within which an audience views the events or space they engage with; thus the symbolism of sound can either engage or alienate potential audiences and consumer markets.

In my recent work called 'Voices of the Asylum' for London College of Fashion I created the music and concept to aurally enrich the visions and aesthetics across the varying collections and to synergise the concept behind the show's delivery. I imagined that the only sounds that one might hear in the silenced boxes of an asylum would be noises made by the voice. Everything that was heard during the forty-minute show was produced by the human voice connected to each garment, exploring the sound of breath, screaming and vocalisations encompassing noise, singing, human beatbox and sound's multifaceted relationship to image in the form of sound installations, interactive electronics in surround sound and live performance coupled with catwalks, lights, models and dancer installations.

In short, a new performance space and market is gradually generating itself, stimulated by technology and greater demands for exclusivity of experience. The new collaborations cross pre-existing artistic borders and are perhaps the forerunners of holistic sensory experiences and future dreams coupling sight, touch and sound, partially driven by the pluralised artistic and social globalised physical and aural models and the consumer's desire to be submerged within more elaborate fabricated performance spaces.

Backwards/Forwards
Betty Jackson

I started our company, along with my husband David, in 1981, and at the beginning we worked out of two tiny basement rooms in Meard Street in the centre of Soho, having moved sewing machines and cutting tables in with the help of the transvestites who lived and worked in the club opposite. I had previously worked with Wendy Dagworthy and then for six years as one of the designers at Quorum, so it was very exciting to be starting something for ourselves.

London was buzzing … in music and the arts, as well as in fashion, and there was a different club to go to every night. The country was in the middle of an economic slump, but that never really gave us cause for concern as we were so confident and sure about what we wanted to do. And in any case, the favourable exchange rate made the collection much more affordable for the Americans.

We showed initially with a small group of designers known as The Individual Clothes Show, who had a joint fashion show and took a collective space at Olympia where the exhibition was held each season, but after three or four seasons, and with loads of American and British buyers clamouring for our clothes, we decided to go it alone!

At the time nowhere else in the world was doing what London was doing. New York was churning out sports-wear, Milan was boring and Paris was still dining out on being the capital of couture, so as far as youth and energy

Betty Jackson: A/W 1982

was concerned, London was uniquely positioned to change everything.

By this time we had moved into our
own building in Tottenham Street,
just north of Soho but still in the heart
of the West End, with a team of ten
people, give or take a few hangers-
on, and we were manufacturing the
clothes in England and in Italy, using
small units who would produce for us
and give the quality we needed to be
on an international stage.

It was a very exciting time: our
orders were doubling every season, I
met the Queen, won Designer of the
Year, and had two children all within
a space of about three years.

And then everything changed as
the exchange rate slumped. One
pound equalled one dollar and the
American buyers fell off a cliff. Their
domestic market had been growing
very successfully and with the emergence of their own home-grown
designers like Donna Karan and
Calvin Klein grabbing the headlines,
there was no need to cross the Atlantic to buy clothes at three times the
price. Or so they thought. Luckily for
us, David had been cautious about
signing a licence deal with Japan,
something that most other designers
had jumped at years previously, and
when the bad times began, he did
the deal and the Japanese filled for us
the huge hole left by the Americans
and we rode the storm. Many other
brilliant people didn't.

Twenty years on from then, London
is still a fantastic place to live and
work. It has provided a constant
supply of creative energy, stimulation
and scope. It has the best music, the
best theatre, the best museums, the
best parties, and the best people. It's
fantastic to be in London.

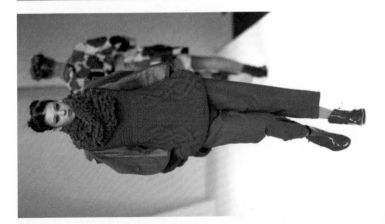

253

Chalk Marks

The London Cut
Alistair O'Neill

It is perversely British that the first city to celebrate the bespoke tailoring of Savile Row in exhibition form would be Florence, Italy rather than London. But then, this is only as peculiar as the fact that the most ardent admirers of English tailoring are not English.

The *London Cut* exhibition was staged in January 2007 as part of the Pitti Immagine Uomo 71 Fair, which showcases Italian and European ready-to-wear menswear collections. The project is typical of Pitti Immagine's directional exhibition projects, which not only complement and promote the trade fairs they stage, but which also anticipate the direction in which the zeitgeist shifts. In this case, it is in the return to made to measure for the menswear market, or *su misura* if the suit is an Italian one.

The reception given to the idea of an exhibition celebrating English tailoring staged by an Italian trade fair for menswear did not escape the international press. When *The Times* noted that 'Savile Row gets Italy hot under the collar', it gleefully reported that Brioni had responded to the premise by installing a giant print of Daniel Craig as James Bond wearing a Brioni suit in *Casino Royale* in its main store in the Via Condotti in Rome. Other Italian tailoring firms and associations were not as wry in their views.

But the achievement of the project did not lie in the staging of the

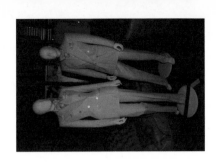

exhibition on foreign soil, but in the collaboration of so many tailoring establishments based in and around the Row for the common cause. Curator James Sherwood termed it 'a decisive historic moment – the first time so many of the leading tailoring houses have co-operated to promote the Savile Row product'. And show they did.

The setting was the illustrious Empire-style apartments of the Duchess of Aosta in the Palazzo Pitti, which are rarely opened to the public since the Duchess's departure in 1945, and Italian artist Luca Trevisani designed the exhibition. What was particularly inspired about the display was the way in which it enmeshed the rem-nant material culture of English tailoring past with the vision of a rekindled present. One of the initial drawbacks to the exhibition was that because the lead time was so short, they were unable to secure loans from international dress collections. But this creative constraint forced many a tailor's hand, so that all manner of illustrious paper patterns were dusted down and wise hands reconstructed from scratch the deft proportions they had once chalked into cloth.

My role had initially been to lend four Tommy Nutter suits for a room devoted to the legacy of the tailor. The centrepiece to the room was two pairs of white suits: the first set had been made for Lord and Lady Montagu in the early 1970s and they had been resurrected from storage

Edward Sexton, British
Ambassador's Residence,
Paris, July 2007

257

especially for the exhibition and were displayed in all their unconserved, stained glory on wooden hangers; whereas the second set were reconstructions of the same garments using the original patterns made by Edward Sexton, Nutter's Head Tailor and now a tailor in his own right, who had made the first set by hand too. The reconstructions gleamed a brilliant white and were displayed on mannequins who were arranged to look like they were about to dance.

The display illuminated something so rare about the nature of bespoke tailoring that I don't think I will ever forget it: that the authority of the craft lies not in the things it makes, or the people they are made for, or the provenance that is bestowed upon them; rather it lies in the act of making those things and in the persistence of those craft skills. It was my great privilege to inform Mr Sexton that I thought he'd just got better with the passage of time.

Chalk Marks

Apprentice — Student and back to LCF
Alan Cannon Jones

The sixties was a great time to be young and in the fashion industry; those times will probably never return. My career began in 1962 when I left school and started an apprenticeship with Nicholson & Co (Coat Specialists) in St Albans. I started in the Trimming Department where all the linings, canvases and internal trimmings for the coats, jackets and trousers were cut and prepared for the workroom. The foreman showed me how to mark and cut out pocket bags, and this was my job for six days a week. I must have showed some promise, as after a few weeks I was then also allowed to cut out the front and collar canvases. After three months the designer called me into his office and informed me that my progress was satisfactory, and in September I would be sent to the Shoreditch College for the Tailoring Trade to study menswear cutting and tailoring. This college was later to join with Barrett Street to form London College of Fashion. By September I had also progressed to cutting out linings and so, with this experience, I commenced a course of study at the college. The courses then were all City & Guilds and the timetable was day release, one day and two evenings each week. This meant that I worked the remainder of the time, including Saturdays.

My first pattern cutting lesson was in room S1 at Curtain Road with Mr Eric Clarke as my tutor. There were twelve of us in the group and between 9.00 am and 12.30 pm the only sounds were Mr Clarke's voice

and the odd pin dropping. Maths was never my strong point at school: straight maths was OK, but algebra was a foreign language to me. It was at that first cutting lesson when my eyes were opened to just how simple maths is, if you understand the application. It was explained that to cut a pattern, you had to have a set of measurements, and for this you worked to a scale based on half the chest measurement. All other body proportions were fractions of that scale, either an eighth, a sixteenth, a quarter, a half, etc. Along with this were other formulas such as height plus chest divided by eight to determine the depth of scye. If only algebra had been explained in the same way, I could have been a nuclear scientist! But it was too late, as I had now found my destiny in life.

The morning classes were always pattern cutting and then in the afternoon we were taught tailoring. This was sitting on the table cross-legged holding a needle and thimble. Mr Nickle, the tailoring tutor, would walk up and down and if anyone did not hold their thimble correctly, there was a swift wrap across the knuckles with a ruler. We learnt quickly and accurately to be proficient with the thimble. The evening classes were for design and textile study. The classes started at 9.00 pm prompt and we were expected to be in class before the start time. The Head of Department, Mr Orange, would be waiting just inside the entrance door from 8.55 pm onwards and if anyone was late, a report went to their employer.

AN INTERESTING LECTURE ABOUT LADIES' CUTTING

BY MR. R. G. BASHFORD

AT one of the recent meetings of the Metropolitan Foreman Tailors' Society a very instructive lecture on the cutting and fitting of ladies' garments was given by Mr. R. G. Bashford. The lecturer was assisted by his wife, who acted as model for the trying-on of a basted jacket, thus making the demonstration practical as well as interesting.

Mr. Bashford began by explaining his method of taking measures. He did not, he said, take the complete circumference of the bust in the usual way, because he thought there was always a tendency for the tape to slip down. His own method was more accurate.

Measurement Check

Holding the tape at the centre back, he measured over the bust prominence to the centre front—the half-bust. He checked the balance by measuring from the nape to side waist, holding the tape there and bringing its end under the arm back to the nape, and recording the "difference." For normal figures this would be about 1½"; for round-backed figures it would be less than this amount; and for erect figures it might be anything up to 3".

Mr. Bashford expressed the opinion that neck sizes did not vary in anything like equal ratio with bust sizes. It was, therefore, not satisfactory to draft the necks on a pattern by a proportionate scale. He maintained that a 3" gorge, back and front, was sufficient for all practical purposes in every coat.

With regard to the location of the shoulder point, the lecturer said that it was always a good plan to fix this at a "half-way" line on the shoulder of the figure.

Smaller Sizes

The practicability of making front darts from the bottom of coat to the bust only was discussed by many of the members. The lecturer said that such a plan was successful only in sizes under 42" bust, because of the amount of "working-up" which would be needed to provide the required bust contours.

Mr. Bashford demonstrated his own method on the board. It consisted of straightening the shoulder a little, shrinking in the front of scye and taking a dart out under the lapel. He pointed out that, before using this method, it was important for the cutter to take into careful consideration the texture and pattern of the material.

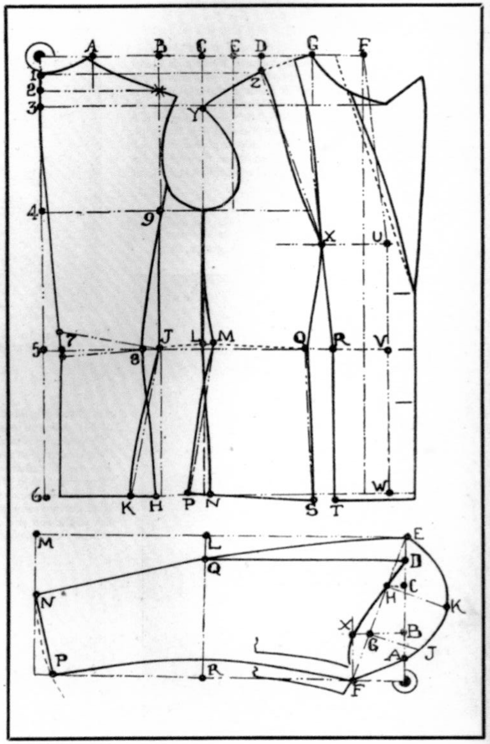

The lecturer concluded by laying down a basic draft (which we are pleased to reproduce here), and showing with what ease this could be applied to a number of different styles.

Measures

Measures: 17" nape to waist, 26" full length, 7" x-back, 19" to elbow, 29" to cuff, 14½" from nape to point of bust, 21½" to front waist, 20" to side waist, 7¾" x-back at base of scye, 11½" front scye, 19" half bust (taken from centre back, under arm, over prominence of bust, to centre front), 28" waist (tight), 38" hips.

Scale=Half bust (19).

The Draft

Square lines O-F-6.
O-A=3".
O-B=½ scale+½".
O-C=½ scale.
O-D=2/3 scale.
E is midway between C and D.
O-F=half bust (19).
F-G=3".
Square down from these points.
O-1=1"; O-2=2"; O-3=3".
1-4=½ scale+2".
1-5=natural waist (17).
1-6=full length (26).
Square across from these points.
Shape centre back, with 1" suppression at 7 and slight round between 3 and 4.
Curve from 1-A, and make back neck 3".
Apply the two half back measures, shape back scye, and draw back shoulder through star squared by B.
Make 8 from 7 ¼ of waist.
Place arm of square ½" below 7, and square down from 8 to H.
Complete the back from 8 through 9.
Follow line 9-J for sidebody, and place arm of square 1" above 7, and square down from J-K, adding slight round for hips.
Follow line Y-L for front of sidebody, with slight spring at N.
Apply front scye measure+½" for ease, and shape front scye to Y.
Place 3" on G, and measure down to X for bust depth, to V for front waist, and to M for side waist.
L-M is half the amount between 8-J; make M-P parallel to J-K.
Apply half bust measure from centre back, through 9 and X to U, adding 1" for ease.
Square down to W, and connect to F for centre front. (Fronts should be bridled about ⅜".)
Make X from U ⅛ scale+½"; R-V ⅛ scale.
Connect R-X and produce line to top, hollowing as shown.
Square down from R-T.
Connect X-Z; with X as pivot, sweep from G-Y for front shoulder.
Measure 7-8, place that amount on J, and measure to L; place that amount on R and measure to V; place that amount on M, and make Q half waist+2".
Measure up hips in the same way, and make S half hips+1".
Complete front seams as shown.
Lengthen fronts ½", and add lapel and button stand to taste.

The Sleeve

Measure up the armhole, and make this the scale, viz., 18.
Square lines O-E-P.
O-A=1/12 scale.
O-B=⅛ scale.
O-C=⅙ scale.
O-E=⅓ scale.
D-E=1/12 scale.
O-F=⅛ scale.
Connect E-F.
Square down from B-G, C-H, and E—M.
Square by F from G, and make J ⅛ scale +½".
Square by F from H, and make K ⅛ scale+½".
Shape crown from F through A, J and K to E.
Place the half back measure on E, and measure to elbow at L and to cuff at M.
Square across M-N ⅙ scale+1".
With D as pivot, sweep from N-P.
Place arm of square on P, and square from N-Q.
Connect Q-E and D.
Shape under-sleeve from F through X and H to D, hollowing ½" between F and X.
Hollow forearm 1" at R, and complete sleeve with false forearm, as required.

B.O.T. NOTICES

Wool Rebate Scheme

THE Board of Trade have now completed arrangements for the payment to clothiers of rebate on stocks of Utility wool cloths unprefixed or prefixed with the letter "S" held by them at the time of the wage increase in the heavy clothing industry in May 1946.

The Board of Trade announced in June 1946, the introduction of higher rates of rebate to offset, in part, the increased costs of making up. At that time, no provision was made under this scheme (as was done when the original subsidy was introduced) for payment to garment makers on stocks of cloths held at the date of the wage increase and on which the new rates of rebate had not been paid.

The Board have now arranged to pay rebate on Utility wool cloths unprefixed or prefixed with the letter "S" delivered to clothing manufacturers during the three months ending May 31, 1946. These payments will be confined, on this occasion, to Utility cloths used in the manufacture of men's, youths' and boys' outerwear.

As before, these payments will be made only to those clothing manufacturers who can certify that they have been unable to recover their full costs of production and sale plus the permitted margin of profit, within the ceiling prices. Payments will be made direct to garment makers, and forms for use in this connection can be obtained from the Wool Control, Bradford.

American Garments

THE sample garments of American manufacture, brought by the Working Party for the Heavy Clothing Industry from the U.S.A., which have been available for inspection recently at the Board of Trade, will shortly be displayed at the Manchester Chamber of Commerce.

It will be recalled that the garments were obtained by the Working Party for the purpose of comparing British and American methods of production. The items may be seen in the Board Room of the Manchester Chamber, Ship Canal House, King Street, Manchester 2, from Monday, May 19 to Friday, May 23 inclusive, between the hours 9-30 a.m. to 1 p.m. and 2.30 p.m. to 5 p.m. Tickets of admission are NOT necessary.

There were examinations at the end of each term and we had to learn all the cutting instructions by heart. No books were allowed in the examination room. The City & Guilds examinations were held every two years: an intermediate exam and then a final exam after four years. They were held on a Saturday, the final one always being on Cup Final day!

I remember those days as being hard work and good fun. I still feel that the balance of working my apprenticeship and attending college part time gave me a thorough grounding in both education and work experience for a career in tailoring and menswear. I did gain both my City & Guilds intermediate and final certificates along with my indenture papers for completing the apprenticeship. Some time later when I was a cutting room supervisor, I returned to college for further evening classes to gain the City & Guilds Full Clothing Technology certificate.

My career continued in the industry working with a variety of menswear companies, and then one day I presented a paper at a conference where the then Head of Department at London College of Fashion was in the audience. After the seminar I was approached to consider joining London College of Fashion to develop the menswear programme. The rest, as they say, is history. I had been an external examiner for City & Guilds, and through this I was offered a position as a Lecturer Grade 11 at London College of

Fashion to develop wholesale tailoring and menswear. My academic career started by teaching Wholesale Tailoring (as it was called then), from which developed an HND and later the first menswear degree at the college. The menswear course has been successful, and I can say this because of the strong presence that the graduates have in today's industry. Those graduates are working with a number of high profile companies including Burberry, Levi Strauss, Donna Karan, Ted Baker, Comme des Garçons, and others. From the tailoring direction we have students working in Savile Row, and now we have also established a degree course in Bespoke Tailoring.

The first Course Director I worked under was Colin Stovell – no longer with us – and I can remember him saying: 'to be able to teach is a privilege'. I have not forgotten that, and when I meet our successful graduates at industry events, it confirms to me that the work we put in with our students does have a value.

YOU never looked in and we were disappointed!

WHERE WERE YOU? That was the painful cry on Thursday last week when the trade's budding youngsters put on their annual show of quality make and styling for the "masters'" inspection.

We reiterate here the same old plaintive moan that has been carried on this page for the last five years: all sections of the bespoke tailoring industry, both London and outside in the provinces—taking in our usual ardent supporters, the woollen merchants—were almost depleted at this year's showing of the Annual Exhibition and Competition of Work by Apprentices, Learners and Students.

Weeks of hard work and prepara-

tion went into this event, first from the youngsters taking part, and by the handful of loyal workers who make up this special committee of the National Association of "Craftsman Tailors, sponsors of the Exhibition. The judging is completed, the winners informed, and the big day for the winning competitors arrives. Sharp at 11 o'clock on that Thursday morning (May 25), the garments were carefully laid out in true exhibition manner for the throng of trade craftsmen who were to inspect, approve, and to offer constructive criticism. But nothing on this scale happened: noon arrives and the few youngsters still waiting feel suddenly hurt by this obvious lack of attention from the trade. But things will be different at 3 p.m. when the presentation of prizes and awards are made!

The time arrives, and the hall in the London College of Fashion, Princes Street, Oxford Circus, fills up with

the youngsters, but with only a very small number that never quite made: the round dozen of trained, trade educated, quality craftsman tailors to add their applause to the winning few.

The *Tailor and Cutter* was disappointed at the response this year—even more so than in early years—and this disappointment was also felt by those bright, smiling, eager faces.

Even the few regular visitors to the event were missing this year, due, we are told, to some unforeseen circumstances. But it is not so much their absence that we are bemoaning, but the general lack of enthusiasm from the British bespoke trade as a whole.

The event produced some remarkable work in styling, cutting and make. They are trying hard to keep up the British standard of quality make set them, and we sincerely trust that this will be the only standard they will emulate.

Picture above from last Thursday's Apprentices' Exhibition shows one section of master tailors and craft-students attending the event.

THE NACT sponsored Annual Apprentices Exhibition for 1967 took place last week. Our photographs below show Charles Hunter (C. Hunter, London) presenting the Awards to the winning students and apprentices.

Top row, left to right: **Alan Berlin** (London College of Fashion) with the Illey "Schools" Trophy; **John Misson** (Kilgour, French & Stanbury) with the Illey "Trade" Trophy; **Colin Harris** (Shoreditch College) with the "Special" Cup; **June Rock** (Martin Sydney, Dublin) with the Stacey Cup. Bottom row: **S. Butler** (Huntsman & Co. Ltd) with the Palmer Cup; **Lloyd Miller** (London College of Fashion) with the Theo. Hewitt Trophy; **Robin P. Botley** (Shoreditch College) with the Garrard Bowl; and **Winston C. Ashley** (Tailor and Cutter Academy) with the Special Prize for trousers.

Discussing a selection from the entries are, left to right: **Anita Brackley**, Westcliff; **H. Ruback**, Margate; and **F. G. Watson**, London.

Chalk Marks

Thom Browne by Matthew Moore

It's his clothes that you notice first. He wears his shirt unironed, fresh from the tumble dryer. It is fitted, maybe a little tight. This doesn't matter, for he is athletic in build; this tightness merely serves to accentuate his masculine physique. The button-down collar remains unbuttoned, his tie falls neatly from his collar, it is immaculately pressed and tucked into his trousers. He wears a single-breasted grey flannel jacket, narrow in the shoulders, high in the armholes and noticeably short in length. There is grosgrain taping under the working buttons of the jacket. His trousers are high-waisted and cropped, and not just a little cropped either: they sit a good three inches above his ankles. These ankles are naked and highlight the strangely cartoon-like oversized brogues that seem to weigh down his feet. But he looks entirely comfortable, dignified, and it all looks right.

His look, although a little humorous at first, is in fact both sexy and cute. There is humour in the design, but it manages to remain youthful and sophisticated. You may think that his clothes do not fit, but on the contrary, when you look closely it all starts to make sense. What was once the anti-fashion, baggy, ill-fitting T-shirt and jeans, has now become the everyday norm for most men. Men have become lazy in their approach to dressing. Their desire for comfort has become their excuse for wearing clothes that hang off the body, unflattering to the physique, and drowning their proportions. The suit has become the anti-establishment.

Thom Browne's clothes set out to challenge this. They hark back to a time when everyone from the businessman to the Beatles and John F. Kennedy (as the Massachusetts junior senator) wore a suit. A time when rock stars could look cool, and politicians look impossibly stylish, both wearing suits. It's Steve McQueen in *The Thomas Crown Affair*, it's about the individual again, and fundamentally it's about clothes that fit in the right way. Thom Browne makes clothes that fit men in a different way. The fabrics are cut close to the body, accentuating the male form. They make you stand differently, like a gentleman, encouraging good posture. They manage to be both well mannered and sexy at the same time. They are young, but not in age, in spirit. They are comforting. It's about being comfortable and creative, about offering men classics but done in modern fabrics and with modern accents. It's about being provocative not conformist.

The shrunken silhouette that Thom Browne creates is so distinctive that by merely wearing his own designs on the streets of New York's Meat-packing District, he managed to create enough interest and a list of clients all wanting the same look. His business was born and he has quickly become acknowledged as a leader in the menswear market. Looking at the current state in menswear one can easily notice Browne's influence. Silhouettes are smarter and slimmer, trousers are cropped and there seems to be more effort in the way

menswear is presented. It's new,
and it all feels incredibly relevant
to London.

London thrives off diversity and
youth, its very soul feeds off young
creativity. It seems fitting that a brand
like Thom Browne is now recognised
and available in London, for even
though it derives from American
sensibility, it certainly emulates a very
British spirit. Think Gilbert and
George at Tate Modern, 'New York
Fashions Now' at the Victoria and
Albert Museum (which features three
Thom Browne suits) and the current
shift in fashion from mass production
to the painstaking fashion of times
past. London, the home of punk and
the birthplace of anti-establishment,
is surely the greatest setting for the
Thom Browne man. It's about fashion
that is handmade for the individual,
and it's more than just suits. It's
about a rock 'n' roll spirit, and more
importantly it's about a new kind of
couture for men.

LC   Your background is in tailoring; what led you to train in this field?

HT   When I was a child my parents' home doubled as my father's tailoring workshop and I grew up around the smell of sewing machines and fabric. I went through my school education, and as most parents, mine wanted their son to do something academic, so I took a business accountancy course. And I was quite good, but it didn't inspire me. I heard about a college called Barrett Street Technical College, which had a men's tailoring course. And having grown up living in a family of clothiers, I applied and took an entrance examination. I had some obvious knowledge about clothing.

I went through a period of time of being dressed quite well by my father. Appearance was important to me. I passed the entrance exam, went to Barrett Street Technical College. Shortly after I joined, only a matter of months, it was closed and moved into what then became London College of Fashion in John Princes Street, probably 1967. And of course I was overwhelmed when I joined John Princes Street, because it wasn't like Barrett Street, which was just about tailoring; it was a design college in general, much as it is today but certainly more than just a men's tailoring course.

My course involved learning fabric construction and pattern cutting, which was what I was mainly interested in. And tailoring. This

again gave me the ability to learn how to make a garment, how to take apart a garment, and know what was wrong with a garment through its pattern, which had been created in the first place.

My tailoring tutor was Mr Thomas, a very good, firm teacher, a good personality. I remember making my own first jacket. It took six months. Made by hand. Every stitch was hand-picked and every inch had to have so many stitches. I did have some benefits, as my mother and father were in the business, so I would get the paddings, wadding and the linings right, I would get some help from them. And pattern cutting was very important. We were very proud because we cut our own patterns and then made our clothes according to that pattern.

Two years later I left with my graduation certificate; we didn't have degrees. I then went to work for a company which was in Great Portland Street. It was a men's outfitter. And really that was the background for the start of my career.

My experience at the college has stayed with me forever, because when I went to work for that company I was frustrated by what they were doing, and I wasn't allowed to design what I thought was right. Then Carnaby Street emerged and the King's Road scene came very shortly after. I was predominantly the pattern cutter for my own designs in the early part of my career. I used to

work with suppliers, manufacturers and factories, getting the product by wholesale, tracking down particular stockists and just trying to get everything right.

We went from hipster trousers, through to Flower Power to what then became 'fashion tailoring'. It was a very big thing for a few years. Then my businesses really took off.

LC   So how did you progress into ladieswear?

HT   I did at one point, through the business, tailored ladies' clothing. And of course the cut is different, the sizing is different, but it was still back-to-basics pattern cutting. And I always went for what I called the more formal business look for a woman's tailored suit. If you look back to the thirties, forties and fifties, they were very strong, very tailored, very structured.

Then in the late sixties I started getting into the more 'soft' product. T-shirts and shirts. Jersey knit and so on. So it was becoming unisex. Gradually I moved into blouses and skirts, ladies' coats as well as men's coats. It was progression; there was no sort of 'oh I'm going to go into ladieswear', there was never 'I am in ladieswear only'.

LC   Inevitably though this progression must have been business led to some degree. You mentioned you studied accountancy when you were sixteen. This must have given you an advantage in being able to combine your practical skills with a business acumen, giving you an understanding of the market you are designing for. So at this point in history you were perhaps unusual because most designers go towards the business end after they do the design studies, but you did it the other way round.

HT   It's an interesting point you've made. If you ask me my preference I'd still do it my way round. I know that some would worry though about losing their flair by undertaking something this disciplined

LC   And looking back, what personal legacy has your college training left with you?

HT   When I first went to Hong Kong in 1969, there were soup kitchens on the streets and only a couple of hotels and I had to go into factories that were making shirts. In those days one of my brands was George Best who was a footballer and his shirts were being mass-produced at low cost. The workers had the machine skills but not the pattern-cutting skills; that is part of what my education at London College of Fashion did for me. I was able to sit down with the pattern cutters in these factories and show them simple little things in order to get the shirt right, teaching them simple markers to be able to follow, cutting a piece of cardboard so that when you're sewing the buttons underneath, it's four inches apart to the next one. These are the things from my days at London College of Fashion that are coming back to me. The fabric and the harshness of certain fabrics, trying to find the better fabric because of the way it has been woven and doesn't pill because something is brushed against it. All of that was part of my education at the college, but my competitors didn't have that because they had never been to college; they were just traders. And today where I am at this junction with Jaeger, people might laugh at me but I walk into my shop and my first instinct is to touch the garment and make sure it feels right.

I am still very involved with the aesthetics, the shop layout and the window displays. You have to have that eye. I am very critical and analyse the displays a lot And it might be because they display a men's jacket and there are two buttons closed on a two-button jacket and I'll be phoning at two o'clock in the morning and saying, 'I've just driven by, get in that window and undo one button, you don't do up the buttons on a jacket with two buttons', and that comes back from being educated into clothing and fashion in the right way.

LC   It's remarkable you are still so involved at ground level and your eye is so finely tuned to detail given the demands of your business empire.

HT   You can't teach someone that; it's either right or it's wrong. Am I getting myself overly stressed, is it really appreciated? Who knows? I walked into a shop not that long ago

271

and I walked through the menswear department and every mannequin with men's suits on with two-button jackets had all the buttons done up, and I was going round undoing the buttons and I thought, 'I'm gonna get thrown out of here, they might think I'm a shoplifter', but I couldn't resist it.

LC   Looking to the future, what would be your best piece of advice to those undertaking fashion-led courses today?

HT   I think the people should understand their love of what they want to be, what they want to design; it could be fabric design, it could be packaging design, it could be graphic art, etc. And I think the tutors need to quickly recognise a talent, encourage it and support it, and back up that encouragement with practical, applicable skills.

I think people get lost if they don't focus. When they come out of a three-year course they can flounder. It's not easy to be definitive and to do what you really want to to do, because the students want to do what they enjoy and the tutors have to push them to see what they are good at and support their passions through training. We need designers to be multifaceted in their skills. It's no good just being a person who draws a picture of the outfit they want to put on the catwalk that blows everybody away and suddenly can't be produced. It's the person that actually is designing colourways and

understands the fabric, then sculptures. It's about the overall picture.

I believe that we really do need to encourage retail businesses to support designers, otherwise we will have no talent. Without the designers, the buyers won't have a job.

LC   Do you feel there is enough support for graduating designers in the UK today?

HT   I think you'll find certain countries will be more aggressive in their support and promotion of emerging designers. Perhaps because they haven't got the history we have here in London. Perhaps we have become a little complacent, having had a London College of Fashion for a hundred years. I think that we need to be constantly developing our approach to training future practitioners in the fashion industries, in order to look to the future and support young talent in the industry.

LC   I understand you are also involved with the food industry through your restaurant businesses. There are current debates around the idea of slow fashion, which is of course a return to those old and traditional methods of tailoring, and investing more in bespoke and handcrafting. This idea of slow fashion of course is a response by some to the idea of disposable fashion, a more eco-led approach to production. How do those issues affect you as a retailer? What are your views on that, moving forward?

273

HT   At the top end you've got people like Ralph Lauren and couture houses, and they can still afford to tailor. In pure manufacturing it's mass-produced, it doesn't come across in the same way. I mean I can tell immediately a tailored suit, a hand tailored suit, or bespoke.

I would like to think everybody genuinely believes in ecological debates in the fashion world for whatever reasons. There is something in me that says, 'you've got to do something to save the planet'. But I'd be disappointed if this huge publicity currently about eco-friendly clothing suddenly just disappears. I believe in it and I am working on something at this present time.

To continue our reputation in the industry for the next hundred years we require investment and a lot of money. London is not the most economic place in which to live, but it is a city where we do create the finest talent. We often don't appreciate just how much all of our lives, our jobs and businesses are dependent on design and it's easy to think only of the well-publicised designers. In reality we need graduates each year to join us. I'm a great believer that we do create huge talent. People don't – you know I'm on my soapbox here – people don't realise how much desire and passion London has. And it always seems to be at the front end of retail that we can realise that ambition.

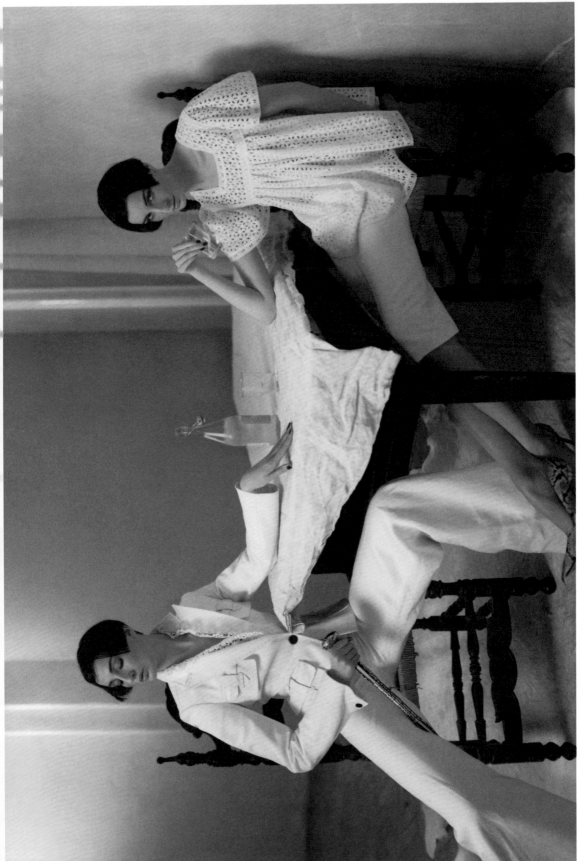

Shelley Fox's designs are woven from stories found behind boxes and beneath forgotten albums. Looking through her website leaves the impression that she has spent a good deal of time rifling through old stuff. Found histories, uprooted stories separated from their original owners, have been turned inside out: reworked into conceptual contemporary clothing and shown live on catwalks, modelled in videos, hung in galleries, repeated through photographs and displayed interactively over the internet. The sources of inspiration behind her collections vary immensely, from the simplicity of raised shapes and codes that create the texture of Braille, to the meticulous diary of a Philadelphia florist. Fox draws from thought-provoking concepts.

Faith in the value of original sources, and an addiction to the thrill of the hunt, drive Fox's research, and have brought her through a cacophony of flea markets. As an urban scavenger, Fox laments that fact that times have changed, and that it is now more difficult to find the cheap thrills that were once an almost certain reward after a long day of second-hand scouting. Today antique hunting is more difficult, as charity shops and market dealers have become much more discerning and now take on the work that Fox considers her role: finding the good stuff at a good price.

Fox maintains an astute awareness of the time in which she is working, and how it affects what she is doing and what she has done. Growing up in a small northern town, access to design and other creative industries was limited. Fox travelled to see bands play. She would buy second-hand patterns and old furnishing fabrics to create one-off outfits for nights out. This was not unusual for a time in which the only way to get a great outfit was to make one. Even then, the element of reworking items with a pre-existing history played a central role in her philosophy.

During her youth a trip to London was a big deal, and Fox remembers her first visit to the Victoria and Albert Museum; and in particular Rei Kawakubo's Comme des Garçons jumper with holes in it. Seeing this garment live inspired an interest in the notion of absence, what has been left out of a garment. This has become a common theme running throughout her collections.

Today, travel in and out of London is easy, and UK towns are far more in touch with fashion, music, art and culture generated in London, and worldwide. Access to information has changed creative environments by bringing an awareness of style and design into homes everywhere, and therefore making originality more elusive. 'What would it be like to be in the mind of a teenager today,' Fox wonders, 'and how much more difficult would it be to come up with new ideas?'

The nature of Fox's work brings her into the company of others who

Philadelphia florist diaries,
May 22, 1939

Y MORNING, MARCH 22, 1939

FORTY-NINE DOROTHY JAMESES

Miss Dorothy James, daughter of the Governor, embraces the huge bouquet of 48 "Dorothy James" roses named for her by Robert Pyle, West Grove floriculturist, who presented them yesterday at

277

share an interest in the nature of fashion and its presentation in London, and internationally. In a seasonal and trend-focused city such as London, working unconventionally is risky, but creates a network of like-minded individuals collaborating on innovative fashion-based projects. Fox's website was a collaboration with Digit, as a part of her most recent project for the Stanley Picker Fellowship for Design. The site's presentation of her work in three sections – Collections, Projects and Exhibitions – illustrates her approach to fashion design, along with the site's emphasis on the sources of her inspiration.

After graduating from Central Saint Martins in 1996, Fox spent eight years showing her collections seasonally. In 2004 she stepped away from selling collections in a commercial environ-ment and moved into uncharted waters. Her first project following this shift was an installation at Belsay Hall, where she spent twenty one days (over a three-month period) working alone, listening to Radio 4, creating and hanging her installation. 'At the time it was like nothing I was used to; it was calm and quiet and in this big castle surrounded by fields and sheep. It was a very strange job to do, having just come from running my own production-centred company.'

The Belsay Hall project was one of the many collaborations in which Fox has participated. In 2002 the film *Shelley Fox 14* was made and produced with SHOWstudio, launched at the ICA in 2002 and then shown at the 2006 London Fashion In Film festival. In March 2007 the film travelled to New York City and, in June 2007, it will be screened at the Arnhem Mode Biennial. *Memories*, a short film by D-Fuse, was inspired by her own family photographs, along with those of artist Ross Tibbles, sound artist Scanner and D-Fuse. Fox has design-ed costumes for Michael Clark's dance company, and has worked with graphic designers Rebecca and Mike to distribute postcards and packaged scarves throughout the shops along Charing Cross Road. She has shown in exhibitions by curators such as Judith King, Andrée Cook, Judith Clark, Alistair O'Neill and Valerie Steele.

Each project has raised different considerations about clothing, demanding attention to certain details such as strength, longevity, history, tangibility, value and worth of a garment. By showing her collections through non-traditional formats of presentation, Fox has adjusted our attention to focus on things that we might usually over-look when viewing fashion.

Stanley Picker Gallery: Installation
images from *Philadelphia Florist,*
October 2006

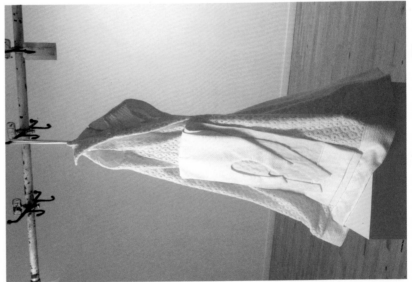

Chalk Marks

A star and his stripes
Ian Mankin

I grew up in London to the sound of Bow Bells: a proper Cockney. I was at London College of Fashion from 1950 to 1952 when it was called Barrett Street Technical College. I originally studied dress-making – what was known as court dressing, which was literally making clothes for people presented at court.

Originally I wanted to go on to make a career from it at couture level and got a job in a couture house. As an apprentice I was earning £6 12s and 6d, which was less than I had been getting in the army. It really was quite a hard time to enter the industry. My father had a textile trimmings business and someone persuaded me to work for him. I did that for seven years.

I got married in the sixties and I had my head down, working hard. Many people worked really hard at that time; it wasn't just parties. That was the time I was building up my business, from 1961 to 1968. I was beginning to develop quite a large workforce.

Then I saw a slate tie in Jaeger's window that cost 2 guineas, and I thought 'I can make those'. The first order I received was from Kew Gardens and then Aquascutum and Austin Reed, and I eventually got involved with Jaeger where I had seen the tie originally. I decided I couldn't make a living out of this and I slowly started making clothing – menswear. Again we had very, very high standards. I was amongst half a dozen people around the world making that level of very high quality leather clothes. I had a work-shop in Berwick Street at the time.

Because I had made ties, it was an easy step going to the same clients to show them clothing. The first American order I got was from Saks Fifth Avenue for sweatshirts. As time developed, I think I had about forty accounts around America at Neiman Marcus and five accounts on Rodeo Drive. And every one had different stuff – they all wanted to be exclusive. Then I made some clothes for The Beatles for a film. They all asked me to make clothes for them, which I did. This was in the 1970s and I was supplying in Europe and all over America. I saw a picture of Bob Dylan once and he was wearing one of my jackets. That was a nice thing.

Then I went into luggage. I made hand-made attaché cases with hand stitching. And there is no doubt that all the hand stitching and fine detail has stuck with me. Part of it goes back to my childhood. My dad used to go to warehouses in Manchester and buy whole boxes of fabric – calico and stripy materials – and I started going up there with him. I spotted some black and white material. It was different and I saw the potential in it.

When I opened the shop in 1983, you couldn't buy cheap, quality fabrics. We started selling things such as calico and ticking at about £2 a metre. It was a time when everyone had festoon blinds and we showed that, although calico is a very basic cloth, it can look incredibly sculptural if

you use a lot of it. By 1986 we had a
set client base, and I guess by 1989
we were on the map worldwide.

I found an English mill to produce
the fabric, shrink it and colour it, and
that's how it started. People say you
can't get anything made in England,
but it's not true. I manage to get 90
per cent of my fabrics made in the
UK. The big mills have gone because
they weren't willing to adapt.

We don't have anything in half-
primary colour, there are no fabrics
that date and all of them are the
same as my clothing. My clothing is
so good that it has lasted forever; it
doesn't wear out. And a lot of my
fabrics last for a heck of a long time
too. I'm quite proud of that. I know
it may not be great business sense,
but it's full of honesty, and the integrity of the product is very important.
For me the key to longevity and success is to keep things simple and not
expand too quickly. Looking back,
what I believe I have achieved is to
make quality fabric available to the
general public: I'm proud of that.

I find it very difficult to say I'm a
designer. My training was not in
textiles or weaving. I'm happier de-
scribing myself as a 'fabric retailer
who designs his own fabrics'. A lot
of work goes into what appear to be
very simple designs; the designs don't
just come from nowhere. For instance
the last time I was in France staying
in a hotel, I very nearly cut a piece
out of the ticking of the mattress in
my room; it was so wonderful. But I
managed to restrain myself.

I see a good stripe being all about
colours that go together and what
artists call the 'white space' you
create around them. I can still
remember the ticking on my school
mattress. It was black and white.
Funnily enough when I opened the
shop decades later, black and white
ticking was one of the first things I
introduced. I could never do an
abstract design – it wouldn't look
natural. I want the flowers I design
to look like flowers.

I am not anti-technology, but I don't
have a mobile phone and we do our
stock books manually; it's a standard
joke here that the day the pencil on
the stock file disappears will be the
day this company falls apart. We

Textile Samples from Ian
Mankin, 2007

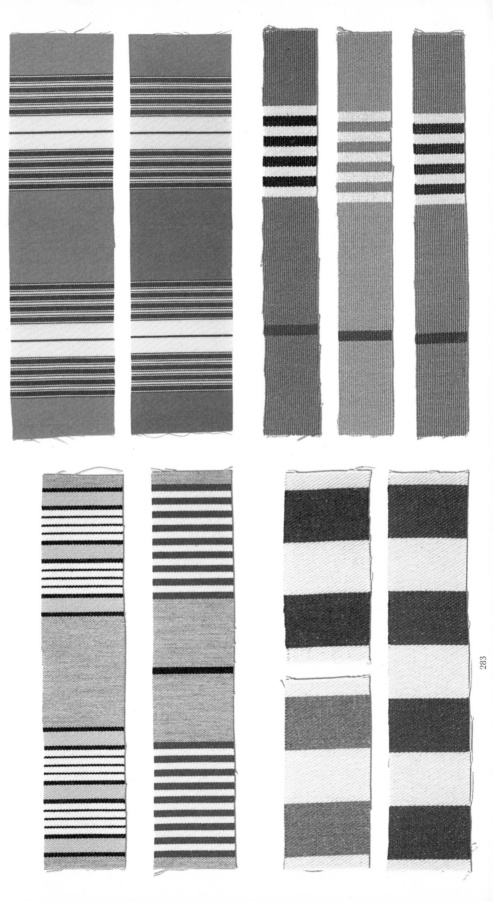

were the only business in the street
that continued to function when
power cuts struck in 2003/2004,
so there is some merit in this.

The advice I would give to those
entering the business is to pay your
bills on time: most young designers'
businesses fail because they don't
keep to this rule. Credit is not something I offer anymore; everyone has
to pay up front, and in turn I pay my
suppliers on the dot. The secret of
long-term success is not growing too
quickly and keeping things simple.
The overall integrity of the product
and the business is very important.

I find it hard to think about retirement because I feel I'm at my peak
in design terms, and most of all I
love what I do, which is all any of us
can hope for.

Ian Mankin's shop, 2007

London Bejewelled
Vivienne Becker

I may well be biased, as I spend my life in a jewel box, but to my mind London, always a gem of a city, has become the City of Gems, and jewels are now the talk of the town. Take a walk along Bond Street, glossily transformed over the last few jewel-addicted years, and you will find it tantalisingly sumptuous, scintillating with treasure, pulsating with the undeniable power of gems and jewels. Bond Street is now one of the most important jewellery centres in the world, surpassing even the classic elegance of place Vendôme and rue de la Paix in Paris, or Geneva's glitzy rue du Rhône.

What makes London so very different is the fact that folded in amongst the great master jewellers of the world, the grand jewel houses like Cartier, Chaumet, Tiffany, Boucheron, Bulgari and Van Cleef & Arpels, you will find those quintessentially English antique jewellers like the formidable S. J. Phillips, totally impervious to the fast-changing outside world, or Bentley & Skinner, whose craftsmen recently made Damien Hirst's attention-grabbing, diamond-dusted *vanitas* skull. Not only that, but alongside the sprinkling of sparkling names, both international and British, like Chopard, David Morris, De Beers, Ritz Fine Jewellery, and Adler, pearl king Mikimoto, the arch-modernist Georg Jensen, or flamboyantly individualist de Grisogono, London now presents the newest phenomenon in the international world of jewels. This is the highest of *haute joaillerie*, the rarest and most ravishing gemstones on the planet, with their other-worldly beauty and price tags, offered by names like Graff, Harry Winston, Leviev and Moussaieff.

Harry Winston, once known as the King of Diamonds, recently decided London was right for a roll-out of their particular brand of glamour. London jewellers Moussaieff, one of the most important diamond dealers and couture jewellers of our time, with a centuries-long heritage of gem trading, had been hiding their lustre and light under a bushel in a corner of London's Park Lane Hotel, before giving their creations a window on Bond Street. Leviev, again one of the most powerful names in the diamond industry, a long-term secret in the trade, with an almost impossibly rare and beautiful choice of gobstopper-sized coloured diamonds, chose London as the venue for their first ever retail boutique.

This may well be a sign of the times, a reflection of the super-wealth that is infiltrating London, breeding a new era of supreme connoisseurship and hyper-luxury. Yet London has a rich heritage as a jewellery capital of the world, as a Mecca for great collectors and connoisseurs. Think of the dashing, bejewelled maharajahs who brought their family heirlooms to London to be reset in contemporary style in the 1920s; or even further back, the belle époque beauties, in town for the Season, with American tycoons in tow, for whom jewels were an essential accessory, like a fine

Bentley & Skinner:
Art Noveau Pendant

Bentley & Skinner: Panze

house or a carriage, an indispensable badge of entry into society.

There is still another important element to London's life in jewels. Tapping into the city's own vein of subversive, eccentric artistry, its way of pushing boundaries and challenging conventions, London has a history too of nurturing originality and ingenuity in jewellery design, lifting jewellery to the level of an art form. London today is home, and sanctuary, to the iconoclastic designer-jeweller, Solange Azagury-Partridge, to Stephen Webster, quintessential rock-star jeweller, and to some of the world's leading artist-jewellers, including Kevin Coates, a modern Renaissance man, whose masterpieces, layered as they are with cultural, musical and magical references, challenge, provoke and thrill. And in his eyrie, the Glasshouse in the Sky, hung high over the city of London, artist and true English eccentric Andrew Logan still creates his subversive smashed-glass ornaments, so evocative of '70s fashion, and enjoying a revival today.

The newest, avant-garde talent is showcased in galleries like the unique Electrum, one of the first in the world to promote the work of artist-jewellers, or at the annual, much anticipated Goldsmiths' Fair, held in the grandeur of the Goldsmiths' Hall in the City (with its own links, via the Assay Office, to London's long history of jewels), where clients have the opportunity to view a whole panoply of styles and, most importantly, to meet their makers, understanding that essential, personal quality inherent in jewellery, setting it apart from any other of the decorative arts.

There is a rather laboured misconception that British people don't buy lavish jewellery, that we are all reticent about outward shows of adornment. I don't buy into that theory, believing a love of jewels to be in our DNA, to be a deeply embedded human impulse. The Victorians had a voracious appetite, and deep pockets, for the grandeur of fine jewellery, and a love too of the most whimsical or imaginative fantasy jewels. In an era of fast-growing prosperity and new technology (much like now), the Victorians were great jewellery consumers. Women were

walking shop windows for their husbands' success, and social etiquette decreed that they change their jewels, along with their clothes, according to the occasion and time of day. Jewels, then, as now, were the ultimate symbols of power and status – the most powerful expression of individual style.

At that time, too, London was home to great jewellers, both home-grown and imported: Hennell, sadly no longer in existence, but one of the oldest jewellers and goldsmiths in London; Asprey, which received its first warrant from Queen Victoria in 1862; Garrard, celebrated as the Crown Jeweller; Hunt & Roskell; Robert Phillips, who worked in the archaeological revival style; and Hancocks, the creators of the Devonshire parure, a vast and magnificent suite of 'Holbeinesque' jewels.

Art-jewels, a new concept at the time, were welcomed wholeheartedly by London society. Carlo Giuliano first came to London in the 1860s to manage the Frith Street, Soho workshop of the great archaeological goldsmiths Castellani, and he stayed to open his own exclusive, elitist shop in Piccadilly in 1874. This was a destination boutique for the wealthy but aesthetically-inclined intelligentsia of the day, who looked at jewels as works of art, not as gemmological wonders of intrinsic value, just as today's trendsetters might head towards Solange Azagury-Partridge's darkly sensual jewel-box shop in Westbourne Grove for an alternative jewellery experience. And, on the subject of jewel-box-like shops, does anyone remember Charles de Temple, with his gold-wrapped baroque pearls, and his tiny, equally baroque fantasy boutique in a Piccadilly arcade, hosting soirées and parties like a society salon? Or the avant-garde, ruggedly concrete Jermyn Street corner shop of quintessential 1960s designer-jeweller Andrew Grima, who launched a brave new era of free-thinking, free-form modern jewellery, perhaps the last cohesive jewellery style of our times – and encouraged an entire new generation of art-school educated goldsmiths, whose mission was to create jewels with a soul, deeply imbued with the spirit of their age.

One of the most important influences on all contemporary twentieth-century jewellery was the extraordinarily emotive work of the greatest art-jeweller of them all, René Lalique. At the turn of the century London was enlightened and insightful enough to invite Lalique to exhibit in London. This genius of art nouveau, arguably the greatest art-jeweller known, who changed the course of jewellery history, exhibited his divinely decadent, poetic masterpieces in the Grafton Galleries in 1903, and then at Agnews in 1905. Queen Alexandra was known to treasure her swan pendant made by Lalique. In 1987 I was privileged, and honoured, to be asked to curate and write the catalogue for the exhibition *The Jewellery of René Lalique,* held at the Goldsmiths' Hall. It was the first retrospective showing of his jewels since his own exhibitions at the turn of the century. London once again was first in embracing and celebrating the art of the jewel.

Even now, London is spearheading the renewed global appreciation of the intensely personal nature of jewellery, a recognition of the vitality and diversity of the genre, as we see an eclectic fistful of creative, individual jewellers, like the exquisitely ethnic, eco-conscious Pippa Small, or the quietly conceptual Jacqueline Rabun, setting up shop, opening their own boutiques, and studding London with yet more tempting trinkets. So behind the dazzling façade of Bond Street's breathtaking gems lies a rich story of tradition, heritage, originality and artistry. Embrace and celebrate London's life in jewels.

Objecthood Johanne Mills

I have always had a fascination with London and wanted to live here since coming down as a teenager in the '80s, visiting the markets and the club scene. I have been living and working here since beginning an MA at the Royal College of Art in 1995. London was new and exciting; I went out every night. I was inspired by its art, music, contemporary dance scene and architecture. Within my work I examined the relationship between body, architecture and space. I have continued to work across disciplines since college.

After graduation I worked on various projects from textiles to accessories or styling and art direction. I travelled frequently with consultation for Donna Karan, but always felt at home in London. I have very much enjoyed working with London-based clients and collaborators including Giles Deacon, Mr Pearl, Isabella Blow, Stuart Vevers and Luella.

My interest in the Arts and Crafts movement and craft in general is a very important aspect of my work. The sense of craftsmanship and wit injected into the original collections remains, consistently lending a sense of experimentation and playfulness to the jewellery. I continue to explore new methods, creating unique pieces that combine tradition with a distinctly modern and fresh sensibility, which is definitely a reflection on my being based in London.

In a recent collection I put together inspiration from punk, the jewellery of Mrs Simpson and medieval armour. Voluminous and natural forms are created using handcrafted techniques such as marquetry, *passementerie* and knotwork. I spend a lot of my time in workshops and studios in London experimenting with new processes. Within my current work I have used rubber, brass, Swarovski, leather, chrome, silk, cork, silver and semi-precious stones and explore how they can be combined with each other or formed on the body. I gather materials and push them beyond conventional characteristics, working with both contemporary and traditional techniques and I enjoy putting iconoclastic things together.

I also work closely with London-based stylists such as Katie Grand, Lucinda Chambers and Sarah Richardson and this gives me an arena to create new and exciting work. The beauty of living and working here is that I can source materials and research very easily. Everything is on my doorstep and I can turn around projects very quickly; it is a very spontaneous place.

Research is an essential part of my creative process. London's resources have always helped me to develop ideas and push techniques further. I constantly find new places or revisit old haunts, spending time in charity shops, textile fairs and markets.

Visiting the V&A, the William Morris Gallery or the British Museum has always been a passion of mine; I grew up spending the summer

British Vogue, March 2007: Raw silk mini-dress with fold detail, Sportmax; leather wedge sandals by Hermes; Swarovski crystal and wooden necklace by Johanne Mills

British Vogue, March 2007: Poplin vest top and matching skirt, Dior by John Galliano at Christian Dior; shell pendant necklace by Johanne Mills

Following page: British Vogue, May 2007: Embroidered lace wedding dress with jewelled headdress, Christian Lacroix Haute Couture, Paris; chrome bustier by Johanne Mills

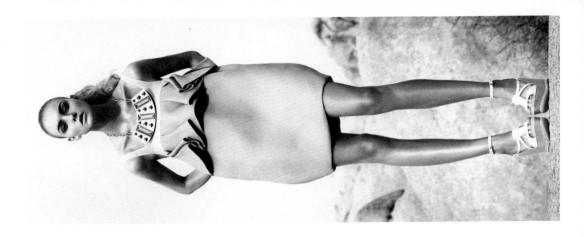

holidays in museums and junk shops in Leicester with my mum. While at the RCA I would be able to pop in to the V&A and this very much influenced my work.

The Wallace Collection has also been a favourite place of mine; I always see things differently each time. Its richness of decoration has always drawn me back to the works of art, furniture and arms and armour. The boulle marquetry furniture and the opulence and beauty of the oriental and European armour have also been reflected in my designs. Influences also come from modernist and art deco jewellery that I first discovered at Alfie's Antiques Market, another place I enjoy pottering around.

I am still as happy living and working in London as I was when I first moved here. I find it challenging and creative; fashion here has a certain irreverence and often a sense of humour and it's always original.

Objecthood
Husam El Odeh

Husam: Cap glasses: leather and perspex, 2007

I came to London in 1999 after having seen the infamous *Sensation* exhibition which travelled to Berlin at the time. It was one of those few moments when a collection of work had really excited and touched me at the same time. I knew I had to come to London; that was where it was happening! I now feel it was almost childish to act on an impulse as I did, but I have never really regretted it. In London I swapped the canvas for the body and began making jewellery.

My work essentially is rooted in my fine art background and I often see my change of career as a change of context rather than content. There are certain threads of themes that have always interested me and are reflected in all my work: I have an almost obsessive relationship with the directness of the body, its directness towards itself, e.g. the body being the initial source of all experiences, and also the power of the direct touch and trace. For me placing my work on the body is an incredibly tactile affair and lifts my work out of the realm of distance and pure observation. It creates a direct tension and an intimacy. It is sometimes almost like repeating the daily interaction and influences I experience with my environment, and translating them into objects. The image created is involving and immediate.

For a few years now I have worked in the context of fashion. I like the way fashion can pretend on the surface to be important, but retains a certain irony about its own function. It is very fast moving and changing yet essentially revolves around the same needs. A lot of my work happens in collaboration. These collaborations all have their individual character and focus. They put my work in context and also appeal to my flexibility as a designer. I consider it a great luxury that I have been able to work with designers whose work I value very highly and who have interests and a focus that resonate with aspects of my own work.

Marios Schwab and I have been working together since his degree show. I admire his almost sculptural approach to the female form. He has a highly sophisticated understanding of the body and strikes an elegant balance between tender, sexual and empowered. His designs are raw and refined at the same time. We have developed an intense and finely tuned dialogue over time. I interpret his approach into my specific materials. He is also probably the designer with the strongest vision I have ever encountered: his attention to detail is meticulous and has made my work for him challenging, but very rewarding in the outcome.

I met the menswear designer Siv Stoldal through her stylist Thom Murphy, who has worked with her for years. Siv Stoldal's playful approach is both refreshing and uncomplicated. Her designs are young and full of innovation, yet wearable and masculine, even classic. My love for playing with material and meaning complements this

Husam: Braces with ballchain; elastic, blackened silver 925, stainless steel, 2006

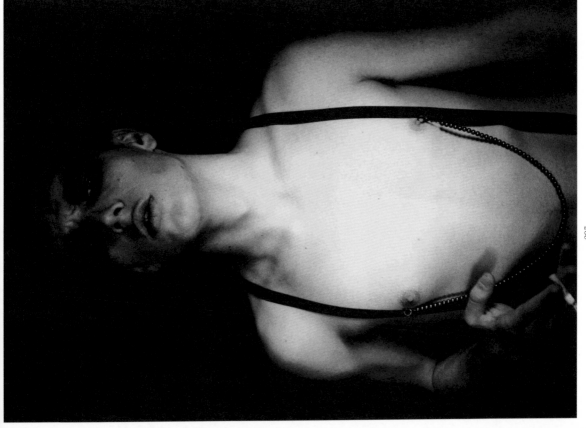

freshness. Her collections are a great context for the fun elements of my work. Our creative exchange enables me to develop ideas alongside her fascination with functionalism and tradition in a modern and un-compromising way. I have designed collections for Siv Stoldal for three consecutive seasons and have worked with her on the Lens collection created for Topman.

Ann-Sofie Back was a great influence on me when I was a student and I was extremely flattered when she asked me to work on her S/S 2007 mainline collection. Her radical and idiosyn-cratic approach to beauty and style resonate with a facet of my creative personality where the constant questioning and constant readjusting of the viewpoint is key. She is a very strong designer with an open mind but sharp focus. The pieces I created for her collection were themed around hard and industrial references broken up by a sense of irony. The materials I used for her collection were wire mesh and distressed metal.

Mihara Yasuhiro is a Japanese designer who has been designing his own line for Puma since 2001; he also has a mainline menswear and womenswear collection. His work is characterised by the experimental use of material and patterns whilst retaining an elegant and classic urban chic. He asked me to design a series of hairpieces for his menswear A/W 2007 show held at the Palais de Tokyo in Paris in February. The concept of making metal hairpieces

for men that would be classic and modern looking was intriguing. I worked on basic shapes of combs, one of my favourite functional objects, and replaced parts of classic hairstyles with highly polished sur-faces. The outcome was a variation of a traditional object with a slightly futuristic twist. The pieces reflected the sharp and classic lines and the modern use of materials of Yasu-hiro's collection. The pieces were displayed exclusively at l'Eclaireur in Paris during the menswear shows in Paris in June 2007.

I am also currently involved in three projects with Topman and am designing a special range for Kickers.

Apart from these design collabora-tions I have had the great fortune to work with some of the best stylists in the field on editorial designs, such as Jane How, Tal Brener, Nicola Formichetti, Thom Murphy, Patti Wilson and Jamie Surman.

I put together my own mainline collection twice a year, working along the fashion calendar. I must admit that I feel I have a greater freedom with my own line as it evolves less around trend-oriented ideas. I always feel my pieces should last longer than one season; they should always look modern and classic with an edge.

I like it when a piece surprises me: I love it when people who would usually never make a comment about a fashion item stop me and ask. My signature of recontextual-

Husam: Silver watch cuff: sterling silver, 2007

ising objects and symbols is born out of the same impulse of absorbing things around me and rearranging them to form a direct relationship with the wearer. A lot of the process is intuitive and almost random; just as I experience reality as random, I do not claim to be able to give answers or conclusions – neither interest me; I am more interested in questions and questioning. If only one of my pieces manages to make one person realise there might be another way of looking at the smallest detail of the world, I would consider it a success.

Husam: Crystal glasses: perspex, basemetal with silverplate, 2007

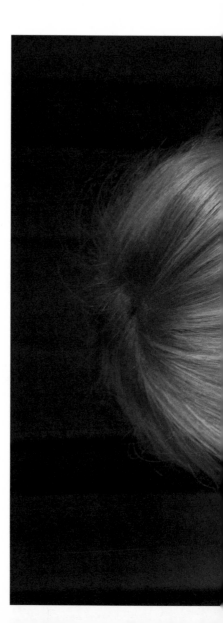

Husam: Metal visor: basemetal with silverplate, 2007

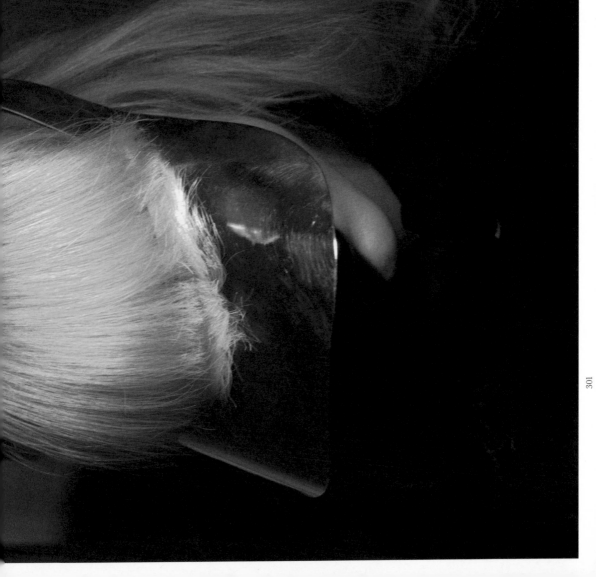

I arrived in London in 1994 with dreams but never imagined that I would start my own business in fashion, never even dared to think about it.

As a teenager, then a young adult, I grew passionate about the arts, from photography to cinema, from performing arts to jazz and classical music, to literature also. I was a very lonely child as my sister had died at a very young age and I was raised by my grandmother, who was a bit of a feminist! I was greatly impressed by female artists, by Gena Rowlands in *A Woman Under the Influence*, by Charlotte Rampling in *The Damned* and *The Night Porter*, by French actress Arletty in *Hôtel du Nord*, by Jeanne Moreau in *Lift to the Scaffold*. I worshipped artists such as Barbara Hepworth, Cindy Sherman, Diane Arbus, Louise Bourgeois, Nan Goldin. I listened to Billie Holiday and loved her style.

These women shaped me and helped me define my sense of style much more than any fashion designer. I did not know much about fashion, but through my grandmother, a dressmaker, I had heard the names of Schiaparelli, Coco Chanel, Madame Vionnet, Paul Poiret, Jean Patou...

At eighteen I started to buy magazines about cinema and fashion mainly; I discovered Yves Saint Laurent, Claude Montana, Thierry Mugler, Jean Paul Gaultier... But fashion happened in Paris and I was living in provincial Lyon, where I felt

I was suffocating; I was trapped and not permitted to be who I wanted to be. With a media degree I left for London, hoping something would just happen.

London felt like a place where I could be my own person, dress as I wished without being put into a category, where my personality would not be trapped within the way I looked, where I could learn, meet exciting people from all horizons, have lots of experiences. I was a bit stiff and quite serious, sometimes snooty – that had to change! I knew I wanted to do something in the creative field and I knew deep down that I would not design or make; it would be more about promoting.

My very first introduction to jewellery and body adornment happened this way: I saw in a small jewellery boutique off Brick Lane a few pieces that were for me more sculptures than jewellery; they touched me, they questioned my perception of jewellery, of identity, of fashion ... I discovered the name of the designer, Naomi Filmer, and I went looking for her for months until I managed to meet her and was able to promote her beautiful, sensitive and intelligent work.

I worked for a few years as a jewellery buyer promoting new talents such as Shaun Leane, Scott Wilson, Bless among others, until I became disappointed by too many restrictions and a lack of support. I then set up my agency, encouraged at first by one stylist Francesca Burns, now fashion

Clockwise from above: Lilian
Harvey, 1933, solarised portrait
New York Studio; Honey & I;
Charlotte Rampling, Paris,
September 1985; Arletty
(1898–1992); Barbara Hepworth
with sculpture, 1967, *Three Forms
Vertical (Offering)*, 1967;

Naomi Filmer, Chocolate Mask;
Florian Ladstätter, Jet Collection
2005; Gena Rowlands, *Gloria*,
directed by John Cassavetes, 1980

editor at *i-D*. I met amazing people, talented, forward-thinking and like-minded people, people with very strong visions … these people also made me who I am. My agency has now been going for more than two years. We have gone through lots of successes and it has been a real learning process; we have learnt from our mistakes, but on the whole we have collaborated with truly fine people.

I am still the same as when I arrived in London – I like talent and individuality, and I want to get people to meet and connect. I love to share views on films, books, exhibitions … I am totally curious and eager to discover, experience … Will I still be in London in ten or twenty years? I really can't tell – if you had asked me thirteen years ago if I would be in London in 2007, I would not have known either.

London for me is definitely a place with energy, and also a place where you get challenged daily, a place where you face irony and a certain dark sense of humour that you would not get anywhere else; neither in Paris, nor in Milan nor in New York, the three places for fashion otherwise. Being able to laugh and being able to realise that I am privileged to do something I have great passion for and something that can appear rather frivolous. Because in the end I am not saving human lives!

I would love to open my own space/ gallery/ home where I could show things I feel passionate about, things that have changed who I am … This place would be like a cabinet of curiosities; a place that would breathe individuality, sincerity and generosity.

Natalie Brilli, 2006

Florian Ladstäetter: Florian
Window installation, b Store, 2005

Florian Ladstäetter: Florian Jet
Collection, 2005

Scott Wilson's idea
of Glamour Pop, 2005

NH   Let's start with fashion. You've always been an artist, essentially a sculptor, but somewhere along the line you fell into the fashion world. I gather you were tripped up by some dirty feathers…

DR   Yes. It was not long after I graduated from college that I was messing around in my local park and came across some decomposing feathers that had been stripped almost to the bone. I loved their look, started playing around with them and assembling them into structures. I had a mannequin in my place at the time, which ended up with these objects, mask-like forms constructed from the feathers, on its head. Because I'd studied at Saint Martins I knew quite a lot of fashion people, who saw the pieces and harassed me to go and show them to a stylist, so I showed them to Katy England, who was Alexander McQueen's stylist at the time… He saw them, liked them and he commissioned me to make fifteen pieces for his spring/summer collection in 1997. I did that and literally within six months of the shows it just went mad, crazy. Like the whole fashion industry got hold of it. Suzy Menkes from the *Herald Tribune* ran a story on my work, about how these feathers in the park ended up on the catwalk at McQueen's show. It became this sort of fashion fairy story.

NH   Cinderella's rags got to go to the ball … What was the initial impetus behind the feather masks?

DR   I'd always been interested in the idea of creating a physical space around women through hats, inverting the tradition where hats were used to seduce and draw men in. I wanted to go somewhere else … assembling these quite large, aggressive structures that created a space around you when you wore them, that made an impact when you just walked into a room; forcing people to interact with the wearer as a viewer would with a work of art … I mean the things were gilded in silver, sometimes with very sharp edges, full of threat. If the wearer moved, you moved too…

NH   So was the intention to celebrate a more muscular, Amazonian-style ideal of the feminine?

DR   It was liberating, in some respects. In fashion the woman is passive, a thing in the hands of designers, who are predominantly male, who dictate what she is to look like in the world at large, which is also largely male dominated … so I liked the idea of these pieces of mine empowering women, putting them in control, in a very direct, physical way.

NH   Did the intent survive the transition onto the catwalk and into the shops?

DR   Yes. I think that's why McQueen picked them, because they worked and they created these strong, powerful images, and at the end of the day really strong images is what fashion is about. Within months of

starting up the business I had twenty-six stockists: Bergdorf Goodman, Marcus Sax, Liberty, Harvey Nics… They all wanted the pieces and the whole thing just snowballed…

NH   Was it weird, suddenly being engaged in this commercial world of producing product lines?

DR   It was weird, but we were quite clever, making these expensive pieces, £7,000 sometimes, and alongside them much more accessible neck pieces and small head pieces…I'd send the team out to Trafalgar Square to pick up feathers, bring them back, flock them and we'd end up selling them in Harrods or whatever for £20 a piece. They cost me nothing but we were selling like 15,000 of these so it was just mad… To be honest we were; like, taking the piss in some respects, we just thought, well if people are stupid enough to buy these, then let's just go with it.

NH   Is that why you have a very ambivalent relationship with fashion?

DR   Yeah…My mum used to have a saying which was, 'you can't educate pork' and I believe it!

NH   Er…Can you break that one down for me?

DR   Well it's like if people are pigs… fashion is about truffle hunting, they go out and they pick what they think they should be picking, because they have been told what to pick. There is no integrity really, no intellectual rigour to what they buy.

NH   Did you despise the fashion world at the time, at the height of your success in the field?

DR   No, I was intrigued by it because I really liked the immediacy of it. I liked the fact that you could make something one day literally and then a couple of days later you'd see it on MTV. And the global excess of it was fantastic, the fact that you'd get clients coming from all over…

NH   But in the end you closed down your fashion career very self-consciously…

DR   Well, in the first five years it was quite fun, but then it got more

serious and then you increase stockists, and then you are working more towards pleasing the buyers and the further you dig in, the more you are dictated to, and we just weren't interested in that game at all. So ten years down the line we just thought, come on let's just drop this.

NH   And with your last collection you did…

DR   So, yes, for a finale we created a last collection for London Fashion Week that was a political statement against the fashion industry. It was titled *No More Useless Beauty*, taken from an Elvis Costello album, and was a collection of twenty-six outfits, like twenty-six accessorised looks, which weren't for sale. All the world's press and buyers were there but no one knew what was coming until they sat down and the first girl came out…

NH   And what was the first girl wearing?

DR   A dress with '*Vogue* is the Devil' emblazoned across it. Another carried the legend 'No Celebrities Required' because two days before the show started, Nicolas Coleridge, head of Condé Nast, sent out an email to all the designers asking what celebrities they had coming to their shows so they would know what to cover…and we just thought this is a fucking load of bollocks, what's this got to do with our sales or keeping us afloat as a business? So we created looks that used politically loaded images taking the narrative of subversive subcultures as a silhouette. There were lots of punks and Teddy boys wearing utilitarian kind of garments bearing these subversive statements, like 'Made in Wales not Taipei', or 'Woven in Scotland not China'. It was really in your face. And we changed the passive role of the model. We sent them all out with cameras, and they stayed on the catwalk after they came out, standing around, spitting and throwing gum at the audience, and then walking into the audience, taking photos of them, which really frustrated the cameramen because they were no longer in control.

What I was saying with those garments was everything the industry couldn't talk about, like highlighting the cheap production of clothes in

Dai Rees: *No More Useless Beauty*, London Fashion Week, S/S 2001

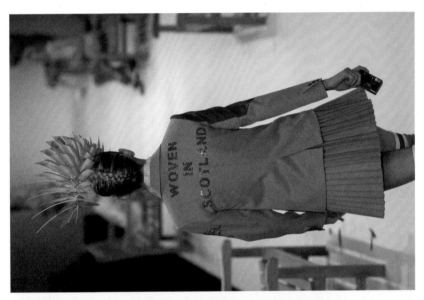

developing world countries, about the control of the magazines that the big brands wield ... London Fashion Week was selling itself on the talent of a few truly avant-garde designers, but then it wasn't supporting us in any way ... So that was it. It was my kind of like, BYE BYE!

NH   Like a rebirthing technique?

DR   Well I didn't have any kind of escape plan, I didn't have something to fall back on, so it was a bit of a risky thing to do, but I like to throw myself in at the deep end not knowing what's gonna happen.

NH   And then did you very consciously have to redefine yourself, again perhaps, as an artist?

DR   It was important that I got back to where I wanted to be and the only way that I could do it was by saying, 'I can't go back in now'. I've cut my legs off kind of thing.

NH   But your sculptural works, for example those in your current show, Carapace, which are wall-hung forms, made from leather, that resemble bovine carcasses, maintain a formal link with fashion design ...

DR   Well my work has become much more abstracted as time has gone on ... but in general I'm quite interested in mixing things up, and throwing things into a pot and seeing what spits out. So I chose three disciplines to interact with: the butcher, the tailor or dressmaker, and the mortician. They are all practices embracing elements that we covet ...

NH   Do we?

DR   Well, food we have to eat, we buy meat ... there is a ritual to the butcher's cutting-up of a carcass and his presentation of it in the butcher's window. The tailor creates our clothes and then there's the mortician, the last one ... it's the last thing perhaps that we do covet; we expect to be a good product in the end, and we all want a good death.

NH   Death is present in the materiality of the works. There is a Bacon-like engagement with the representation of flesh ...

DR   Francis Bacon has been an

influence, not in a direct sense, but I really like his ability to create the impression of bulk, of material presence ...

NH   Aside from your artwork, you are at present setting up a new MA course at London College of Fashion. What is its purpose?

DR   The course is called Fashion Artefact and the intention is to create an environment where people with a similar way of thinking to me can use fashion as an environment where different objects can be shown. The interesting thing for me about fashion is that objects can exist within its world which can have a fifteen-second existence, be it either for a photographic shoot or a piece used as a styling tool ... I'm really intrigued by these objects that lack a direct commercial purpose ... I want to create an environment where people can work within this area, and learn hard skills to create products which can be viewed within a gallery context, even if they come from a background of fashion.

NH   What do you think the fashion world has to give the art world?

DR   Well I think the first thing is that there has to be a refinement of the word 'fashion'. Too often we confuse the word fashion with clothing. I think there is the clothing industry and then there is the fashion industry. Fashion is about image, it's about the distortion of the silhouette, it's about the way that the figure carries a garment. It's very abstract with designers like McQueen, Balenciaga, John Galliano, Viktor & Rolf playing with that idea of the silhouette. For that's what fashion is, beyond the mere manufacture of clothes.

Dai Rees: Exhibition: *Carapace*; Solo Touring Show; (British Council) Musea, Experemental, Mexico City, 2007

Objecthood

Philip Delamore in conversation with Suzanne Lee

SL   Perhaps you could start by framing the project you are involved in?

PD   I guess it all came about with me discovering what rapid prototyping and 3D scanning technologies were, which was in about 2001, quite prophetic I suppose! I just chanced upon an article about rapid prototyping, and I misunderstood it because I was working in digital printing and I saw something about 3D printing, and at the time I was interested in trying to print 2D images onto 3D objects. I read this article and thought no, that's not what it means at all. It means you can actually print the object. Wow! And quite soon after that I read about the work that Janne Kyttannen had done and he was, I think, one of the first designers who actually engaged in that technology apart from Ron Arad. It was quite mind-blowing to me, this idea that you could actually print an object. So I was completely captivated by it and determined to have access to a machine to play with, and I've now started to look at what I can do with this.

SL   What have you been printing so far?

PD   Very simple things actually because its also about developing a new mindset. I've moved from a world of 2 dimensions to a world of 3 dimensions and while I had some knowledge of Photoshop and Illustrator (2D applications) a 3D

application is a whole other world. And for me to start all over and learn again all the 3D applications is actually quite daunting.

SL   But it must be easier for you as someone that has some sort of training in 3D, because you have created clothing in the past. That requires you to think in a 3D way.

PD   Its funny actually because when you talk to other designers, textile designers, a lot of them do not think in 3D.

SL   Really! I personally struggle to do the reverse. I find it hard to get from a flat pattern to a 3D thing.

PD   I always struggled with (2D) pattern cutting at college. I found it very mechanical, I disliked rulers and reducing things to lines. There seemed to be a lot of cheating going on.

SL   And you create things when you drape that you wouldn't have done had you gone at it with a pencil and ruler.

PD   Exactly, and I think what is exciting with the development of 3D technologies is the potential and what I'm excited about is that everything will be in 3D, not 2D. So you could potentially capture all that interest in something that was draped.

SL   So will your project going forward be looking at that right from

Mixed Reality; 3D Drawing using real-time capture, 2007

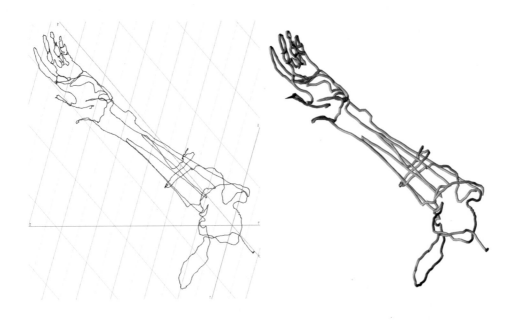

the start to the end of the process? Will you actually design things using haptic tools? Are you going to create a space that allows you to use your 3D model which is then printed in 3D?

PD   Well that's the idea, but potentially the thing that is always missing with this technology is the front end. It's really how a designer uses these tools. And the thing about learning a 3D programme or a piece of software is that you have to sit at a keyboard, and a keyboard is not something that a designer wants to work with. And the only other tools available are haptic ones like a 3D mouse or pen.

SL   That's the closest thing isn't it?

PD   Yes, I think there is a real lack of digital or translation tools that let you move between the real and the virtual. Although the virtual seems to have moved on in leaps and bounds as computer graphics and processor speeds now allow real-time move-ment and real-time cloth movement, and you have virtual worlds like Second Life opening up a whole new dimension to fashion. Where the real and the virtual meet you begin to get some interesting questions raised, and people are using the term 'mixed reality' now. It seems that we will soon have a new web that exists around a (3D) virtual world, rather than a (2D) web page, so that we may see and interact with others who are visiting the same places. Our persona will then have a virtual identity and that is obviously interesting for all sorts of reasons, like the fact we are not limited by the constraints of the real world.

PD   One of the things I was going to ask you was why you think fashion is so scared of the future? Because we still seem to be living in the '60s vision of the future, the future de-scribed by Courrèges and Paco Rabanne. We haven't moved on. Whereas every-thing else that fashion uses – its branding, its marketing, its packaging, its production – is right on the edge of technology. The fashion products that we consume, we want a new phone every 6 months and we want the new technology to go with it.

SL   Yes but it's taken the fashion industry a very long time to grasp that a phone can be a fashion object. It's only recently that we have seen Prada produce a phone, and at the end of the day, no matter what they say, it's still design coming from the electronics angle. As production which fashion companies are actually investing in projects like yours?

PD   None. That is to say there are designers I work with, and that I talk to who are engaged by the technology, designers like Hamish, and Gareth and Hussein. But most of the technology doesn't make it beyond the catwalk, unless it goes straight into a museum collection. In fact to a historian of the future it will look like fashion had engaged with technology much more than it actually has, as all the archives will be full of this stuff, but it was never consumed: it just bypassed the stores and went straight to the museums!

SL   So are fashion companies engaging in any contemporary technologies and what might be the next stage in production? I think fashion might actually be the last industry to engage with any new technologies. I mean, look at the uptake of designers who have created websites. Who acknowledged that the Internet was a space for selling? I mean, when Net.a.porter first went to design houses and said we would like to sell your collections online, they said why? And now suddenly everybody wants to be on Net.a.porter because they realise they are reaching a global market and they can even have a shop within a virtual shop. You know, it's a window to a whole customer base that they didn't even know they had. But it took years for many to come around to that point of view.

PD   Are we just banging our heads against a brick wall here?

SL   No, I think maybe people like you and I are perhaps doomed to always be too far ahead in terms of actually capitalising on it. There are generations behind us who will use what you are pioneering and won't even think about it. The bigger question is whether the market is actually ready to embrace that. And that is certainly the big issue with wearable electronics in clothing area. We can actually do a great deal now;

Assisted Self Portrait; 3D Drawing, 2007

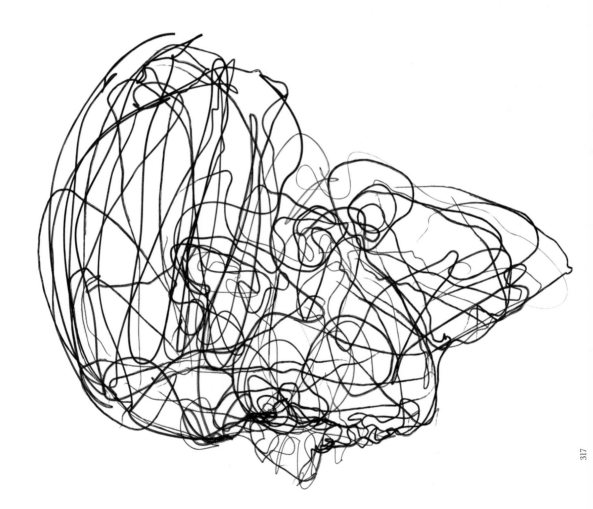

we can make a garment smarter, more intelligent. But the fashion industry is still disinterested; it remains a tiny niche for high-end sportswear manufacturers. Occasionally you get a company like Levi's trying to test the water with a pair of jeans and an i-Pod controller, but you talk to anybody from high fashion and they are extremely sceptical if not completely derisory about the whole idea. For the man in the street, too, it's a huge leap to suggest that a jacket can go from being this woven wool thing that has existed for hundreds of years to something that could receive a phone call or give you a hug.

PD I think as well that people are scared of the notion that everyone is trying to put them in some sort of second-skin suit. And if you look at what clothes we were all wearing 50 years ago compared to clothes we are wearing today. I'm trying to think of the technology that has changed in those 50 years. I suppose Lycra is the only significant change.

SL Well anything else that comes along seems to end up as a gimmick and be sidelined. There is a surface engagement with technology, but the consumer isn't interested in reading labels that explain the tech in their jacket and they don't want to pay the add-on cost of it. I think that's one reason that people are slow to embrace new products. Because nobody wants to pay the extra cost!

PD That's true and also because retailers haven't addressed how to approach retailing technologies. Interestingly, I recently went into the new Adidas store in the Champs-Elysées where they have an innovation centre showcasing new technologies and customised products, and it's such a compelling environment. They have people there to draw you in, to involve you and to explain what it is to you. People loved it. It looked really good, futuristic, and there were many people there. It's like an experience really, educating people in the possibilities that these new technologies have. People can't be sold to in the way that they were sold to through the mass media of the last century. Everybody is working on communities in MySpace and it's all about the flow of ideas and recommendations. The niche

and this idea of the 'long tail' and all of those things that have happened through other media have now filtered into how we consume design. And I think that's potentially a great thing because you can pursue something quite niche and still hope to reach an audience.

SL It's a source of hope, I think, for small companies and young designers who don't have massive resources at their disposal.

PD Absolutely. I think from the time that I left college to now the potential to reach an audience, as a small independent designer has never been greater. But people need to be equipped to be able to capitalise on it. What I think is exciting about these new technologies is the potential to allow you do that. If you have a 3D printer in Japan or the States or wherever, someone can come online and go to their local manufacturer and have it produced. It wont be very long until people have that on their desktop. Now everyone has a 2D printer; soon everyone will have a 3D printer. You can actually go and get a 3D desktop printer now for about £5,000. But like any type of technology the price will come down. So I think in 5 years time, a significant number of people will have them on their desktops.

SL So, tell me – the scope of your project, what's the near-term goal?

PD It's a very short project so it's about scratching the surface of 3D printing textiles – it's more about demonstrating. I'm trying to get some prototypes together that demonstrate the possibilities so hopefully we can go and explore it further. To look at the design interface, the materials and the construction of a set of prototypes is a huge undertaking. I'm looking at, what existing materials are out there that I can use. So really looking at the existing materials, proposing developments on those materials and whether there is a system or a combination of materials that would work. Whether we could throw out some new types of textile structure, as we are not limited to having to weave or knit or bond the fibre together, so there is no reason why different types of structure couldn't be suggested.

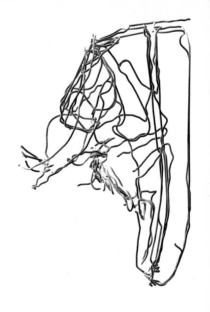

SL   And is the goal still aimed at a fashion context or is it for any textile application, maybe interiors or even architecture?

PD   I think the joy about it, is that it's completely scaleable. There are now 3D technologies which work on the nanoscale and there is a team in the States who are trying to rapid proto-type buildings! So I'm somewhere in the middle.

SL   I guess that's a good place to start because you can then go into the microworld.

PD   It's all about the internal and external: I think it's really interesting, the similarities between body and architecture. You know, classical architecture is based upon dimensions of the body and the fact that you can then scale up or scale down. That's really exciting because we are working in a sort of body-related area purely because of size. We have machines that we can only build to a certain size at the moment.

SL   But ultimately surely it is a highly sustainable mode of manufacture?

PD   Well, yes it is. Especially if you look at what it can save you in terms of the number of physical prototypes you have to make. Just shipping things around the world. I mean, you're still shipping machines and raw materials, but actual data can just be sent on the net and then your design can be built anywhere in the world that has a machine.

SL   Well that's a good question in terms of what the impact and significance of this project is. What are the implications?

PD   Well there are many, but the most significant are that we will have new approaches to design, and design disciplines that cross boundaries, and that we will have new materials and ways of realising these designs. It's very exciting: companies are designing car engines around the flow of air and liquid so its kind of designing backwards in terms of the way that we used to design.

SL   How soon before you see the first 3D – manufactured garment on the catwalk, and what label?

PD   Me in 18 months I hope! I plan to exhibit these prototypes in some way. Whether putting them on the catwalk is the right context – my guess is that it probably isn't. I like the idea of mixed realities, how things can stay in a virtual state for longer and longer now, or if they become real at all. I am enthralled by the Second Life phenomenon: The Emperor's New Clothes. I love the idea of people spending real money on things that don't exist. I mean, for me that is the ideal forum for disposable fashion. Go to a virtual Topshop.

Engineered digitally printed leather suit for Tristan Webber, 2002

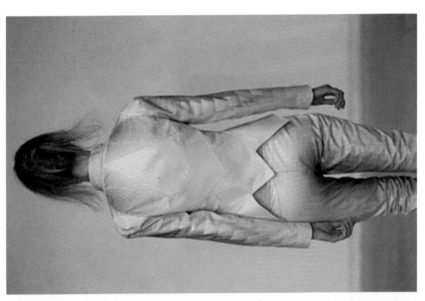

Objecthood Walter Buchholz

My work is very personal. I find it difficult to express myself without exploring a part of who I am. To me, it seems risky not to work like this. It is strange to try and imagine what something must feel like and then base any work on that.

I am obsessed with process. Processes are sincere. Outcomes and conclusions are often forced on to the end of a lovely process. This frustrates me because I am in a (fashion) situation where you cannot wear a process. You have to make clothes.

Nietzsche understood my predicament well when he wrote: 'Sometimes in conversation the sound of our own voice distracts us and misleads us into making assertions that in no way express our true opinions.'

Processes are my true opinions and trying to find conclusions is a distraction. Finding a *fashion* conclusion to a part of me is difficult.

My current project, *you touched me*, is a series of journeys that are in a way extensions of my fears and curiosities.

With *you touched me* I wanted to simulate (through clothes) the way I think people accumulate and assimilate memories. I wanted to create stories and experiences for clothes, something that logically cannot exist, almost like having a past before you are even born.

To do this, the fabric used for each garment had to go on journeys.

I had to be personally involved in each one of these journeys. I had to go outside myself and face my own fears of public embarrassment, confrontation and failure to make these journeys possible. Only by doing this could the processes and the necessary outcomes become personal and sincere.

These journeys ranged from begging people on busy streets to touch my fabric to asking people to walk over some fabric on busy pavements, to climbing on a Henry Moore sculpture opposite the Houses of Parliament and draping the fabric over it, and befriending a beggar at Old Street Tube station and trusting him to take some fabric away and bring it back for ten pounds.

These little journeys are also my miniature processes that, when joined, become a huge invisible web. This is a web of many memories that lie just under the surface of each garment I make.

Through this way of working the garment is not really an outcome but rather a part of my process where I store my own and other people's memories. The garment is there to remind me of parts of myself. In this way my work remains personal; I am both involved in and affected by it.

I seldom break my work into separate and completely new projects. Instead I try to address new issues through the same ongoing process.

Walter Buchholz: *you touched me*, Betty Jackson, 2007

Walter Buchholz: *you touched me*, Patricia Field, 2007

Walter Buchholz: *you touched me*, Judy Blame, 2007

Walter Buchholz: *you touched me*, Pete Doherty, 2007

One development is always just an overflow of the previous one.

In this way I think my awareness of my body led to the collection of little journeys into public humiliation with my fabric. I am 2.04 metres tall. I am always visible and as a result always a topic of discussion. I am public property through no fault of my own. I am made aware of my height every day I set foot outside my front door.

A life of being pointed at and stared at has made me extremely anxious and introvert when I am in busy places. Talking to strangers in public and humiliating myself by asking them to hold a piece of fabric is something I would never do. That is why I decided to do just that. I needed to expose myself to achieve a sincere process.

I remember as a teenager wishing that I were fat instead of extremely tall. I reckoned that at least after a while of being fat I could simply lose the weight and just be seen as normal. I started to obsess about wearing only horizontal stripes because apparently they made you look shorter.

I created a collection based on these body insecurities called: *we all have to wear our bodies.* I created some trousers that could be worn before and after massive weight loss and some that had extremely long legs. I used bright colours that would attract as much attention as possible.

My work will continue to be one big, erratic process, discovering parts of me: insecurities, memories, loves, hates and as yet unknown phobias. Along the way I will have to produce outcomes but they will be for the most part sincere and personal.

Walter Buchholz: *you touched me,*
Walter Buchholz, 2007

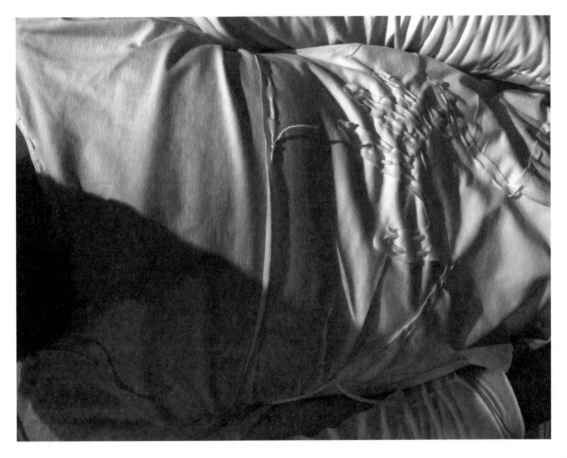

Exhibitionism

Fashion Curation
Judith Clark

'The exhibition-maker's job is to arrange this encounter between people and what puzzles them in such a fashion that they will derive the maximum benefit and pleasure from it .' Robert Storr

In a recent essay called *Show and Tell*,* the Director of the 2007 Venice Biennale Robert Storr describes what the multiple roles of a contemporary curator might be, and in doing so, chooses to use the term 'exhibition-maker'. The runaway term curator can then be reascribed to those who keep – look after and conserve – a particular collection. The exhibition-maker instead makes decisions about 'architectural layout and sequencing of works', lighting, signage, labelling, brochure, text panel design and content', and 'every other detail, large or small, that substantively conditions the encounter between the viewer and the work'.

The MA in Fashion Curation was established in 2004 under the Directorship of Alistair O'Neill and is a timely response to what could be considered second generation curating or exhibition-making. Like second generation feminist art it has shifted from being something rooted in practice (in our case the museum) to a more theoretical position re-hearsed both inside and outside the institution. It rests on the shoulders of those who treated dress as material culture and now has the luxury of taking its value, its capacity to act as historical testament, for granted. A more complex language is being developed that can play

anachronistic games which are seen as such, not as betrayals, or indeed as mistakes. The course reflects this position: it does not take for granted venue nor medium – we have had to embrace virtual reality – encouraging students to participate in this re-definition. It does, however, maintain dress as its central concern, encouraging students to treat it as a specialised, not a generalised practice. It is a vocation that can be learned through the handling and classification of real objects.

Both in practice and in teaching I have attempted to make explicit – literally build into the exhibitions – some of the questions raised within this second generation of curating fashion; it lies between theory and practice, exhibition design and selection, sequencing and documentation. The encounter that Robert Storr refers to in his text starts prior to the exhibition in the encounter between exhibition-maker and practitioner or archivist, exhibition-maker and graphic artist, for example, where common interests are established, and what might be 'puzzling' is spelled out.

The experiments around exhibiting dress that I work on started in a small gallery I opened in London's Notting Hill in 1997 – Judith Clark Costume Gallery – and continued at the Victoria and Albert Museum with Spectres: When Fashion Turns Back and Anna Piaggi – Fashion-ology. It was in London in the late 1980s and 1990s that I found the exhibitions,

the texts and the collaborators that I required to create a gallery that would meet a very specific need, a gap in the discipline: curators and academics and artists who could describe fashion in new ways, conjuring allusions, were constantly generating references for potential exhibitions. In the process a revisionary history of dress was and is being worked out.

* Paula Marincola (ed.), What Makes a Good Exhibition? (Philadelphia Exhibitions Initiative, 2006)
Both in practice and in teaching I have attempted to make explicit – literally build into the exhibitions – some of the questions raised within this second generation of curating fashion: where it lies between theory and practice, exhibition design and selection, sequencing and documentation.

Richard Grey, *Morpho-illogical* display in the *Anna Piaggi: Fashion-ology* Exhibition Curated by Judith Clark, Victoria and Albert Museum, 2006

Exhibitionism

London College of Fashion Archives and Special Collections
Katherine Baird

At the heart of the London College of Fashion Archive is the collection assembled by Ethel Cox. Ethel Cox was the first headmistress of Barrett Street Trade School, which opened in May 1915. She finally retired in December 1950. Before this appointment she taught English at Shoreditch Technical Institute Girls Trade School (opened 1906), forming a unique link between the two foremost 'needle trade schools' which were eventually brought together in 1967 to form London College of Fashion and Clothing Technology on the purpose-built site in John Princes Street. An initial enrolment of forty students to the Barrett Street Trade School in 1915 was built up to an annual enrolment of over 750 full-time students with about 720 part-timers studying dressmaking, tailoring, embroidery and hairdressing.

As an English graduate and keen Shakespeare scholar, Ethel initiated an annual production where the girls played all the parts and created the costumes and wigs. Evening classes in Dramatic Literature and the Influence of Historic Costume appeared in the prospectuses by 1920 and the same year saw the start of day classes for salesmen and saleswomen engaged in the textile distributing trade. These early roots formed the basis of the strengths of the curriculum of the college today and reflected the technical needs of the couture and ready-to-wear clothing trade, creating a college that was in the vanguard of technical education.

By 1926 the school had grown sufficiently to create a Junior Technical School for girls aged fourteen to sixteen, studying dressmaking, embroidery, hairdressing and ladies' tailoring, and a Senior Technical School for girls aged sixteen plus, studying hairdressing, dressmaking and embroidery. The evening class curriculum reflected the needs of the trade with classes in flower making, manicure, face massage and permanent waving and by 1930 there were afternoon classes for ladies' maids. The expansion of the wholesale clothing trade in the 1930s saw the Senior Technical dressmaking students being trained to become under-cutters or under-designers, design cutters, saleswomen or buyers, and in addition students were taught French modelling, cutting and fitting for the West End retail trade and drafting, making patterns and cutting methods for high-class wholesale houses.

Interviews with pupils of this time (including Megan Davies – Junior Technical Dressmaking Course 1929–31) reveal a very strict school where uniform inspections were held on a regular basis: gymslips had to be exactly one inch off the ground when the girls were kneeling and hats had to be worn at all times when outside the school in uniform. Hand inspections were carried out every day and pupils had to keep their eye on their work at all times; glancing up or being distracted meant that their buttonhole thread was cut and they had to start again. The quality of the work from both the dressmaking and

embroidery pupils is revealed by the samples donated to the archive over the years by ex-pupils and staff, adding to the core collection donated by Miss Cox. Cuttings, prospectuses, photographs, ephemera and samples give a rich picture of college life; a picture broadened by materials from both Shoreditch College and now Cordwainers College.

When Cordwainers College joined London College of Fashion, their archive included a wonderful historic shoe collection of some 700 items. These were catalogued by Miss June Swann, photographed and digitised for publication on the AHDS Visual Arts website allowing easy access to the images and data. The same website provides access to around 2,000 images and metadata from the London College of Fashion Archive, and now, with the help of the Heritage Lottery Fund, the Woolmark Archive of over 1,000 black-and-white couture and ready-to-wear fashion photographs from the 1940s to the '80s.

Digitising the collections has been an ongoing task necessitated by the fact that the collections were scattered across the college sites and largely unavailable, but it also allows researchers to study the collections in their own time and protects the originals from damage by constant handling. The programme continues with a collection of over 700 commercial dress paper patterns dating from the 1920s to the '80s currently being catalogued. The last collection that has been made available digitally is the EMAP Archive of some 700 volumes of journals like Menswear, Drapers' Records and Shoe and Leather Records dating from the 1880s. These have been catalogued and major articles indexed and made available through the University of the Arts London library catalogue

There are other small special collections such as the Korner Dress Collection, the Hayes Collection of Textiles, the Gala of London Portfolio of Advertising, the Promostyle Archive and the Mary Quant Cosmetic Collection which are not appropriate or too small to digitise, but for the first time they have been brought together on the third floor of the John Princes Street building along with all the other archives and special collec-

tions held by London College of Fashion. The college has appointed a member of staff to develop, promote and make them accessible to students and researchers, making this eclectic but fascinating range of resources available for the first time. Ethel Cox would surely approve.

André Courrèges dress and jacket, 1965

Henry C. Miner's Liquid Stockings, 1941

Charles Creed suit, 1953

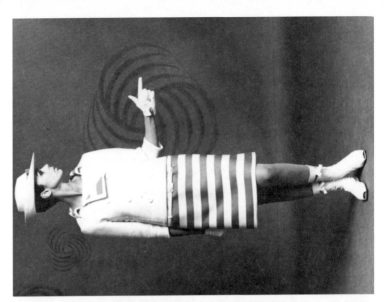

Charles
Gad
1963

Exhibitionism   NJ Stevenson

Why do people look at fashion? Is fashion simply a dialogue between entertainment and merchandising – pretty girls selling pretty frocks – or is there more to it?

Working as a stylist in London, I went out of my way to make my editorial work interesting. The photographers and I spent hours coaxing live snakes to lie round models' shoulders; we chased models wearing wire masks and numbers on their backs round Walthamstow dog track, hung out of hot air balloons, learnt the dance routines from *Cabaret*, and on one memorable occasion spread a ton of sweets on the studio floor as a backdrop and almost asphyxiated from the sugar fumes.

We wanted readers to pick up our fashion pages and laugh at the humour, recognise the references and, hopefully, remember the images. The key strength of fashion is having a captive audience, and as such the opportunities for creativity are limitless. Fashion is not art; it is a commercial transaction – but one that on the journey from drawing board to wardrobe via the shop floor utilises several strata of artistic endeavour. Designers, stylists, photographers, art directors, illustrators and visual merchandisers apply their talents and skills on a form that is not the preserve of the elite, but belongs to us all. As soon as fashion is produced it is in the public domain to purchase, interpret, adapt and copy as we wish. Clothes are barometers of our moods and keepers of our memories. The way we dress documents our times.

Why then, I wondered, as I tried to convince a model to throw a flamenco shape in the middle of the road in Barcelona at three o'clock in the morning when I was five months pregnant, is it that fashion is so often dismissed as frivolous? Isn't it time that the creative processes behind the scenes of the fashion industry are celebrated as relevant in their own right?

Fashion interacts with film, music, dance and design within popular culture and contributes to and reflects sociological development. Fashion can be used as a research tool to trace points in history. Curators working on exhibitions in museums and galleries are employing fashion to capture the imagination of the public.

The value of fashion in this way, and in contemporary forms of display, has become an attractive medium to me, which I'm currently exploring as an extension of the crafts that I've learnt as a stylist and writer. There are obvious parallels, some which I had failed to anticipate when I found myself wrestling to detach the arm of a mannequin from her body at three o'clock in the morning after my first show. It would be a conceit to see an exhibition as merely a bigger page, but people do look at fashion. In the gallery, they will have the chance to look at it in a different way.

Fiona Freund: Fencing shoot for *Guardian Weekend Magazine*, 12 August 2000

Exhibitionism
Alison Moloney

Fashion, although deeply imbued with personal identity, also holds within its fibre the history and cultural heritage of a people. Whether it is the Ikat textiles of Uzbekistan, the traditional embroidery of the Ukraine, or the indigo tie-dye patterns of northern Nigeria, the unique symbolism and techniques inherent to these countries' textiles and fashion production is a fertile medium for discourse.

It is for this reason that fashion, and the industries which it encompasses (photography, styling, art direction, show production, journalism), are an important element of the British Council's international Design & Architecture strategy, and the arts programmes of our colleagues in 109 countries around the world.

As the United Kingdom's international agency for cultural relations and education, the British Council endeavours to create dialogue with practitioners and students from the UK and those overseas. Fashion's popularity the world over is the perfect impetus to begin these conversations. Fashion can be the most exclusive of the design industries – few are able to experience the work of the world's leading fashion designers as we can the publicly visible work of architects. But the ubiquity of the sewing machine and the low-cost, low-tech infrastructure needed to produce the simplest of garments makes fashion a palpable channel for cultural exchange all over the globe.

It is London's outstanding reputation on the international fashion stage which makes us a valuable partner and contributor when sharing our expertise and best practice. The breadth and exceptional talent of our designers, photographers, journalists and stylists and our unique system of design education enables us to enhance Britain's reputation as a creative and vibrant nation.

London is a hotbed of young talents who gravitate to the capital for its insatiable network of creatives working across all disciplines of the arts; and it is from London that we pool many of our own networks of designers for our exhibitions and workshops. London prides itself in being home to communities from all around the world and, undoubtedly, this rich cultural mix helps to inform and inspire our designers – who in turn produce such multiplicity of work.

Our exhibition *Import Export* illustrated this cross-fertilisation of cultures by showcasing the work of designers from overseas who have made London their home. Slovenian-born Lara Bohinc, Brazilian-born Inacio Ribeiro of design duo Clements Ribeiro, and Wakako Kishimoto of Eley Kishimoto from Japan, were enticed to the UK by the design education and have remained and established their businesses.

It is Britain's willingness to welcome this influx of designers from around the world; the inquisitive nature of our own designers – continually

Oman: Jeweller Lina Peterson at the opening of *Alchemy*, 2007

seeking to absorb new cultures to inspire and expand their own practice; and the desire to inspire others that together enable the British Council to run a rich and varied fashion programme.

Textiles designer Kate Lewis spent a week in Buenos Aires working with fashion students whose brief was to transform a denim jacket, donated by Lee, using the traditional textile processes of Argentina. The students drew on emotional and political responses to national identity and the finished garments, worn by the students, were photographed by London-based photographer Gavin Fernandes in locations chosen for their emotive or visual relevance to the idea behind the work.

Gemma Bunston, one of Topshop's in-house designers, and freelance designer/weaver Jacqueline Ednie led a workshop in Uzbekistan to encourage dialogue between the fashion designers of Tashkent and the weavers from Margolin in the Fergana Valley. Over the week-long workshop the designers began to develop a range of textile designs and fabrics, to be incorporated into the fashion collections, which have their basis in traditional Uzbek designs while satisfying contemporary international tastes.

This was part of a wider programme of events in Central and South Asia as part of our New Silk Road series of design workshops based on the traditional materials and production

techniques of these five countries: felt in Kazakhstan, textile printing in Iran, bamboo and jute in Bangladesh, and textiles in Pakistan and Uzbekistan. The designers who led these workshops were selected for their ability to incorporate innovation with heritage, a trait inherent to many British designers. The campaign continues with the expansion of Colin McDowell and IMG's Fashion Fringe platform into Central and South Asia: the British Council is organising a series of inspirational visits for the four 2007 finalists.

Alchemy: Contemporary Jewellery from Britain was developed for five countries in the Middle East. The eight jewellers within the exhibition challenge conventional parameters of jewellery design by experimenting with materials, references and scale, and by questioning our inherited notions of value, identity and adornment. By comparing our own pluralist notions of consumption with the firm traditions of value within the Middle East, we aim to open the debate about value and adornment in the twenty-first century.

Included in the exhibition is the work of Naomi Filmer, Scott Wilson and Shaun Leane, each of whom made their names on London's catwalks through inspired commissions from Hussein Chalayan and Alexander McQueen. Those designers' visionary approach to fashion and its presentation saw the potential of jewellery to enhance and complete the story of the season. The sensitive

Uzbekistan: Fashion and textiles workshop in Tashkent, led by Jacqueline Ednie and Gemma Burton, 2007

exhibition design by Judith Clark, London College of Fashion's Senior Research Fellow in Fashion Curation, captures the uniqueness of each jeweller's practice while promoting the importance of high quality and imaginative exhibition design.

We are soon to launch a new award to celebrate the achievements of young fashion entrepreneurs in emerging economy countries. Our own entrepreneurial innovators – among them Sir Paul Smith, Terry and Tricia Jones and Joan Burstein – are inspirational figures who have managed to capture the essence of British fashion and culture and transform it into new possibilities for fashion as a business. We will be working with our colleagues in ten countries (including Mexico, India, Indonesia and China) to find young entrepreneurs who are working to develop the fashion sector in their country. Each finalist will spend two weeks in the UK meeting with specialists from all fields of fashion. This study visit will stress the importance of fashion as a compound in which many elements create a complex machine with economic and cultural force.

During the ten years of our programme – exhibitions, collaborative projects, educational initiatives and specialist visits to the UK – we have worked with a number of London College of Fashion's lecturers. It is a privilege to contribute to this centenary book, not only because of our long history of collaboration with the college but also as a recent graduate of the MA Fashion History and Culture course.

Argentina: Argentinian students wearing the denim jackets which they re-worked during a textiles workshop led by Pete Lewis, 2004

Exhibitionism

London and Fashion as Visual Arts Practice
Wessie Ling

Wessie Ling:
National Dress, 2005

Wessie Ling:
Authentic Dress, 2005

Wessie Ling:
Dollar Dress Suitcase, 2005

With 300 languages spoken among its 7.3 million residents, London can lay claim to being the world's most diverse and multicultural city. Home to a highly diverse range of people, cultures and religions, this cosmopolitan city is marked by a multicultural character. London today is considered to be an international creative centre and diffuses a global vision to its creative industry. It is a critical zone of creative interchange embodying ethnically diverse and historically rich ideas, all of which make the city a magnet to foreign artists and designers choosing to base themselves outside their home countries.

Artists and designers from all around the world play a crucial role in generating London's dynamic and vibrant creative industry, as their relationship with London sees the intersection between their background (of multiple cultures) and the city (as a multicultural site). Since so much of creative practice implies an activity which draws on various cultural traditions, and benefits from an international experience, London provides a space where creativity meets individual style, enabling freshness to be brought to the world. It welcomes new and challenging ideas, and is where impossibilities can be assayed. Its openness encourages many London-based foreign artists and designers to highly value their ability to cross boundaries, to transgress cultures in their creations, to introduce the unseen to the world. The fact that the city's creative talent injects new ideas into London and vice versa manifests new creative forms and movements. More than a source of inspiration, London collaborates with a diverse pool of talents; both keep feeding each other as they reshape and redefine creativity. Not only is it a foreground to experiment with challenging ideas, but also where they flourish.

Approaching fashion by means of visual arts practice is a challenging yet ambitious project. Many factors facilitate its materialisation. Fashion has been united with everyday culture and individual lifestyle to the point that it can no longer be seen as a separate entity. As a topic of exploration, fashion deserves an equal share when food, tourism, consumerism and globalisation are frequently visited in contemporary arts. London's openness and acceptance of new ideas form the roots of the project. In the past decade a range of vibrant contemporary arts has arisen. Despite severe competition among emerging artists due to insufficient funding, contemporary arts in London present a wide variety of works characterised by internationalism. Many of them challenge traditional norms by finding their way to define new forms and movements. London allows new forms of arts to grow, thus permitting exchanges between different cultures, acting as a springboard for artists from around the globe to meet and collaborate. For many London-based artists the capital has become an asset on a multiplicity of levels.

Wessie Ling: *Game On: The World Fashion Conquest*, 2006

Incorporating academic research and visual arts practice, my work challenges traditional perceptions within visual art and situates fashion as a core practice. The relationship between fashion, cities and identities is taken for critical inquiry. Inclusion of a place, a space, or a locality plays a major role in my examination. London is an interesting site to explore the interaction between fashion and visual arts. The project's experimental approach finds its grounding in a capital city where a sense of adventure is appreciated. As a foreigner based in London, I am aware of the sense of difference, and the different identities I am seen to take on as I move between different worlds leads me to question the way I perform creative work.

The study of the Chinese dress, the cheongsam, is the result of referencing the place I was once at home with and where I question identities. The development of the cheongsam expresses a blend of the ancient/ modern, Western/Eastern that partly sets it into a constant evolution. A marker of Chineseness, the dress has a cross-cultural appeal and has circulated and travelled globally through many decades. Looking at it from a distance enables me to consider the different perceptions of it by Chinese and Western audiences. British audiences' familiarity with the dress dates back to its heyday in the late fifties, Suzie-Wong style. Yet twenty-first century London continues to retain colonial perceptions that contribute to the multiple identities that have in turn been internalised by Chinese communities. The cheongsam that we recognise now continues to evolve and has entered the fashion vernacular on a global scale. It has become a popular inspiration for contemporary fashion designers who then promote their interpretation of cheongsam, lifting its Chinese origin for their affiliated styles and shifting the perception of a Chinese dress. Through a series of cheongsam-art installations, this ongoing project questions the identities of the cheongsam, its representation and social practices.

Questioning cultural identities on the one hand, while on the other visualising fashion from a variety of global perspectives, London also provides inspiration for projects that map international audiences. *Game On: The World Fashion Conquest* (2006) is a board game shaped like a catwalk that mimics the glamorous world of fashion yet uses this context to explore how fashion has been exploited to achieve various objectives, ranging from city branding to generating tourism. Inspired by the classic board game Risk, *Game On* makes a theoretical examination of the phenomenon of the 'fashion week'. By deconstructing the fashion week's objectives, the exhibit acts as a critique of globalisation. Are cities slaves to fashion or do they enslave fashion for their own objectives? Is fashion week an image-making exercise? What does fashion week sell? Is there any difference between fashion week in Tunis and Asunción?

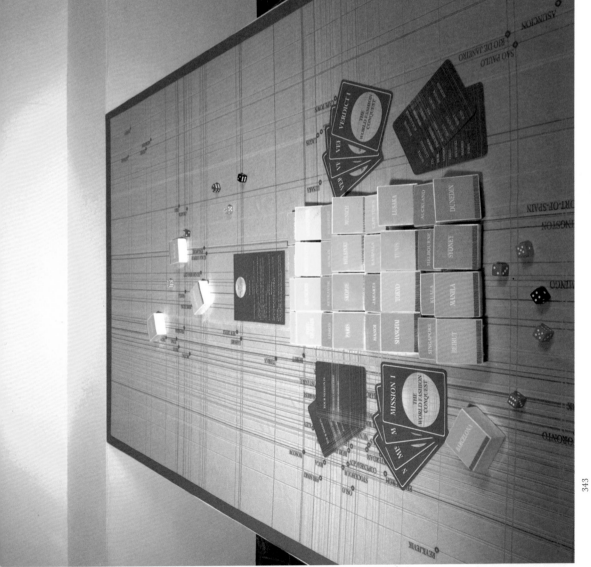

These interlinked questions are represented in the board game and its army of pawns, compressed T-shirts in the form of white cubes, each representing a city that boasts a fashion week. Inside each is a plain white T-shirt. The uniformity and banality of these T-shirts reflects the content of the eighty-five fashion weeks in as much as most new-rise fashion weeks are organised in much the same way as the established ones in Paris, Milan and New York, only that they attract significantly less buyers, journalists and designers. Some even have no fashion-show schedule at all. Rather, fashion week brings modernity to these cities: hosting a fashion week signals their readiness to be included in the international calendar, to join in the global competition. Inside this competition is a gigantic network stretching from one city to another. The map in *Game On* shows no territory, boundaries, regions and continents, only the cities that hold a fashion week.

Audiences identify with the nature of the board game and the exploratory journey of identities, while London aligns international audiences to these projects. The city interconnects like minds and suggests a discussion of topics arising from these works. It might only be a small step away to put fashion firmly on the agenda of visual arts. London is seen as on the move.

Wessie Ling:
Game On: The World Fashion Conquest;
map on textile, 2006

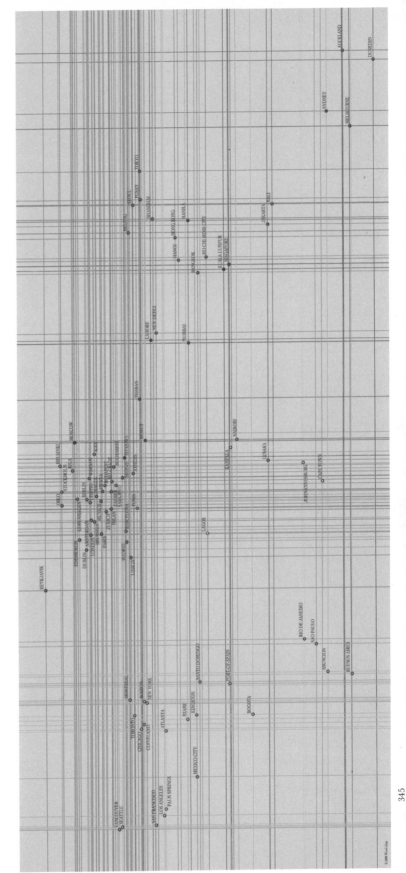

Exhibitionism

Simon Thorogood

I think of myself as a product of an almost traditional school of hybridised or cross-fertilised ideas in the arts. This legacy helped to establish a framework in which it was acceptable to explore fashion's frontiers with other disciplines, be it architecture or painting or whatever. As well as being an industry-led concern, fashion for me and many others could enjoy a lively and productive conversation with almost any other subject it wanted for speculative and artistic intent.

Almost certainly, my design philosophy and practice were reinforced by my exposure to the varied culture that London has tendered since I first came to the city as a student in the late '80s. Surrounded by so many types of people and diverse artistic, intellectual and technological developments, London provided me with a space to try to be something other than the defined and labelled commodity much of my earlier education had been about. This process of edification was fuelled not only by the city itself but by the very calibre and mettle of my contemporaries who were likewise drawn to the city. They were citizens, not borne of a certain class, status or background but of an open, enquiring mind and a desire to change and enhance the landscape of fashion before them.

London became and has remained for me a chimera, in all definitions of the word – a figment, a fantasy, an unrealistic idea, impractical, composed of composite parts. Yet as a contradiction and an inconsistency, it nonetheless embodies all that I hold dear in both day-to-day life and in creativity, to be lost and found at the same time. It is this belief that interesting discoveries are to be found on the cusp of chaos and cohesion that fuels my work and thinking.

As a place of continual change, it is hard to maintain any kind of ownership with the capital. However, for me it is this perpetual adjustment, transformation and promiscuity of the social, the abstract and the physical that creates a place of belonging and not belonging and a peculiar yet dynamic sense of unfinishedness. Unfinishedness, therefore, is something that I have perpetually tried to capture in my design work. It is something that I have inherently applied to the design of garments as well as to the design of interactive installations.

I have been motivated by the idea of design, not necessarily as having a conclusion as a finished object or garment but as a trigger for having design experiences. How can I provide opportunities for audiences to have their own experiences and to partially determine their own results from a design process rather than providing complete or finished experiences?

Similarly, physically travelling around the city reinforces for me how important it is to try to reflect a sense of creative travel within fashion. As has long existed in fine art for example, a shift in the position of audience

Simon Thorogood: Material/izations,
Unit-f Gallery, Vienna, May 2002

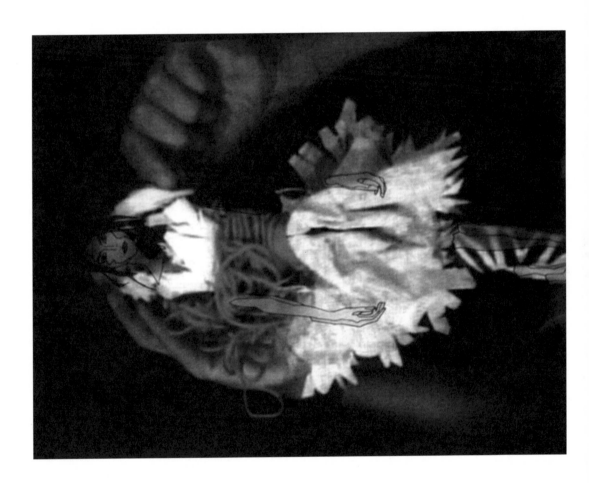

responsibility is now opportune for fashion where consumers should become increasingly responsible to themselves rather than to any label or trend. Whilst this certainly occurs in the styling of clothes, it is less evident in the actual design of clothes.

A handful of my projects, such as 'Digital Runway', 'Material/izations' or 'SoundWear', have sought to allow an audience a degree of interactivity and co-authorship so that one can contribute and become an active participant in a design process rather than remaining a spectator. Can this approach encourage the designer and consumer to work together as part of a design practice, where the whole is greater than the sum of its parts?

'SoundWear' looks to endorse this attitude, employing music as a starting point to prompt shape and colour for possible fashion design. By following a series of instructions, a user will be able to establish a 'vocabulary' of colours, shapes and motifs that contribute to a fashion story or process. This research considers how the interaction of an audience and a system might introduce arbitrary form, layering, colour and pattern into a conventional design procedure, that of sketching on paper, copying existing garments or draping cloth on a stand. Through an active blend of invention and event, can prospective methods of designing complement, augment or update the traditional ways of creating fashion?

This methodology finds further correlation for me with the city. As I look to find and apply a blend of convention and contemporary transience for fashion design, of being creatively lost and found, so too do I see this viewpoint reflected in my relationship with London. I have a history and a certain understanding of the place, but that is tempered by its continual evolution, a future that is exciting, ambiguous and partially alienating. But unquestionably, it is this peculiar chemistry that binds and compels me. London will always be for me, and for so many others I daresay, an extraordinary cultural laboratory and a champion of diversity and innovation.

Simon Thorogood: *SoundForms*, *SoundWear*, 2004 onwards

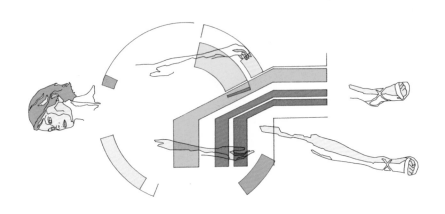

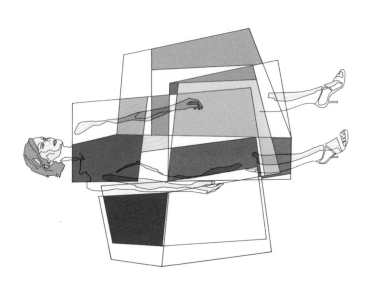

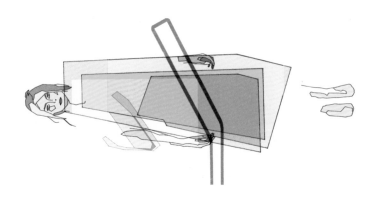

Exhibitionism
Graham Dolphin
by Alistair O'Neill

Graham Dolphin is an artist who uses fashion imagery as source material for his works. His work is unconcerned with that weary academic debate about whether or not fashion can aspire to the condition of art, or vice versa – it's much more hands-on. By this I mean that his work is about crafting things from the material culture produced from the world of goods represented, from the material reality bound into magazines.

As an investigation it's rather archaeological – scraping through sedimented layers to reveal otherwise hidden depths – but it's an excavation that corrodes as much as it conserves. And this is its discordant beauty. The piece *Dust* (1998) involved tipping the contents of a vacuum cleaner bag over a cover of *i-D*. Its assurance as an image lies as much in what it conceals as in what it frames, but beyond these compositional concerns, it deposits the relentless pace of a magazine culture that regularly smothers its own image in pursuit of its next.

So the work is as much about the cover of the magazine as it is about its temporal logic. It was with this picture in mind that the symposium *The Death of Taste* was born, staged by London College of Fashion and the University of the Applied Arts Vienna in 2006. The event sought to examine the work of making, styling and fashioning taste within the context of increasingly speeded-up fashion trends and the constant plundering of the recent past.

Following page:
Model hands, 2006

Poster for *The Death of Taste* conference, Original artwork
Graham Dolphin, 2006

The Death of Taste:

unpicking the fashion cycle

24-25 November 2006 Institute of Contemporary Arts, London
22-23 June 2007 University of Applied Arts, Vienna

It remains for me a rare confluence between a set of academic ideas and an existing image.

When I approached Dolphin again about the possibility of writing something for this publication, he supplied a series of drawings he has been working on, which are carbon traces on paper. Once again a process of layering and accumulation is in evidence, but this time it is looser and inexact. These works trace the imprecise, multiple outlines of consumer products we think we recognise, but without their seductive visual 'fill' they deny us the right to possess them and their detail. Yet conversely the repetitive outlines claim possession of what we wish to desire, engraved in the trace of the product's circumference. Just as the triplicate invoice receipt creates more than one record of commodity exchange through its carbon papers, so these drawings represent another process of exchange, but one replicated in representation.

It is these kinds of attentions to the material surface of fashion imagery that claim Dolphin as an artist disinterested in the onslaught of the digitally seamless image but drawn to an earlier, handcrafted vision of the commodity. His recent carbon drawings are, for me, reminiscent of Michael English's preparatory drawings for his airbrush paintings of crushed Coke bottle tops and empty bottles of Heinz Ketchup from the mid 1970s. The Rubbish Prints, as they were known, were some of the most popular poster images of their time. What was so attractive about them was that they celebrated an iconic product with a hyperreal clarity not at its moment of perfection, but at its nadir: as litter.

Like English, Dolphin draws our attention to the visual accumulation of printed material culture cast off by fashion and the world of goods. And just like English he asks us when is it that these things are at their most seductive? I have a feeling that the answer is unlikely to be found in the next issue, more likely in the stack of back issues.

Graham Dolphin:
Guerlain Perfume, 2006

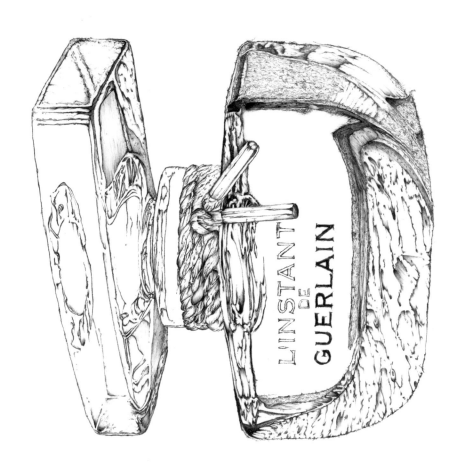

L'INSTANT DE GUERLAIN

Close

Paul Smith

London is a goldmine of talent and ideas and it has been for as long as I can remember. We seem to have the ability to think more freely than other cities, be more willing to experiment, and through this new ideas come.

Probably the explosion of unusual ideas was at its height in the 1960s. Two generations after the horror of war, at last young people in the '60s could express themselves in an honest way. This was not confined to fashion but included many creative fields: graphics, photography, music. The music industry in the UK was bursting with ideas and creativity at that time which was only rivalled by the USA.

Our colleges have contributed greatly to this self-expression and from the creative, but not necessarily well-organised days of the 1960s, we have continued to teach students from all over the world but with a greater balance of both design and business.

Our colleges allowed the students freedom and let them really express themselves. Unfortunately this was not always linked with the understanding of the world they were entering into. Many designers and their designs fell by the wayside. It has always been hard for English designers to find business partners that really understand design. Many of our best creatives either work abroad or for foreign companies. Maybe this is not a problem but it is sad.

The 1970s saw English students

Shop at 13 Park Street, Borough, London

Paul Smith: A/W 2007

calming down from such extravagant
fashion that had been linked with
the music industry, maybe taking
more influence from Europe,
especially Italy.

As the years went by and travel became easier we all observed what
each other was doing and with more
and more design and fashion magazines, the industry became more
mature. London College of Fashion
always kept its feet on the ground
and balanced creativity with the importance of pattern cutting, business
and how things worked.

The 1990s through to today has seen
the industry grow massively with
competition enormous. Communication is so fast that a large low-price
brand can see a designer show on the
Internet thirty minutes after it has
happened; taking key looks immediately, making and delivering to
their shops before the designer label
has delivered to its own shops. Big
brands from the top level to the low-
cost commercial ones, which are
mostly large public companies with
lots of money to spend on promotion
and new shops, have put a lot of
pressure on independent brands and
designers, and now a designer cannot
just rely on the clothes but has to
consider much more the personal
image as well as the company one,
and really understand that you have
to try to create a loyalty from your
customers because of the huge
selection available.

In the '60s and '70s you would have
said it was not necessary for a
designer to be aware of business and
marketing and it's a shame they now
have to be; they should just be
allowed to design, but sadly that's not
enough in today's highly competitive
world. Today's colleges have to equip
their students not only with design
skills but also awareness of the other
aspects of the business.

Paul Smith Mini Cooper, 1997

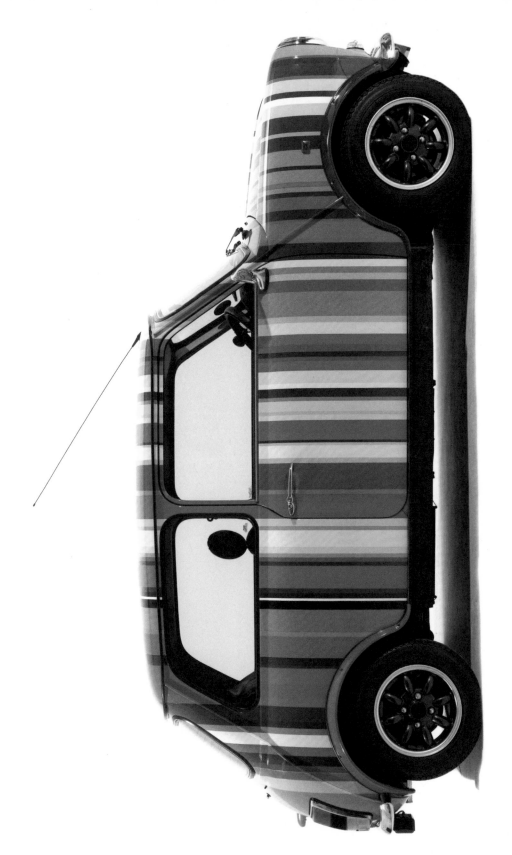

Contributors

Katherine Baird
Librarian
After training as a librarian, Katherine Baird's first job was at St Martins School of Art in 1968, where she became College Librarian ten years later. On the formation of the London Institute she moved to London College of Fashion, becoming their Head of Learning Resources in 1989, a post she held until her retirement in 2006. She currently works part-time managing London College of Fashion's archives and special collections.
http://ahds.ac.uk/visualarts/index.htm
http://www.arts.ac.uk/library/opac.htm

Vivienne Becker
Jewellery Historian and Writer
Vivienne Becker is a jewellery historian, journalist and author of several books on antique and twentieth century jewellery. She writes regularly for the *Financial Times' How To Spend It* magazine, for the *Saturday Telegraph* magazine, and is the Jewellery Writer for *Harper's Bazaar* (UK). She began her career working in the antiques trade in the 1970s, buying and selling jewellery, before embarking on journalism, first as assistant to the Fashion Editor of *SHE* magazine, and then as a writer on *Antique Collector*, where she was able to develop her speciality of jewellery. Becker has been involved in broadcasting projects; has written television scripts; has curated several jewellery exhibitions, including Jewels of Fantasy and Costume Jewellery at the Victoria and Albert Museum; has contributed to a number of jewellery books; and works as a design and marketing consultant.
www.goldinspirations.com

Belle & Bunty
By Alice-Louise Shreeve and Hannah Coniam
Fashion Designers
Alice-Louise Shreeve and Hannah Coniam met and became friends while studying at London College of Fashion. In April 2003 they launched Belle & Bunty at London Fashion Week. Both Shreeve and Coniam graduated in 2002 from a BA (Hons) Surface Textiles course specialising in embroideries. Individually they have worked with designers such as Paul Smith, Pepe Jeans, Replay Jeans, Caroline Charles, Tracey Boyd and the Jasper Conran, John Rocha and John Richmond labels at Debenhams. Since its launch Belle & Bunty has received impressive media attention; the duo has been named 'The Label to Watch' by Drapers Record in 2005 and received the NatWest Every Woman Artemis Award for 'most inspirational women

running a business who are aged under 25'. Their celebrity clientele includes June Sarpong, Victoria Beckham, Kate Bosworth, Myleene Klass, Fearne Cotton and Ana Matronic of the Scissor Sisters.
www.belleandbunty.co.uk

Wendy Bevan
Photographer and Jewellery Designer
Wendy Bevan is a photographer and jewellery designer whose work lies between fashion and art. She received her BA (Hons) in Fashion Photography from London College of Fashion in 2004. Bevan has photographed for *i-D, Russian Vogue, Qvest, Exit, The Independent, 10 Magazine, Nylon, V Magazine, POP* Magazine, Italian *Marie Claire, Lula, Œ0,* Magazine, *Tank, Wig* and *GQ Style* and has worked with a number of leading stylists, fashion editors and fashion directors. Bevan's sculptural costume jewellery has been commissioned specifically for collaborations with stylists including Edward Enninful, Katie Grand, Kate Phelan, and Nicola Formichetti, and has been photographed by Stephen Miesel and Bruce Webber amongst others.
www.wendybevan.com

Celia Birtwell
Fashion and Textile Designer
Celia Birtwell studied Textile Design at Salford School of Art in Manchester. It was there that she first met Ossie Clark, who she married in 1967 and worked with until 1973 when their marriage ended. Birtwell and Clark dressed celebrities such as the Beatles, the Rolling Stones, Bianca Jagger, Jimi Hendrix, Paloma Picasso, Talitha Getty, Patty Boyd, Twiggy and Marianne Faithfull. After taking a break from the industry to raise her children and teach, Birtwell began designing again in 1984 and opened a shop in Notting Hill's Westbourne Park Road, selling fabrics for the home. Birtwell's designs adorn interiors of a prestigious international clientele, ranging from The Grand Hotel in Leeds and The Dubai Hilton to interiors for Zoffany and Cacharel Allders. Her work is currently being collected and archived by the Victoria and Albert Museum and she is current-ly launching her third collection for Topshop.
www.celiabirtwell.com

Manolo Blahnik
Footwear Designer
Manolo Blahnik was born in the Canary Islands, studying languages and art in Geneva

before moving to Paris in 1965, were he decided to become a set designer. He was encouraged by Diana Vreeland, then editor-in-chief of American *Vogue,* to concentrate on his shoe designs, which he decided to do. Blahnik returned to London where his shoes were used by designer Ossie Clark, and where he opened his first shop in Chelsea in 1973. Blahnik has received several awards from the Council of Fashion Designers of America in the United States, from the British Fashion Council and from His Majesty Juan Carlos I, King of Spain. In 2003 the Design Museum in London exhibited a retrospective of his work. Blahnik has also been featured in two books by Thames & Hudson: *Drawings* in 2003 and *Blahnik by Boman* (photographs) in 2005. He designed shoes for Sofia Coppola's 2006 film *Marie Antoinette,* which won an Academy Award for Best Costume.
www.manoloblahnik.com

Judy Blame
Stylist, Jewellery Designer and Art Director
Judy Blame is a stylist, jewellery designer and art director whose work has appeared in various forms throughout high fashion and pop music. Blame has styled, designed for and art-directed celebrities such as Neneh Cherry, Björk, Massive Attack, Boy George, Baaba Maal, Iggy Pop and Kylie Minogue. He has collaborated with designers such as John Galliano, Rifat Ozbek, Christopher Nemeth, Jessica Ogden, Philip Treacy, Comme des Garçons, Louis Vuitton and photographers such as Nick Knight, Glen Luchford, Juergen Teller, Mark Lebon and Jean-Baptiste Mondino. His jewellery designs are stocked in selected boutiques worldwide and have been featured most recently on the catwalk of Gareth Pugh. Blame is currently consulting for clients such as Superfine and Fred Perry.

Pippa Brooks
Fashion Retailer, Model and Singer
Pippa Brooks was raised at the seaside in Gosport, Hampshire. She studied at the Coventry Lanchester Polytechnic before moving to London in 1989 where she met Max Karie and worked at Venus designer sale shop in Covent Garden, all the while making and playing music. In 1994 she opened her first Shop in Frith Street and, and a year later opened her second Shop on Brewer Street. In the same year she formed the band Posh with James Dearlove and Richard Evans. In 1998 Brooks and Max created the label Shopgirl and, a year later, she

and Dearlove formed a band by the same name. In 2000 Shopgirl designed a range for *Playboy* featuring Swarovski crystal bunny heads, later undertaking collaborations with Babycham and Dunlop. In 2006 Brooks and Dearlove formed the band All About Eve Babitz and she and Max opened Shop underneath Maison Bertaux at 27 Greek Street.
www.shopatmaisonb.com

Thom Browne
Menswear Designer
Thom Browne attended Notre Dame, Indiana as an undergraduate, where he received a business degree. After college he moved to Los Angeles in search of work as an actor. However, he was far more interested in the work of his friend Johnson Hartig (now co-designer at Libertine) who reworked vintage clothing. After abandoning his acting dreams, he moved to New York in 1997, where he began working in Giorgio Armani's showroom. From there he moved to Club Monaco, owned by Polo Ralph Lauren. Lauren picked up on Browne's talent and transferred him to Club Monaco's design and merchandising departments. Browne left Club Monaco in 2001 to launch the Thom Browne label, but could only afford to make five suits, which he would wear around town. Today Browne's upscale suits are sold in only sixteen stores worldwide. In 2006 the Council of Fashion Designers of America named him Designer of the Year.
www.thombrowne.com

Walter Buchholz
Fashion Designer
Walter Buchholz completed his first degree at the University of Stellenbosch, South Africa in 1993. From 2000 to 2003 he completed City and Guilds certificate courses in dressmaking and design at Southgate College, and then moved to London College of Fashion where he obtained a BA (Hons) in Fashion Design Technology. Since then his work has been shown at Futuremap 2006, and he is in the process of completing an MA in Menswear at London College of Fashion.

Joan Burstein, CBE
Browns Founder and Buyer
In 1970 Joan and Sidney Burstein purchased Browns from Sir William Piggott-Brown and opened the first Browns shoe store on Molton Street in London. The pair quickly acquired more property along the street, opening Browns Living in 1975 and Browns Menswear in 1976. It was Burstein's courageous and fine buying that recognised some of the world's greatest designers, bringing them into London for the first time. Some of the labels she has stocked include Calvin Klein, Ralph Lauren, Armani, Missoni, Comme des Garçons, Azzedine Alaia, Sonia Rykiel, Byblos, DKNY, G-Gigli, Jil Sander and Gianfranco Ferré. Burstein was the first one to spot John Galliano at his degree show, and famously gave young Manolo Blahnik a job in her jeans department. In 2006 Burstein was awarded a CBE in the Queen's birthday honours.
www.brownsfashion.com

Alan Cannon Jones MSc. FFCDE
Director of Programmes, London College of Fashion
Alan Cannon Jones is both an academic member of staff at London College of Fashion and a practitioner within the fashion industry. He is the Principal Lecturer and the Director of Programmes for BA (Hons) Fashion Design Technology Menswear and BA (Hons) Bespoke Tailoring at London College of Fashion. His additional recent work includes research for the DTI on Italian and British tailoring and collaborations with TPC (Hong Kong) in parametric pattern cutting and realisation. Cannon Jones has worked with Dirk Bikkembergs, Dockers,

Hardy Amies, Daniel A. Hanson, Ocha and Garth and John Rocha, for whom he is currently working on the menswear ranges. He is the General Secretary for the Federation of Clothing Designers & Executives.
www.fashion.arts.ac.uk

Jimmy Choo, OBE
Footwear Designer
Jimmy Choo was born in Malaysia where his father was a reputable shoe designer. He began working as his father's apprentice and moved to London in the 1980s to study footwear at Cordwainers College. In 1986 he established his own couture label, which has included an extensive range of hand-beaded; hand-stitched and personalised shoes ranging from slippers, sandals and mules to boots. In 1996 Choo launched his ready-to-wear line with the late Mr Tom Yeardye. He subsequently sold his share of the ready-to-wear business in November 2001 to Equinox Luxury Holdings Ltd, who manage the line while he continues to operate his couture line. Choo is currently an ambassador for footwear education at London College of Fashion and a spokesperson for the British Council in promotion of British education to foreign students.

Pamela Church Gibson
Cultural Historian
Pamela Church Gibson was brought up in Oxford, and read English at Cambridge. She is currently Reader in Cultural and Historical Studies at London College of Fashion and has published widely on film, fashion, fandom, history and heritage. Her three co-edited anthologies include: *Fashion Cultures: Theories, Explorations, Analysis* (2001), *The Oxford Guide to Film Studies* (1998) and *More Dirty Looks: Gender, Power, Pornography* for the British Film Institute. She was co-founder of *Cinema* magazine and helped to run a community theatre group in Bermondsey before becoming a lecturer at Barnet College and studying for an MA in Film and Television at the Polytechnic of Central London, now the University of Westminster. Following the birth of her two sons she has worked part-time in publishing, editing and organising lecture programmes for international students in Oxford, where she currently resides.
www.fashion.arts.ac.uk

Judith Clark
Curator and Exhibition Designer
Judith Clark is a curator and exhibition designer specialising in costumes and fashion. She attended the Architectural Association Graduate School, London from 1990 to 1991, after receiving her BSc Degree in Architecture from the Bartlett School of Architecture, UCL, London. She has curated and designed exhibitions for the British Council, the Victoria and Albert Museum, the Barbican Art Gallery, the Hayward Gallery and the Millennium Dome, amongst others. Clark was the curator and founder of the Judith Clark Costume Gallery (1997–2002); is currently launching the website judithclarkcostume.com, an experimental online exhibition space; and is co-curating and designing an exhibition on the Italian couturier Donna Simonetta at the Palazzo Pitti, to be shown at the Museo del Costume, Florence. She is the Co-director (with Amy de la Haye) and is the Fixed Term Senior Research Fellow of MA Fashion Curation, London College of Fashion.
www.judithclarkcostume.com

Louise Clarke
Curator and Editor
Louise Clarke is an editor, curator and arts consultant. Since graduating from the MA in Fashion Curation at LCF her work has focused upon viewing distance and filmic techniques

and their affect on our experiences of visual culture. Recent exhibitions include the screening of *Curating Madness* (Victoria & Albert Museum, 2005), *Beyond the Hide* (Truman Brewery, 2005) and *Case Study* (London, Plymouth, 2006). She is Curator of commissions and board member for the Fashion and Film Festival 2008 (Tate Modern, London). Clarke's work has been published in New York ID magazine and *Image and text*. She has worked as art consultant to uber-collector David Roberts, helping build and promote his contemporary art collection and is currently a Lecturer on the MA Fashion, Design and Enterprise course at Westminster University. She has been awarded a University of the Arts Studentship to undertake PhD study at London College of Communications to work on The Stanley Kubrick Archives: project title *Raising the Celluloid*.
www.louiseclarke.com

Dr Frances Corner FRSA
Head of College, London College of Fashion
Dr Frances Corner has been Head of College at London College of Fashion since October 2005. She was previously Head of the Sir John Cass Department of Art, Media and Design at London Metropolitan University and has over 20 years experience within the Higher Education sector on both a national and international level. Dr Corner believes London College of Fashion's dedication to widening participation and commitment to research and employability, combined with its links with the associated industries, make it a strong model for 21st century Higher Education. Dr Corner is currently Chair of CHEAD with a special interest in social inclusion and employability research in art, media and design. Her own research projects have examined issues such as lifelong learning, employability and skills as well as teaching and learning methods, whilst her professional experience includes work for a number of bodies supporting the creative and cultural industries.
www.fashion.arts.ac.uk

Patrick Cox
Footwear Designer
Born in Canada, Patrick Cox moved to London to study at Cordwainers College in 1983. His career accelerated quickly, launching his own line in September 1985 for which he quickly gained a reputation as 'the shoe guru'. In 1991 he opened his first boutique and in 1993 he created the diffusion line Wannabe. The British Fashion Council awarded him Accessory Designer of the Year in both 1994 and 1995, and in January 2003 he was appointed Creative Director at Charles Jourdan, where he spent two years rejuvenating the brand before leaving to concentrate on his own business. His shoes can be found in museum collections internationally, and have attracted an extensive celebrity clientele. He has collaborated with Fender to produce a limited edition guitar and is currently Chairman of the Amnesty International Creative Committee.
www.patrickcox.com

Giles Deacon
Fashion Designer
After graduating from Central Saint Martins College in 1992, Giles Deacon worked for Jean Charles De Castelbajac in Paris for two years. From 1998 to 2002 he was a designer at Bottega Veneta and the Gucci Group. In February 2004 Giles showed his first collection at London Fashion Week. The collection was featured in American, British, Japanese, Italian and French *Vogue*, as well as *W, Harper's Bazaar, POP* and *i-D* and was sold at Harvey Nichols, Liberty and Selfridges. Giles has been awarded Best New Designer at the British Fashion Awards 2004, Best New Designer from *Elle* in 2005 and

British Designer of the Year in 2007. His illustrations have appeared in *Interview, The Face, Pop, i-D, Dutch* and *Arena Homme Plus* and form the basis for some prints in his collections.

Terry de Havilland
Footwear Designer
Terry de Havilland is a footwear designer born in East London. With a talent for design and pattern cutting he joined the family shoemaking business; his designs quickly attracted the attention of Paul Smith, who became his first client, and Annie Traherne, the fashion editor of *Queen* magazine. In 1972 de Havilland opened his first boutique on the King's Road in Chelsea, Cobblers to the World, which he would briefly reopen in 1999 in Camden Market. He has designed shoes for movies such as Tim Curry's *Rocky Horror Show* and Todd Haynes' *The Velvet Goldmine*, which won a BAFTA for best costume design. He has provided footwear for runway shows by Zandra Rhodes, Alexander McQueen, Anita Pallenberg, Anna Sui, Paco Rabanne, Lainey Keogh, David Fielden and French Frost. In 2005 he relaunched the Terry de Havilland brand and introduced the diffusion range D-Havz.
www.terrydehavilland.com

Philip Delamore
Fashion Designer
Over the last fifteen years Philip Delamore has developed new approaches to fashion design through a combination of art, science and technology. From 1992 to 1999 he ran a successful womenswear label partnership, showing in London and Paris, and selling internationally. For the last seven years he has done freelance design and consultancy, working collaboratively with other designers, artists and clients in the area of design technology and innovation. Delamore currently holds a Research Fellowship and is director of the Digital Fashion: Make studio at London College of Fashion, where he is developing the use of 3-D technologies for the fashion industry.
www.fashion.arts.ac.uk

Carmen dell'Orefice
Model
Carmen dell'Orefice is a model of Hungarian and Italian descent. She began her career at 14, after being discovered on a bus in New York. She went on to have an exclusive contract with Condé Nast, appearing on her first cover of *Vogue* at age 15 and on six more *Vogue* covers throughout her career. Dell'Orefice has been shot by top photographers including Irving Penn, Richard Avadon and Cecil Beaton; she has been muse to artist Salvador Dali and Donald Cammell, and has modelled for designers such as Carmen Marc Valvo, Christian Dior, Jean Paul Gaultier, Hermès, Moschino, Pierrot and Donna Karan. Her other achievements include acting in the movies *Celebrity* and *The Age of Innocence*, as well as writing the book *Staying Beautiful: Beauty Secrets and Attitudes from my forty years as a model.*

Valery Demure
Jewellery Dealer
Valery Demure was born in Amsterdam and raised in France. She studied History of Arts in Strasbourg and obtained a degree in Media Studies in Lyon. After graduating she worked at the Press Office of Cultural Affairs of Lyon for two years, promoting jazz festivals, short film festivals, theatre, performing arts and cinema. In 1995 Demure moved to London where she worked in fashion retail, and then spent four years as a buyer for a jewellery store in Soho where she developed an interest in non-traditional jewellery by designers such as Naomi Filmer, Shaun Leane, Scott Wilson and Betony Vernon. In 2005 she set up her own agency, where her first clients were Florian

Ladstätter, Sonja Bischur, Natalia Brilli and Scott Stephen. Today Valery Demure is one of London's top jewellery agencies.
www.valerydemure.com

Graham Dolphin
Artist
Graham Dolphin lives and works in Newcastle upon Tyne, UK. He graduated in 1994 from the Bath College of Higher Education with a BA in Fine Art specialising in Painting. His work engages with many aspects of popular culture, from music lyrics to magazine pages, and involves meticulous manipulation of mass-produced and culturally loaded objects. Works such as *Every Word in Vogue* (2004) and *500 Images of Kate Moss in 60 Seconds* (2001) have drawn from sources such as magazine and catwalk runways, which inspire similar obsession and idolisation. Dolphin has exhibited extensively, in both solo and group exhibitions in the UK and internationally, including the Mark Moore Gallery in Los Angeles, Seventeen in both Miami and New York, the Whitechapel Gallery in London and the Mori Art Gallery, Tokyo.
www.grahamdolphin.co.uk

David Downton
Fashion Illustrator
David Downton studied graphics at university and worked for fifteen years as a freelance illustrator before an art editor sent him to Paris for the Couture shows. It was there that Downton discovered his interest in fashion illustration and Couture. Since then he has illustrated some of the world's most beautiful women, including Erin O'Connor, Dita Von Teese, Jade Parfitt, Linda Evangelista, Marie Helvin, Jerry Hall, Carmen dell'Orefice, Anna Piaggi and Paloma Picasso. His work has been included in books such as the V&A 150 Year Anniversary album and *Made for Each Other;* in exhibitions such as *100 Years of Fashion* (The Fashion Illustration Gallery) and *David Downton: Couture Voyeur* (London College of Fashion); and in magazines such as the *Telegraph, Cent* and *Annabelle's,* and the *Evening Standard.* He is currently working on a limited edition art book entitled *Pourquoi Pas? A Journal of Fashion Illustration,* due to launch in October 2007.
www.daviddownton.com

Husam El Odeh
Jewellery Designer
German-born Husam El Odeh studied Fine Art at the Hochschule der Künste in Berlin, where he worked successfully as an artist until he relocated to London in 1999 and began making jewellery. Since graduating from Middlesex University in 2005 he has been awarded New Generation sponsorship from the British Fashion Council and from FashionEast. El Odeh has collaborated with designers Marios Schwab and Siv Stoldal; has contributed to the b Store artbook; is involved in projects with Topshop and Kickers; and is currently working on future collaborations with Ann-Sofie Back, Marios Schwab and Mihara Yasuhiro. His work has been featured in Italian *Vogue, Pelle Vogue, i-D, Purple, Dazed & Confused, AnOther Magazine, AnOther Man, Ten Magazine, Numéro* and *Elle.*
www.husamelodeh.com

Gavin Fernandes
Curator, Photographer and Art Director
Born in Kenya, Gavin Fernandes grew up in the United Kingdom. His degree in Graphic Design at Middlesex University was followed by studies at the Royal College of Art, London College of Communication and a recent MA in Fashion Photography at London College of Fashion. Currently working as a photographer and art director, Fernandes has also worked as a curator. In 1993 he participated in the *Street Style* exhibition at the Victoria and Albert Museum, and in 1999 co-curated *000zerozerozero* at the

Whitechapel Gallery, London. His first solo exhibition was at the Institute of Contemporary Arts in 1998, and in 2002 Fernandes' second solo exhibition, *Englisheritage*, was shown at Ashley Gardens, London. His commissions include new work for the exhibition *Photo London* at The Photographers' Gallery; researching, editing and photographing the book *Unclasped: Contemporary British Jewellery* for Black Dog Publishing; new work for the British Council, Rich Mix Cultural Foundation, Browns and David Stewart.
www.gavinfernandes.com

Patricia Field
Fashion Designer and Stylist
Born in New York City to Greek and Armenian parents, Patricia Field opened her first boutique in 1966 in Greenwich Village. In 1986 she styled Michael Mann's TV series *Crime Story* and continued to work in TV and film, winning her first Emmy in 1989 for Disney's *Mother Goose Rock n' Rhyme*. As costume designer for *Sex and the City*, Field was nominated for five Emmy Awards, of which she won one, and for six Costume Designers Guild Awards, of which she won four. Her TV series include *Spin City*, *Hope & Faith* and the pilot episode of *Ugly Betty*. Amongst others, she has designed costumes for *Miami Rhapsody*, *Big City Blues*, *The Secretary* and most recently *The Devil Wears Prada*. She is the owner of Patricia Field Boutique.
www.patriciafield.com

Shelley Fox
Fashion Designer
After receiving her MA in Fashion from Central Saint Martins College, Shelley Fox's collection was purchased by Liberty. She went on to launch her own line, which showed at London Fashion Week for eight years, and established her reputation for designing experimental and innovative womenswear. Fox's collaborations include the design studio Tomato, SHOWstudio, sound artist Scanner, Michael Clark Dance Company and Wayne McGregor of Random Dance. Her work has been included in exhibitions at the Victoria and Albert Museum, Design Museum, Barbican Art Gallery, Modemuseum, Crafts Council, Antwerp Landed 2001, FIT in New York and internationally through the British Council. Fox received the Jerwood Fashion Prize in 1999; the Peugeot Design Award for Textiles in 1999; the Crafts Council Development Award; the Stanley Picker Fellowship for Design; and is now a Senior Research Fellow at Central Saint Martins College.
www.shelleyfox.com

Joshua Galvin
Hair Stylist
Joshua Galvin was born into an established hairdressing family and, from 1953 to 1955, attended Barrett Street Technical College (a constituent college of London College of Fashion), where he trained in men's and women's hairdressing. In 1960 he began to work at Revlon in New York, where his celebrity clients included Judy Garland, Julie Andrews and Liza Minelli. Upon return to London in 1961, Galvin joined Vidal Sassoon's Bond Street Salon. His career with Vidal Sassoon lasted fourteen years, during which time he covered numerous senior positions within the company, set up the first Vidal Sassoon School, eventually becoming General Manager of Europe in 1973. In 1980 he opened his own London salon, in 1984 he founded the British Hairdressing Awards and in 1988 he established the Joshua Galvin Training Academy. Galvin has received many awards, including a Fellowship of British Hairdressing Lifetime Achievement Award in 2002.
www.centraltraininggroup.com

Paul Gorman
Music Writer
Born and raised in London, Gorman began his career as a news journalist before becoming the West Coast Bureau Chief for *Screen International* in 1990. From 1993 to 1998 he was Contributing Editor at *Music Week* in Los Angeles; between 1994 and 1999 he was Contributing Editor at *Music Business International* and in 1994 he worked with Brian Eno and his wife Anthea Norman-Taylor on their War Child charity project. He has contributed to a wide variety of publications from the *Evening Standard*, *Screen International*, the *Daily Telegraph* and *Radio Times* to *Word*, *Heat*, *Mojo*, *Garageland* and *Music Week*. He has written many books such as *The Look: Adventures in Rock & Pop Fashion* (2006), *Straight* with Boy George (2005), *Nine Lives* with Goldie (2005) and *In Their Own Write* (2001).
www.paulgorman.com

Tim Gutt
Photographer
Tim Gutt was born and raised in The Hague. He graduated in 1997 with a BA (Honours) in Photography from The Royal Academy of Art – The Netherlands. His work uses humour to capture and comment on the eccentricities of daily life. Gutt's photographs have been published in French *Vogue*, *Dazed & Confused*, *Kilimanjaro*, *032c*, *Re-Magazine*, *Colette – 10 Years of Collette S/S 2007*, *Art Review*, the *Observer* Magazine and *The Independent on Sunday*. Gutt's commissions include look books for Adidas and Emma Cook, work for the Pet Shop Boys, exhibition catalogues for the Henry Moore Institute and advertising campaigns for Skoda and Holsten Beer.
www.timgutt.com

Nick Hackworth
Gallerist and Art Writer
Nick Hackworth is a gallerist and art writer. He studied at Oxford University and the Courtauld Institute. He has been the Contemporary Art Critic for the *Evening Standard* since 2000 and was Art Editor of *Dazed & Confused* magazine. In October 2006 he started Paradise Row gallery, which shows emerging contemporary art.
www.nickhackworth.com

William Hall
Graphic Designer
William Hall studied Graphic Design at Central Saint Martins, graduating in 1997. He worked for the minimalist architect John Pawson for five years before establishing his London office in 2003. Quietly challenging convention – his projects include a website without buttons, a book with an invisible spine, and stationery that has no printing at all – Hall's work is often described as effortless, but this undermines its considered typographic rigour and sensitive use of materials. His client list includes Calvin Klein, the British Library, Tate, London College of Fashion and the Henry Moore Institute.
www.williamhall.co.uk

Shona Heath
Art Director and Set Designer
Shona Heath was raised in the countryside, but now lives and works in Dalston, London. As an art director and set designer Shona Heath has worked on editorial, fashion and advertising sets, as well as designing costumes for a wide variety of subjects. She works in fashion, art and film. Heath has worked on fashion sets for Emma Cook, Topshop and Gibo on show pieces for Atsuro Tayama and Marcus Lupfer on launch parties for Moschino and Selfridges; and windows for Colette and Martine Sitbon. Her advertising credits include Atsuro Tayama, Cacharel, and Church's shoes, as well as Dax, Dockers, Donna Karan, Fay Coats, Harvey Nichols, Margaret Howell and Tiffany, and her editorial work has been featured in *AnOther Magazine*, British *Vogue*, American *Vogue* and

Dazed & Confused. Heath works with photographers such as Nick Knight, Craig McDean, Tim Walker, Serge le Bon and others.
www.clmuk.com

Wayne Hemingway, MBE
Designer
Wayne Hemingway was born in Morecambe and graduated in 1979 with a Degree in Geography and Town Planning from University College London. Three years later he founded Red or Dead with his then girlfriend (now wife) Gerardine. Creating innovative and affordable designs, Red or Dead blurred the lines between high-street fashion and designer wear. The label was a three-time winner of the British Fashion Council's *Street Style Designer of the Year* award. After twenty-one consecutive seasons on the catwalk at London Fashion Week, the pair sold Red or Dead and established Hemingway Design, which specialises in affordable and socially conscious design. Today Hemingway is the Chairman of Building for Life, a Doctor of Design at Wolverhampton, a writer for architectural and housing publications, a judge of international design competitions, a TV design commentator and has just received his MBE.
www.hemingwaydesign.co.uk

Betty Jackson
Fashion Designer
Born in Lancashire, UK, Betty Jackson studied at the Birmingham College of Art, after which time she worked as a freelance fashion illustrator (1971–73), design assistant (1973–75), and Chief Designer with Quorum (1975–81). Jackson launched her first collection in 1981 and in 1985 was awarded British Designer of the Year. In 1987 she received an MBE, and was awarded Contemporary British Designer of the Year in 1999 at the London Fashion Awards. In 1999 she was also appointed visiting professor at the Royal College of Art. Since its inception Betty Jackson has grown to include the BJ Beach line and BJ Knit line. Jackson has designed ranges for both Marks & Spencer and Debenhams, has produced a capsule collection for Freemans Mail Order Catalogue and has launched her own diffusion line.
www.bettyjackson.com

Terry Jones
Editor and Publisher
Terry Jones was born in Northampton, England, and is the Editor-In-Chief, Creative Director and Publisher of *i-D*. He studied graphics at the West of England College of Art in Bristol. For more than twenty-five years Jones has established himself as one of the most innovative creative directors of his generation, from the covers of *Vanity Fair* and *Vogue*, where he was Art Director from 1972 to 1977, to the innovative designs of *i-D*, which he founded in 1980. The magazine celebrated its 250th edition at the end of 2004 and its twenty-fifth anniversary in 2005. Alongside *i-D*, Jones' Instant Design studio has produced several books, as well as catalogues, TV, graphics, advertising and exhibitions. Jones has also created and curated a number of *i-D* events and exhibitions which have toured internationally.
www.i-dmagazine.com

Nick Knight
Fashion Photographer
Nick Knight is among the world's most influential photographers and is also Director and Founder of SHOWstudio.com, the fashion and art internet broadcasting channel. He has won numerous awards for his editorial work for *Vogue*, *Dazed & Confused*, *W* magazine, *i-D*, and *Visionaire*, as well as for fashion and advertising projects for clients including Christian Dior, Alexander McQueen, Calvin Klein, Levi Strauss, Yohji Yamamoto and Yves Saint

Laurent. On 24 October 2006 Nick Knight was awarded the prestigious Moët & Chandon Fashion Tribute for 2006, which he celebrated by throwing a masked ball at Horace Walpole's Gothic revival treasure, Strawberry Hill. Knight's work has been exhibited at institutions such as the Victoria and Albert Museum, the Saatchi Gallery, the Photographers Gallery and Hayward Gallery, and recently Tate Modern. He has produced a permanent installation, Plant Power, for the Natural History Museum in London.
www.showstudio.com

Suzanne Lee
Senior Research Fellow – Central Saint Martins College
Suzanne Lee is Senior Research Fellow in Fashion at Central Saint Martins College, London. Her book, *Fashioning the Future: Tomorrow's Wardrobe* is published by Thames & Hudson. It imagines a future wardrobe based on contemporary technology R&D. She has exhibited her own work internationally and has curated fashion for the British Council. Her current research project, *BioCouture*, investigates the possibility of growing clothing using biocellulose. She is a creative consultant for several London-based fashion designers.
www.csm.arts.ac.uk

Wessie Ling
Visual Artist
Wessie Ling is a London-based visual artist currently working as a Senior Lecturer at London College of Fashion. She was born in Hong Kong but received her art and design training in Paris. Incorporating academic research and visual arts practice, her work focuses on the relationship between fashion, cities and identities. Interactivity is central to her practice. She uses installation as a medium to turn theoretical interpretation into a tangible phenomenon. Ling has exhibited nationally and internationally: her work has been shown at the Hong Kong Arts Centre, at MAK – Austrian National Museum of Applied Arts/Contemporary Art, at the London Design Festival and at the Museum of the Chinese in the Americas, New York. She is the author of *Fusionable Cheongsam* (2007).
www.fashion.arts.ac.uk

Ian Mankin
Textile Designer
Ian Mankin attended London College of Fashion from 1950 to 1952. He worked for six months in a couture house before spending seven years working for the family textile business. In 1961 he started a leather business and in 1970 made his first order for Saks Fifth Avenue, which was quickly followed by orders from speciality shops across the USA. Mankin has designed clothing for the Beatles, for their film *Help!* and for Michael Caine in *Deadfall*. In 1983 he opened his Regents Park shop, which received much attention from the press, most significantly in a four-page article for *The World of Interiors* in 1986. In 1989 Mankin stopped making clothes to focus on textile design, establishing a mail-order catalogue for the store in 1996. In 1997 he published the book *Natural Fabrics*. Today Mankin produces more designs than ever before, and is currently issuing his seventh catalogue.
www.ianmankin.com

Penny Martin
Writer, Curator
Penny Martin, Editor in Chief of SHOWstudio, is a fashion and photography curator and writer who has lectured internationally. Since studying at Glasgow and Manchester Universities and the Royal College of Art, she has worked as a curator at The National Museum of Photography, *Film & Television* and The Women's

Library, and as a Researcher and Lecturer at Manchester Metropolitan University. Martin curated the *Vogue* Laid Out exhibition at the V&A in 2000 and is an interviewer for the National Sound Archive. She has also contributed to *AnOther, Beaux Arts, Blueprint, Contemporary, Frieze, i-D, Numéro,* British *Vogue* and Japanese *Vogue* magazines and *The Independent* and *La Repubblica* newspapers.
www.showstudio.com

Dan May
Stylist and Photographer
Dan May became a photographer after enjoying a career as a semi-professional rugby player and personal trainer. He returned to university to take a course in styling and photography at London College of Fashion. He then worked assisting *i-D's* Edward Enninful and *The Independent's* Sophia Neophitou, who brought him to *The Sunday Times Style* and on to Russian *Vogue*. He was fortunate to have been there when Sophia started *10* Magazine and subsequently *10+Men*, where he is based now full-time as fashion editor of both the women's and men's quarterly publications. May has worked with photographers such as Tierney Gearon, Tom and Jenny Betterton, Alex Cayley, Satoshi Saïkusa, Paul Wetherall, David Bailey, Allesandro Dal Buoni, KT Auleta and Jason Nocito.
www.10magazine.com

Craig McDean
Photographer
Craig McDean is a fashion photographer whose elegant, conceptual approach to fashion photography is multifaceted and ever-evolving. His work has appeared in magazines including *W,* American, French, and Italian *Vogue, AnOther Magazine,* and *The New Yorker,* and in bold campaigns for Armani, Gucci, Yves Saint Laurent, Hugo Boss, Armani Cosmetics, Estée Lauder, and Anna Molinari. He has created music videos and TV commercials for Versus and H&M. His pared-down celebrity portraits of cultural figures such as Madonna, Edward Albee, Gwyneth Paltrow, and Hilary Clinton have been era-defining. McDean's first book, *I Love Fast Cars* (1999), edited and designed by the Parisian design duo M/M, describes the atmosphere of drag car races and the culture that surrounds the sport. His book *Lifescapes,* in the first title of the new Dangin/Steidl series, reveals a novel and exciting technical and aesthetic turn for McDean.
www.artandcommerce.com

Colin McDowell
Fashion Journalist
Colin McDowell is the author of sixteen books; he is the Senior Fashion Writer for *Sunday Times Style* and founder of Fashion Fringe. McDowell was visiting lecturer at the Melbourne Fashion Festival in 1998 and 2001; he speaks regularly for the Costume Society of Great Britain and the Royal Society of Arts and is a visiting professor at University of the Arts London. As a radio and television broadcaster McDowell has appeared on *The Late Show, Newsnight, Kilroy, The Jamieson Show,* the *Antiques Roadshow, Women's Hour* and *Radio 3.* He wrote and presented a programme on Christian Dior for *Channel Four* and commentated on a documentary examining the life and death of Gianni Versace. Colin McDowell's most recent books include *Fashion Today, a visual look at the past fifty years of fashion,* and the official biography of Ralph Lauren. He has written the biographies of leading international designers including Galliano, Manolo Blahnik and Jean Paul Gaultier.
www.fashion-enterprise.com

Suzy Menkes
Fashion Writer
Suzy Menkes is Fashion Editor of the *International*

Herald Tribune. Trained as a historian at Cambridge University in her native England, Menkes looks beyond the immediate trends to analyse changing style in a social context. Her incisive reporting includes the jousting of fashion tycoons and industry facts and figures for the *IHT's* financial pages and reviews of museum exhibitions in the arts section. She is based in Paris, France, but travelling both in the caravanserai of the international collections and as a reporter, Menkes' beat includes New York, European capital cities and Asia, from Tokyo and Hong Kong, through Beijing, Shanghai and Singapore. Two other areas of expertise and fascination are jewellery and the British royal family, on which she has written several books.
www.iht.com

Johanne Mills
Fashion Designer
London-based designer Johanne Mills graduated from the Royal College of Art with an MA in Mixed Media Textiles. The Donna Karan Company purchased her graduate collection and hired her as a freelance consultant, where she worked for five years. Mills has consulted on textiles and accessories for a range of other clients including Louis Vuitton, Marc Jacobs, Luella, Hugo Boss and Matthew Williamson. She has worked as a stylist on projects for Selfridges, Burberry, Issey Miyake and Bulgari and for magazines such as *W*, Japanese *Vogue*, *View On Colour*, the *New York Times* magazine, *V* magazine and *Viewpoint*. In 2006 Mills was invited to make a piece to be included in the Swarovski Runway Rocks catwalk show. A recent collaboration with Giles Deacon has inspired her to begin her own jewellery collection.
www.kabiri.co.uk

Alison Moloney
Design Curator and Project Manager
Alison Moloney is a Design Curator and Project Manager in the Design & Architecture Department of the British Council. As part of the British Council's international programme of events she has managed the tour of the Barbican's Communicate exhibition to China, Smile *i-D* to Latin America and has worked on the Foreign Office Architecture exhibition at the Venice Biennale in 2002. She has developed workshops in Kenya, Nigeria, Ukraine, Estonia, Pakistan, Uzbekistan, Mexico, India, Oman and Qatar. She has recently co-curated Alchemy: Contemporary Jewellery from Britain, which is touring to five countries in the Middle East where she is currently on secondment as Acting Regional Arts Manager. Before joining the British Council she worked with Judith Clark at Judith Clark Costume, as well as writing on fashion for both trade and commercial magazines. She recently graduated from London College of Fashion's MA History and Culture.
www.britishcouncil.org

Chris Moore
Fashion Photographer
Chris Moore was born in Byker, Newcastle Upon Tyne, in 1934. His first job after moving to London was at a photographic studio in Show Lane. Two years later he was working as a photographer's assistant at Vogue Studios, assisting photographers such as Cecil Beaton, Henry Clarke and Clifford Coffin. He then moved to Camera Press where he quickly became one of its most successful in-house photographers. Moore spent time freelancing before starting his own business, making his first trip to the Paris couture shows in 1967. With the advent of ready-to-wear shows in Paris, and soon after in Milan, London and New York, and the creation of the 1980s catwalk circuit, Moore was soon covering catwalk shows full-time. *The Sunday*

Times, *The Guardian*, the *Observer*, *The Independent*, and the *International Herald Tribune* are among the publications that have been commissioning Moore since he left Camera Press.
www.catwalking.com

Matthew Moore
Print Designer
Matthew Moore received his BA (Hons) Fashion Design with Print from Central Saint Martins College in 2003. That year he was awarded the Arts and Humanities Research Board Scholarship to pursue further studies in fashion. In 2005 he completed his MA in Fashion Textiles at Central Saint Martins College, during which time he was shortlisted for both the Chloé and the Burberry awards. Moore is currently working as a freelance print designer and as Assistant Manager at The Shop at Bluebird, where he represents the Thom Browne Brand.

Olivia Morris
Footwear Designer
Irish-born Olivia Morris graduated from Cordwainers College in 1996. Two years later she began designing and producing shoes under her own label, Olivia Morris, which launched in 2000. Her shoes are currently sold internationally in the US, Japan, the Far East and Europe. Morris also provides a design consultancy service and works collaboratively with designers to provide shoes for their catwalk shows. Her clients include Faith Shoes, Matthew Williamson, Topshop, Evisu Donna, Donna Karan, Evisu Jeans, Luc Berjen, Erdem, Aquascutum, Preen, Pringle, Anthony Symonds and Boyd.
www.oliviamorrisshoes.com

Sarah Mower
Fashion Critic
Sarah Mower is a fashion critic and a contributing editor to American *Vogue*, she reviews shows for style.com and writes a column for the *Daily Telegraph*. Mower has been obsessed with clothes and the reason we wear them since she was taken as a child to the Museum of Costume in Bath, where she was brought up. She fell into writing about fashion after entering the *Vogue* Talent Contest, landing the fashion editorship of *The Guardian* at the time that BodyMap, John Galliano and Katharine Hamnett were stars of the London runways. Mower lives in London with her husband and three children.

Matthew Murphy
Fashion Retailer
Matthew Murphy was born in Strood in Kent and now lives in South-East London. He is the buyer and owner of London's b Store. Before starting b Store in 2001 Murphy was a contemporary menswear buyer for a small chain of independent stores in Kent, buying brands such as Helmut Lang, YMC and Dirk Bikkembergs. He has also worked as UK Sales Manager for the contemporary Italian fashion brand Victor Victoria. In 2005 Murphy was invited by the British Fashion Council to scout new talent and to be part of the New Generation sponsorship panel. He has worked as a creative consultant for the concept boutique Lens, is currently working with young designers in Topman at Oxford Circus and is a panel member for the Man catwalk show at London Fashion Week.
www.bstorelondon.com

Phillip Neil Martin
Composer and Producer
Phillip Neil Martin is an internationally award-winning composer whose work crosses the divide from experimental concert music and installations to film, dance and fashion. After graduating with distinction from the Royal College of Music, his work has received international

recognition and awards. His innovative approach to music has led to collaborations with fashion designers, artists, architects, film-makers and dancers. As music creator in residence at London College of Fashion (2006–07) he has recently collaborated with London Fashion Week, Cannes Film Festival, Fashion TV, Dsquared2, Premier Models, SMC Europe, KDS, Intercontinental Hotels and F-Diamond Cruise. His concert music is performed and broadcast throughout the world by top musicians.
www.phillipneilmartin.com

Tracey Neuls
Footwear Designer
Born and raised in Canada, Tracey Neuls realised her passion for footwear at a young age. After establishing a career in clothing design, she decided to shift focus and moved to London in 1996 to study footwear design at Cordwainers College. She has been the recipient of several awards, including the Royal Society of Art Award, the Absolut Cobblers Award and winner of the Blueprint/Vitra design competition. In 1998 she graduated and started her own company; TN_29 was launched at London Fashion Week, where she received the New Generation Award. Her current client list includes L'Eclai reur and Onward in Paris, Via Bus stop in Tokyo and Tootsi Plohound in New York. Neuls has collaborated with John Rocha Couture, Tracy Mulligan, Gimme Shoes and Rigetta Klint, Nicola Finetti, Maria Chen-Pascual, Nothing Nothing and Russell Sage.
www.tn29.com

Erin O'Connor
Model and Vice Chairman of the British Fashion Council
Erin O'Connor was raised in Walsall, England and was first discovered by a Models 1 scout at The Clothes Show in Birmingham. She first appeared in *i-D* in 1996, photographed by Juergen Teller. Her unique appearance has been credited with launching an 'alternative concept of beauty'. O'Connor has modelled for designers such as John Galliano, Christian Dior, Donna Karan, Prada, Versace, Miu Miu, Giorgio Armani, Julien MacDonald, Jean Paul Gaultier, Badgley Mischka, Dolce & Gabbana and Ermanno Scervino. She has worked with leading fashion photographers including Patrick Demarchelier, Steven Meisel, Steven Klein, Nick Knight, Mario Testino, David Sims, and Jonathan de Villiers, and has featured in magazines including *Vogue, W, Elle, Nova, Harper's Bazaar, Harpers & Queen, i-D,* and *Visionaire.* In 2002 she appeared on the cover of British *Vogue.*

Glenn O'Brien
Editor and Writer
Glenn O'Brien graduated from Georgetown University, majoring in English and Anti-War Demonstrations, before attending the graduate film programme at Columbia University. He has worked editorially for Andy Warhol's *Interview* magazine, *Rolling Stone,* Playboy's *Oui* magazine, *High Times* magazine and *Spin.* He formed the band Konelrad, launched *O'Brien's TV Party,* wrote and produced the film *Downtown 81,* and worked as a stand-up comic before becom-ing Creative Director of Barney's Advertising in the mid-80s. O'Brien has created advertising for clients such as Calvin Klein, Ian Schrager Hotels, Swatch, Dior, Nike, Armani, Fila, Rock the Vote, Song Airlines and Air America. He has contributed to Madonna's *Sex* book, *GQ, Vanity Fair, Italia, Paper, Purple, Self Service, L'Uomo Vogue* and *AnOther Magazine.* His books include *The Style Guy, Soapbox* (essays), and the poetry collection *Human Nature* (dub version). He is editor of the literary magazine *Bald Ego* and has a novel forthcoming.

Alistair O'Neill
Curator and Writer
Alistair O'Neill is a Senior Research Fellow at

Central Saint Martins and runs the Fashion History & Theory pathway of BA Fashion. His first book *London – after a fashion* (Reaktion Books, 2007) considers the relationship between fashion and London in the twentieth century. His most recent exhibition Fashion Lives (The British Library, 2005) promoted the oral history of British Fashion at the library's Sound Archive. He also collects bespoke suits by Tommy Nutter.

Beatrix Ong
Footwear Designer
Beatrix Ong was born in London, England. Ong has studied at Central Saint Martins College, London College of Communication, the Fashion Institute of Technology in New York and Cordwainers College. Before launching her first collection at London Fashion Week in 2002, she interned at *Harper's Bazaar* US and designed for Jimmy Choo. Ong's shoes have been seen on the catwalks in London, New York and Milan through collaborations with Alice Temperley, Tristan Webber, Ashley Isham and Pringle of Scotland. Ong has received commissions from the *Financial Times* and *Buena Vista International,* for whom she created an illustration and pair of shoes inspired by and for its film *Hitchhiker's Guide to the Galaxy.* Most recently she collaborated with illustrator and artist Natasha Law, who created custom designs for Ong's shoe-boxes. In 2004 Ong opened her first boutique in Primrose Hill, London.
www.beatrixong.com

Brenda Polan
Director of Programmes (Media) at London College of Fashion
Brenda Polan is Director of Programmes (Media) at London College of Fashion and also works as a freelance journalist specialising in fashion, design and architecture, media issues and women's topics. She has worked for the *Daily Mail,* the *Financial Times, The Guardian, The Independent,* the *Mail on Sunday,* the *Daily Telegraph* and the *Evening Standard* as well as a variety of newspaper supplements (*You, How To Spend It, Style, Stella, Night and Day*) and glossy magazines (*Tatler, World of Interiors, Harper's Bazaar, Good Housekeeping, Elle, Red*). She was fashion editor and then women's editor of *The Guardian* in the 1980s, fashion editor of *The Independent on Sunday,* associate editor of *Tatler* and style director of *You* magazine, the *Mail on Sunday* and style editor of the *Daily Mail* in the 1990s. She has also worked in radio and television, has lectured at the Rotterdam Art Museum and the ICA and has interviewed Vivienne Westwood many times over the years.
www.fashion.arts.ac.uk

Susan Postlethwaite
Fashion Curator
Susan Postlethwaite is Senior Lecturer in Fashion at Camberwell College of Art and a freelance Fashion Curator. Trained as a fashion designer, she graduated from Central Saint Martins College in 1984 and worked as a womenswear designer for Ralph Lauren, Georgio Armani and Jean Muir among others. She co-curated Fashion at Belsay, Belsay Hall, Northumberland; The Future of Men, ICA, London; Beyond the Hide, Old Truman Brewery, London; and New Directions in Fashion Research, London College of Fashion. Susan's film *The Future of the Costume Museum* was shown at *Spectres* V&A Friday Late. She is researching ideas around the Slow Movement and their application to fashion, and has spoken at the Death of Taste conference, ICA London and at the Royal College of Art in conversation with Dai Rees as part of the College Wide lecture series on Slow Fashion during London Fashion Week. She is currently planning an exhibition about Slow Fashion.

Dai Rees
Fashion Designer
Dai Rees is from South Wales and originally trained in ceramics and glass at Central Saint Martins and the Royal College of Art. His work has been used internationally by photographers, designers and stylists; has been displayed in the windows of Colette, Paris; Liberty, London; Saks and Bergdorf Goodman, New York and has featured in publications such as *British Fashion, Visionaire's Fashion 2001* and *Fashion At the Edge.* His work has been shown in exhibitions at the Judith Clark Costume Gallery, the Hayward Gallery, the Victoria and Albert Museum, the Musée Galliera in Paris and at the Museum of Fine Art, Houston. In 2003 Rees received a Fellowship in the Creative and Performing Arts from the Arts & Humanities Research Board, producing *Carapace,* an exhibition that toured Central and South America with the support of the British Council. In 2004 The University of the Arts awarded Rees the title of Professor, he has recently received an RC UK Fellowship and he is Course Director for MA Fashion Footwear and MA Fashion Artefact at the London College of Fashion.
www.fashion.arts.ac.uk

Serena Rees
Fashion Entrepreneur
In 1994 Serena Rees and Joseph Corre founded Agent Provocateur. Their first store opened on Broadwick Street in Soho, London, and was an instant success, offering provocative lingerie to a demanding clientele. The website was launched in 1999 and the company continued to expand quickly, launching a fragrance in 2000 and slowly opening stores across the UK and in Europe, America, the Middle East, Russia and Hong Kong. Agent Provocateur has been a leader in marketing, producing innovative video advertising campaigns such as *Proof* with Kylie Minogue in 2001 and *The Four Dreams of Miss X* with Mike Figgis and Kate Moss in 2006. Other collaborations have included Damien Hirst's window display and an album entitled *Peep Show* by Joseph Corre and Luca Mainardi.
www.agentprovocateur.com

Zandra Rhodes
Textile and Fashion Designer
Zandra Rhodes was born in Chatham, Kent, UK. She studied at Medway and at the Royal College of Art in London, majoring in printed textile design. In 1967 she established her own retail outlet with Sylvia Ayton, setting up independently in 1969. In 1972 she received the Designer of the Year Award from the English Fashion Trade and in 1974 was made Royal Designer for Industry. In 1975 she founded her own shop off Bond Street in London. Her clients have included Princess Diana, Jackie Onassis, Elizabeth Taylor, Freddie Mercury, Dame Helen Mirren, Kylie Minogue, Debbie Harry, Bianca Jagger and Sarah Jessica Parker in *Sex and the City.* Rhodes is the founder of the Fashion and Textile Museum in London and was made a CBE in 1997 in recognition of her contribution to fashion and textiles.
www.zandrarhodes.com

Sean and Seng
Fashion Photographers
Sean and Seng graduated in Fashion Photography from London College of Fashion in 2004. They currently reside in London, working for clients such as *Zoo, i-D, Harper's Bazaar* Russia, Vivienne Westwood, L'Artisan Perfume and Lane Crawford.
www.seanandseng.com

Jane Shepherdson
Fashion retail advisor
Jane Shepherdson has worked at Topshop since graduating with a Diploma in Purchasing and Marketing from North London University. She

was the Topshop Brand Director between 1999 and 2006, and before that worked as a Buyer and as Buying Director. She is currently Governor at the Fashion Retail Academy, a member of the Advisory Board of University of Westminster and a member of the British Fashion Council.

Alexandra Shulman
Editor, British Vogue
Alexandra Shulman was educated at St Paul's Girls School and read Social Anthropology at Sussex University. She began her career in journalism at *Over-21* magazine and moved to *Tatler* in 1982, where she worked for five years before becoming Features Editor. In 1987 she became Editor of the *Sunday Telegraph*, and then moved to become Deputy Editor of their tabloid magazine *7 Days*. She joined *Vogue* as Features Editor in 1988, moving to *GQ* as Editor in February 1990. She was appointed Editor of British *Vogue* in January 1992.
www.vogue.com

Camilla Skovgaard
Footwear Designer
Born in north Copenhagen, Denmark, Camilla Skovgaard received her BA (Hons) in Design, Marketing and Development (Footwear) at Cordwainers College in 2003. She worked as a footwear designer for both Ilse Jacobsen (Denmark) and BSV International (UK) after launching her own label in 2005. Since then she has developed the Camilla Skovgaard shoe range while simultaneously working for Matthew Williamson as Head Designer of women's footwear. In 2006 Skovgaard graduated from the Royal College of Art with an MA in Womenswear (Footwear) and since then has joined Cordwainers College as a guest tutor for the footwear course.
www.camillaskovgaard.com

Paul Smith
Fashion Designer
Raised in Nottingham, Paul Smith abandoned his dream to become a professional cyclist after an accident hospitalised him. Inspired by a new circle of art school friends, including his girlfriend (now wife) Pauline Denyer, Paul Smith was soon managing his first boutique in Nottingham. In 1970 he opened a tiny shop and started to take evening classes for tailoring. With the help of Denyer's (an RCA fashion graduate), he was able to create the clothes he wanted. In 1976 Smith showed his first menswear collection in Paris under the Paul Smith label. Twenty years later Paul Smith encompasses twelve different collections: Paul Smith, Paul Smith Women, PS by Paul Smith, Paul Smith Jeans, Paul Smith London, R. Newbold (Japan only), Paul Smith Accessories, Paul Smith Shoes, Paul Smith Fragrance, Paul Smith Watches, Paul Smith Pens and Paul Smith furniture and 'things'.
www.paulsmith.co.uk

NJ Stevenson
Stylist and Fashion Writer
NJ Stevenson started working as a stylist and fashion writer in 1993 by contributing to *Blow* magazine. Since then her freelance career has taken her to launderettes in Caracas and industrial estates outside Budapest. She was a regular contributor to *The Guardian* and managed (occasionally by subterfuge) to include at least one charity shop find in each photoshoot. Following a varied fourteen years practising and teaching styling, while simultaneously working as a journalist and fashion consultant, Stevenson is currently studying for an MA in Fashion Curation at London College of Fashion. She lives and works in London.

Mario Testino
Fashion Photographer

Mario Testino was born in Lima where he attended the American School of Lima and went on to study Economics at the Universidad del Pacifico, Law at the Universidad Catolica and International Relations at the University of California, San Diego. From Peru he moved to London and began his formal training in photography. Mario travels extensively shooting for American, British and French *Vogue, Vanity Fair,* and *V* magazine. He has photographed many celebrities and he has contributed to the images of the world's leading fashion houses. His photographs have been exhibited internationally, and he has curated exhibitions at the Andrea Rosen Gallery in New York and at the Royal Academy in London. His exhibition Portraits first opened at the National Portrait Gallery in London in 2002 and still continues its tour across the world. Mario has an Honorary Doctorate from the University of the Arts, London and was awarded the Rodeo Drive Walk of Style Award in March 2005.
www.mariotestino.com

Simon Thorogood
Designer
Simon Thorogood is a fashion designer/artist who exhibits his collections in installation and gallery environments. He established his design practice in 1998 after graduating from Central Saint Martins College in 1992. He terms his design work 'Phashion' (pronounced 'fashion'), a blend of the scientific term 'phase transition' (the transformation of one form or substance to another) and fashion. Thorogood's innovative presentations encourage audience interactivity and critical engagement, exploring the idea that the audience plays a role in determining the course of the event. Most recently his research explores innovation in design technology and its influences on the understanding of traditional forms of fashion education and practice.
www.simonthorogood.com

Harold Tillman
Fashion Entrepreneur
Harold Tillman is one of the most experienced businessmen in the UK fashion and leisure industries. He is currently the Chairman of Jaeger, which he acquired in March 2003, and is the owner of Allders of Croydon, which he bought in 2005. Over his career he has variously run and successfully floated a number of clothing companies on the London Stock Exchange (LSE) and turned around ailing textile concerns. Included in these companies are Lincroft Clothing Company, Sumrie Clothes plc, Austin Reed plc and Baird Menswear Brand. He also has an eye for talent. He was the first person to employ Sir Paul Smith (in 1969), now one of the world's most famous designers, early in his career. He was the founder of Rumours Cocktail Bar in 1978 and has current interests in other high-profile London restaurants.
www.jaeger.co.uk

Marketa Uhlirova
Fashion and Film Curator
Marketa Uhlirova is Research Fellow in Fashion History and Theory at Central Saint Martins College of Art and Design. She is Director and Curator of the Fashion in Film Festival, which she co-founded in 2005 with curator Christel Tsilibaris and costume designer Roger K. Burton. Uhlirova has worked variously as a researcher, curator, oral history interviewer and writer, but is happiest in the darkened rooms of film archives. She has conducted over twenty-five oral history interviews with fashion practitioners for Museum of London's oral history archive and The London Look exhibition (2004–05), and has contributed articles, reviews and interviews to various art and culture publications including *Art Monthly, Detail, Fashion Theory,* and *Scribner's Encyclopedia of Clothing and Fashion.* She is co-founder of SOCK (Society of

Cataloguing Knowledge), an independent group of researchers investigating the history and theory of catalogues.
www.fashioninfilm.com

Alannah Weston
Creative Director, Selfridges
Born in Ireland and raised in Toronto, Alannah Weston received a BA Honours in English at Merton College, Oxford in 1994. After graduating she joined the *Telegraph Magazine* in London, where she soon became Contributing Editor. As a freelance journalist she has also written features for British *Vogue*, *Tatler*, and *The Spectator*. In 1998, she decided to pursue a career in brand development and was recruited as Burberry's Press Officer. After two years she became Creative Director of Windsor and in July 2003, Weston formed Zephyr Projects Ltd, designing books and catalogues for clients in the art world and corporate identities for clients in the luxury sector. Weston has been Creative Director of Selfridges & Co since 2007, Director of Wittington Investments, Canada and Creative Director of Wittington Fashion Retail Group, which includes Holt Renfrew, Canada and Brown Thomas Ltd, Ireland.
www.selfridges.com

Vivienne Westwood, OBE
Fashion Designer
Born in Glossop, Derbyshire, UK, Vivienne Westwood moved to London at age 17. In 1967 she was married to Malcom Edwards (aka McLaren) with whom she opened the shop Let It Rock on Kings Street in 1971. The shop was redesigned in 1972 and renamed Too Fast to Live, Too Young to Die, and then renamed Sex in 1974. In 1981 the pair showed their first catwalk collection. Continuing to show seasonally, Westwood's reputation grew quickly, and the company did the same, growing to include a menswear collection, a Gold Label collection, wedding gowns, the Anglomania Collection and a fragrance. Throughout her career she has received many awards including Fashion Designer of the Year from the British Fashion Council (1990 and 1991); an OBE from Her Majesty Queen Elizabeth II (1993); the first Institute of Contemporary Art Award for Outstanding Contribution to Contemporary Culture (1994); and the UK Fashion Export Award for Design (2003). In 2004 the Vivienne Westwood retrospective was shown at the Victoria and Albert Museum, London.
www.viviennewestwood.com

Val Williams
Writer and Curator
Val Williams is a writer and curator. She is the Director of the Photography and the Archive Research Centre at University of the Arts, and Professor of the History and Culture of Photography; she is also Senior Research Fellow at London College of Fashion. Williams has been Curator of Exhibitions and Collections at the Hasselblad Foundation in Gothenburg, Sweden, co-director of the Shoreditch Biennale and curator of the first *Printemps de Septembre à Toulouse*. She worked with the National Sound Archive on the Oral History of British Photography from 1992 and is currently directing the major UAL research projects New British Photography and ROAD. In November 2004 she received the Dudley Johnston Medal for Curatorship from the Royal Photographic Society and in 2002 her book on Martin Parr won the Photo España prize.
www.arts.ac.uk

Elizabeth Wilson
Writer
Elizabeth Wilson is visiting professor at London College of Fashion, and Emeritus Professor at London Metropolitan University. Her publications include *Adorned in Dreams: Fashion and*

Modernity, *The Sphinx in the City* and *Bohemians: The Glamorous Outcasts*. Her novel, *The Twilight Hour*, was published in 2006.

Yu 'Venice' Xiao
Fashion Designer
Yu 'Venice' Xiao was born in Chungking, China. She studied at the Affiliated School of Sichuan Fine Arts Academy and at the Academy of Arts and Design, Tsinghua University in Beijing, where she completed a BA (Hons) in Fashion. In 1995, her graduate collection won the UNESCO DESIGN 21 International Competition. Venice has worked for Hempel International Group and FIRS Group in China. At her catwalk debut in 1998 at China Fashion Week, she was named one of the 'Chinese Top Ten Fashion Designers'. In 2002 *Fashion China* magazine chose Venice as one of the 'Ten Most Influential Fashion Designers in China'. Since 1998 she has been a council member of the China Fashion Association and a commissioner of the Fashion Art Committee. In 2007 she graduated with distinction from the MA in Fashion Design and Technology at London College of Fashion.

Carla Yarish
Writer and Stylist
Carla Yarish is a fashion and arts writer, stylist and dressmaker. She received her BA (Hons) in History in Art at the University of Victoria and her MA (Hons) in Fashion Journalism at London College of Fashion. She has worked in curation at the Art Gallery of Greater Victoria and at the British Council and is currently working on a small collection of clothing, while continuing to sew bespoke garments for select customers. Yarish's editorial experience includes British *Vogue*, Showstudio, *Amelia's Magazine* as Fashion Editor, and *Art World* magazine where she is currently Features Associate. Amongst others, she has written for Amsterdam Fashion Week, the London Design Museum and *Amelia's Magazine* and London College of Fashion's *The Measure*.

Photography Credits

209.1, 211.1, 213.1
  Alice Hawkins, Courtesy: Agent Provocateur
215.1, 215.2
  Chris Moore
217.1, 217.2, 219.1, 219.2, 221.1, 221.2
  Celia Birtwell
223.1 Pierre Bailey
225.1 Iggy Marianne
227.1 Copyright: The Ancient Art and Architecture Collection
229.1 Courtesy: Company Archive Harrods Ltd
229.2 Hulton Archive; 2005 Getty Images
231.1 Hulton Deutsch Collection; CORBIS
231.2 Photo by RDA/Central Press/Getty Images, Copyright 2007, Getty Images
233.1 British Film Institute Archive
237.1 David Downton
239.1 Robyn Beeche
241.1 Yu-kuang Chou
241.2, 241.3, 241.4, 241.5
  Chris Moore
243.1, 243.2, 243.3
  Courtesy: Belle & Bunty
245.1, 245.2, 245.3, 247.1, 249.1
  Fabrice Lachant
251.1 Martin Brading
253.1, 253.2, 253.3
  Chris Moore
255.1, 255.2
  Fondazione Pitti Discovery
257.1 Courtesy: Edward Sexton
259.1 Hulton Archive, Getty Images 2005
259.1 Hulton Archive, Getty Images 2006
261.1
  Courtesy: Alan Cannon Jones
265.1, 267.1
  Zanna

269.1 Dudley Reed
271.1 Anthony Giocolea
273.1, 273.2
  London College of Fashion Archive
275.1 Zanna
275.2, 275.3
  Andreas Sjodin
277.1, 279.1
  Shelley Fox Archive
281.1, 283.1, 285.1
  Rama Lee
287.1, 287.2
  Courtesy: Bentley & Skinner
289.1,
  Courtesy: George Jensen
293.1, 293.2
  Lachlan Bailey
295.1 Mario Testino
297.1, 297.2, 399.1, 301.1, 301.2
  Courtesy: Husam El Odeh
303.1, 303.2, 303.3
  Courtesy: Valery Demure
305.1 Lee Miller, Lee Miller Archive, England 2007
305.2 Andreas Bleckmann
305.3 Bettina Rheims, Courtesy: Galerie Jérôme de Noirmont, Paris
305.4 Agence Roger-Viollet
305.5 Bowness, Hepworth Estate
305.6 Richard Burbridge
305.7 Peter Garmusch
307.1 Peter Garmusch; Fotofest
307.2 Jonas Unger
307.3 Courtesy: Valerie Demure
307.4 Jean Francois Carly
309.1, 309.2, 311.1, 313.1
  Chris Moore
313.1 Oliver Santana

315.1, 317.1, 319.1
  Courtesy: Philip Delamore
323.1, 323.2, 323.3, 323.5, 325.1
  Photo: Alastair Mucklow
327.1 Photo Courtesy: V&A Photo Studio
329.1, 329.2, 329.3
  London College of Fashion Archive
331.1 Woolmark Archive, London College of Fashion
331.2 Gala of London Archives, London College of Fashion
331.3 Woolmark Archive, London College of Fashion
333.1, 333.2
  Photo: Fiona Freund
335.1, 335.2, 335.3, 337.1, 337.2, 337.3, 339.1, 339.2, 339.3
  Courtesy: British Council
341.1, 343.1, 345.1, 345.2
  Courtesy: Wessie Ling
347.1, 347.2, 347.3, 349.1
  Courtesy: Simon Thorogood
351.1, 353.1, 355.5
  Courtesy: Graham Dolphin
357.1, 357.2, 357.3, 357.4, 359.1
  Paul Smith
361.1 Courtesy: Panagiotis Davios and Priten Patel
363.1 Courtesy: Fabrice Lachant
365.1 Courtesy: Sarah Brittain
367.1 Courtesy: Gemma Stokes
379.1 Courtesy: Linda Stensson
371.1 Courtesy: Panagiotis Davios and Priten Patel
373.1 Courtesy: Fabrice Lachant
375.1 Courtesy: Gemma Stokes
377.1 Courtesy: Rama Lee
379.1 Courtesy: Louise Adolphsen and Sarah Brittain Edwards

Editor's Acknowledgements

With thanks to all those who have contributed their time and energy to participating in the book and for supporting this great cause.

I would like to extend special thanks to the following people:

To Nicholas Barba and James Musgrave at William Hall for their great work.

To William Hall for his stunning design and ongoing skill in translating my ideas into beautiful graphic objects.

To Dr Frances Corner for commissioning this project and allowing it to grow beyond the original brief. Her enthusiasm and visual understanding have been essential to the project's development.

To Anna Millhouse for believing in my vision and supporting me throughout the making of this book. Her unstinting diligence, professionalism and loyalty have made this project possible.

I would also like to thank Alistair O'Neill for his inspirational teaching, his guidance and his endless support. By continuing to champion my work he has shown a belief in me that has given me confidence and has enabled me to achieve things I would never have thought possible.

I would also like to thank:
Victor Archer, Katherine Baird, Emily Campbell, Carolina Campo, Bella Clark, James Colville, Alun Davies, Antonia Deeson, Liz de Havilland, Sophie Dennys, Kate Dooley, Gillian Evans, Sacha Forbes, Joe Fountain, Paul Isaacs, Natalie Kabiri, Fabrice Lachant, Heather Lambert, Jenny Lord, Candice Marks, Cassandra Maxwell, Katie McDowell, Alexandra Milner, Kaylie Mountford, Rebecca Munro, Rosemin Ratanshi, Margaret Rose, Nikki Rowntree, Helen Scott-Lidgett, Anthea Simms, Lorraine Slipper, Charlie Smith, Emma Smith, Jacqui Soliman, Alienor Taylor, Emily Turner, Dyonne Venable, Sadie Watts, Alan Watts, Emma Wheeler, Maisie Wilhelm, Lucy Willis, Chiara Zoppelli

Last but not least, I would like to thank Darian Leader and my parents, Ann and Malcolm Clarke

Colophon

The Measure
Edited by Louise Clarke
www.louiseclarke.com

February 2008
ISBN: 978-1-903455-07-4

Published by:
London College of Fashion
20 John Princes Street
London W1G 0BJ
United Kingdom
enquiries@fashion.arts.ac.uk
www.fashion.arts.ac.uk
Telephone +44 (0) 20 7514 7400

Distributed by:
Thames & Hudson Ltd.
44 Clockhouse Road
Farnborough
Hampshire GU14 7QZ
Telephone +44 (0) 1252 541602
Facsimile +44 (0) 1252 377380

Design: William Hall with Nicholas
Barba and James Musgrave
www.williamhall.co.uk

Typeset in Baskerville, based on a
font used by John Baskerville in 1772

Print: Granite Colour

Project Manager: Anna Millhouse

Consultant Editor: Alistair O'Neill

Proof Editors: Alexandra Milner,
Lorraine Slipper

Picture Researcher: Christel
Tsilibaris

Dr Frances Corner, Head of College
at London College of Fashion

Printed on paper from well-managed
forests, controlled sources and recycled wood or fibre www.fsc.org
Cert no. TT-C0C-002238
© 1996 Forest Stewardship Council